Contents

John Gittings is the East Asia correspondent for the
Guardian. He studied Chinese at Oxford University,
worked in Hong Kong and first visited China in 1971.
He has written books on the Chinese army, on foreign
policy and Sino-Soviet relations, and on modern
Chinese history.

Also by John Gittings

Real China – From Cannibalism to Karaoke

China
through the sliding door

reporting three decades of change

JOHN GITTINGS

TOUCHSTONE

SIMON &
SCHUSTER

TO THE PEOPLE OF CHINA

Renmin wansui!

First published in Great Britain by Touchstone, 1999
An imprint of Simon & Schuster UK Ltd
A Viacom Company

Copyright © John Gittings, 1999

1 3 5 7 9 10 8 6 4 2

Simon & Schuster Ltd
Africa House
64–78 Kingsway
London WC2B 6AH

Simon & Schuster Australia
Sydney

A CIP catalogue record for this book is available from the British Library

ISBN 0-684-85181-4

Typeset by SX Composing DTP, Rayleigh, Essex
Printed and bound in Great Britain by
Caledonian International Book Manufacturing, Glasgow

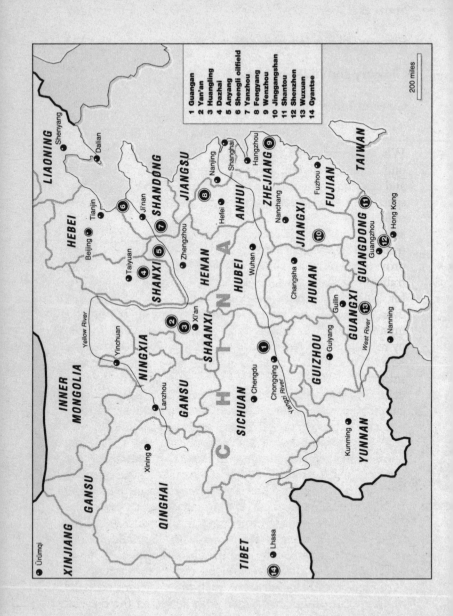

1 Guangan
2 Yan'an
3 Huangling
4 Dazhai
5 Anyang
6 Shengli oilfield
7 Yanzhou
8 Fengyang
9 Wenzhou
10 Jinggangshan
11 Shantou
12 Shenzhen
13 Wuxuan
14 Gyantse

200 miles

LIAONING

Shenyang
Dalian

HEBEI

Beijing
Tianjin

SHANDONG

Jinan
Zhengzhou

JIANGSU

Nanjing
Shanghai

SHANXI

Taiyuan

HENAN

Hefei

ANHUI

Hangzhou

ZHEJIANG

Yellow River

Yinchuan

NINGXIA

Xi'an

SHAANXI

Wuhan

HUBEI

Nanchang

JIANGXI

Fuzhou

FUJIAN

TAIWAN

Lanzhou

GANSU

C H I N A

Changsha

HUNAN

Guilin

Hong Kong

Shenzhen

GUANGDONG

Guangzhou

Chengdu

Chongqing

SICHUAN

Yangzi River

Guiyang

GUIZHOU

GUANGXI

West River

Nanning

Xining

QINGHAI

Kunming

YUNNAN

Ürümqi

XINJIANG

GANSU

INNER MONGOLIA

TIBET

Lhasa

Introduction

Travels in China

When I first visited China in 1971 the Beijing Hotel had the only automatic sliding doors in the country. Beyond the gate and the security guards, small groups of Chinese gaped at the spectacle of foreigners entering and leaving. Most of the onlookers wore cheap Mao suits and carried small khaki satchels with the characters 'Serve the People' or 'Learn from Lei Feng' stencilled on the flap. They were from the provinces, taking a quick peek at the capital while changing trains or perhaps the lucky beneficiaries of a sponsored trip for model workers or peasants. Laden with cameras and over-warm clothing, we and our attachments were as much a mystery to them as they were to us. China had been isolated by most of the West – with the US setting the pace but the Soviet Union more recently joining in – for two decades since the 1949 revolution. It had withdrawn into the self-defining, self-sufficient ideology of Mao Zedong which culminated in the Cultural Revolution. Our two worlds were mutually exclusive: the incomprehension gap was huge.

Beijing now has dozens of international hotels with sliding doors from which to emerge with camera and notebook, and through which ordinary Chinese can walk in the opposite direction to consume foreign food, buy foreign liquor and even foreign newspapers. Every provincial capital has similar facilities, plus ring roads, motorways, modern airports, Hong Kong-style department stores and bowling alleys. The streets once occupied by thousands of bicycles, battered buses and lorries tilting to one side – plus a few mysteriously curtained official cars – are now filled with new cars, taxis and minibuses in traffic jams which have squeezed the bicycles close to the pavement. Instead of the handful of tourists from abroad in the early 1970s – a large proportion apparently from Albania – there are more than a million a year. Instead of the strictly guided tour, with nervous arrangements to clean up anything the foreign guest might see and write about later, there is hardly any restriction on travelling even to the most disadvantaged areas.

Not only is China now 'open' instead of 'closed' (the adjectives used by the Chinese themselves), but it has changed often beyond recognition. To use another Chinese phrase, it has turned 180 degrees. The Maoist insistence on emphasizing human effort and collective work, on putting public before private interest, on restraining personal ambition and initiative, on consciously pursuing a path called 'the transition to socialism', and on opposing 'imperialism' abroad, has been not only abandoned but repudiated. The Cultural Revolution which brought Mao's vision to a climax – horribly distorted by his vindictiveness against colleagues who had crossed him and by the factional fighting of those around him – has been rejected wholesale as 'ten years of madness'. Led by Deng Xiaoping till his death in 1997, China has embraced market economics and Chinese labour has competed successfully in the global market. A new middle class has emerged with a South-east Asian lifestyle and expectations: thousands of Chinese go abroad for business or to study – or even as camera-carrying tourists to pass through the sliding doors of foreign hotels.

In this selection of reports written from China over more than a quarter of a century, I hope to convey both the magnitude of the Chinese transformation and its incompleteness – particularly in political life which remains stained with the blood of the 1989 Beijing Massacre. My visits from 1971 onwards (at least once a year on average since 1976) have taken me to almost every province and have allowed me to witness most of the great upheavals: the Cultural Revolution, the rejection of Maoism, the growth of a consumer society, the repression of political dissidents, the sharpening in-equalities between rich and poor, the struggle in Tibet, and finally the Hong Kong handover in 1997. In recent years I have travelled mostly on my own and far off the beaten track, seeking to understand Chinese realities away from the big cities and the more advanced coastal region. My enthusiasm for official meetings with senior Chinese cadres, sunk deep into padded armchairs and drinking endless tea, waned considerably after witnessing the slaughter on the night of 3–4 June 1989. Yet almost a decade later under the post-Deng leadership, there are some signs of a more open-minded approach emerging, with candid discussion of many of the problems as well as the achievements of China's march to modernization.

China's story – however it is continued now – is one of the great epics of the twentieth century, and the 180-degree turn of the last quarter-century is an integral part of it. But in a world where historical memory is becoming ever shorter, the complexity of the Chinese transformation which I hope to convey in these pages is often overlooked. The Cultural Revolution was not just an act of brutal folly directed by a wilful autocrat in Beijing and his ambitious supporters. Millions of ordinary Chinese believed at the time that they were fighting against corruption and privilege and building a new and better society. The shift to a modern, competitive market society in the 1980s was not universally popular or pre-ordained. There were many uncertainties about how far to go and even some hopes of rebuilding a collective society on a more genuine basis. The economic boom of the mid-1990s has also obscured the degree of gloom into which China was plunged at the beginning of the decade by the Beijing Massacre and the ensuing mood of stultified despair. (And as I write in mid-1998, this same boom has begun to appear vulnerable to the collapse of the Asian 'economic miracle' around it.) Perhaps because of China's physical vastness and cultural difference, we tend too readily to assume that the current situation is both stable and permanent. The last quarter of a century – indeed the last half-century since the 1949 Liberation – demonstrates that this is not so.

During my travels I have sometimes found answers to questions which I had asked in vain ten or twenty years previously. I began to report on China from Hong Kong in 1968, reading between the lines of official publications for clues to the ideological struggle while getting a vivid picture of the physical struggle from Red Guard bulletins smuggled across the border. I belonged to the profession of China Watcher, peering across a border which we could not cross for some insight into Chinese reality (see pp. 19–34).

One day I obtained my first real glimpse. I had spent the day in Macao and was returning in the late afternoon by the slow boat. The sun was already setting over the mountains of Guangdong when, off the mouth of Pearl River, our path crossed almost at right angles with a similar paint-peeled steamer heading out to sea. (The two craft may have belonged to the same shipping company before the revolution.) Its upper deck was lined with young men and women wearing badges and Mao caps, Red Guards who had outlived their political usefulness to the Chairman and were now being packed off to Hainan island in the obscure waters south towards Vietnam. We could not have belonged to more different worlds as we passed within a couple of hundred metres. Where exactly were they going and what would they find there?

It took a quarter of a century before I had the chance to find out when I too visited Hainan, by now a booming Special Economic Zone known for financial scams and sex scandals. With an introduction from a former Red Guard I was seeking out the hillside hamlet where a small group of exiles had been quartered so long ago. This little community was missing out on the 'economic miracle' of the 1990s. Most of its rubber trees, injudiciously planted on slopes too steep to water, had died, and the collection of miserable shacks and dormitories, now sub-divided for separate families, had hardly changed. There was not even TV: the power only came on for special occasions. And yet, insisted the former Red Guard, 'going down to the countryside' in this damp forest had been the happiest time of their lives.

Not only was the idea that Hainan would become one of the frontier zones of Chinese capitalism unimaginable then but so was the very notion of the doors being opened to the outside world.

During my first visit in 1971, I became friendly with our

minder from the China International Travel Service, Comrade Zhang, a young man with serious views on politics and a moody sense of humour. While we were on our travels, somewhere between the Wartime Revolutionary Base of Chairman Mao in Yan'an and the Model Agricultural Brigade at Dazhai, we heard on our shortwave radio some sensational news. A group of American ping-pong players was going to visit China at the personal invitation of Premier Zhou Enlai. This was the first hint of the diplomatic rapprochement which would bring President Nixon to Beijing less than a year later. I discussed this with Comrade Zhang in an airport waiting room. 'Just wait and see,' I teased him, 'before long Chinese ping-pong players will be going to Washington!' His face darkened abruptly. 'Never,' he swore, 'never. They may come here but we shall never go there. It is quite impossible!'

I next met Comrade Zhang sixteen years later in 1987. He was still working for the China International Travel Service but moonlighted as the editor of a popular women's magazine in North-east China for which he wrote articles about interesting topics such as the British royal family. At his request, I sent to him on my return a package of English magazines to consult, ranging from *Good Housekeeping to Cosmopolitan*, for use as 'reference material'.

Most Westerners too found it hard to imagine change in China in the 1970s. Those who were sympathetic – and it was very difficult to visit China otherwise – discovered much to admire in the apparent egalitarianism of a society committed by speech and textbook to the pursuit of socialism. We took Mao's scattered remarks on the need to tame bureaucracy and prevent the rise of privilege and corruption, transforming them into a coherent theory on the famous Transition to Socialism. How would any sort of transition in the reverse direction be plausible? This hypothesis of permanence was reinforced by the sheer weight and solidity of China, its mass of land, its size of population, and the insistence of its official voice which was convincingly echoed in the few conversations which we managed to hold. Besides, those who published forecasts of impending upheaval in

China were almost without exception notorious cold warriors or tame scholars from Taiwan. We refused to believe these tainted sources and took what we saw mostly at face value.

By 1976, on my second visit, there was a different feeling in the air. This was in April, while Mao was dying and the ultra-left faction in the leadership sought to quell an unprecedented wave of protest. In Beijing the protests in Tiananmen Square, where disillusioned ex-Red Guards wrote poems of dissent on the paving stones, had been quelled the day before we arrived.

I visited a heroic couple, the translator Yang Xianyi and his English wife Gladys Yang, in their dark apartment at the Foreign Languages Press. They had each spent four years separately in prison, accused without the slightest reason of being foreign spies, unaware of where the other was or how their children were faring. Xianyi's main regret on being arrested was that he had not thought to put on his shoes, and was wearing a pair of slippers two sizes too large for him.

Though allowed to return to work, the couple were still very vulnerable. This did not stop Xianyi from denouncing 'that woman', Madame Mao (Jiang Qing), as he drank successive glasses of Chinese spirit. 'Do shut up, old man,' Gladys remonstrated, gesturing at the phone which was no doubt bugged, 'or we'll go back to prison.' Xianyi paid no attention.

This was when I first heard about the Gang of Four, except that there was one missing: the ex-worker Wang Hongwen from Shanghai who had been rapidly promoted to the leadership was only identified later as part of the group. He was not regarded with such popular hatred as Madame Mao and her two ideological apparatchiks Zhang Chunqiao and Yao Wenyuan, also from Shanghai. Collectively they were known as the Ten-eyed Three (because two of them wore glasses). Within months they and their supporters would be mocked in cartoons and denounced as conspirators against the state.

In the late 1970s and early 1980s I travelled more widely, visiting my students (I was teaching Chinese history at the

Polytechnic of Central London at the time) in Beijing and at the provincial universities where they were undergoing language training. I began to penetrate into the countryside where the collective structure of Team, Brigade and People's Commune was being quietly dismantled. There was still political nervousness about the rural markets which had been revived after heavy restrictions in the Cultural Revolution (because they were thought to encourage capitalism). I remember vividly passing a huge open-air horse market in the dried-up bed of a river in Anhui province. The local officials looking after me refused to stop the car and let me see it.

In Beijing, I witnessed the appearance of Democracy Wall in late 1978, and its banishment a year and a half later to a small out-of-the-way park when the democracy movement was suppressed for the first time (after it had helped Deng Xiaoping to oust the immediate post-Mao leaders by attacking them in wall posters). Tiananmen Square was still a compelling reference point, full or empty. In April 1980 as I walked around the Martyrs' Memorial, a small group of demonstrators somehow emerged suddenly from across the vast square. They bore a handful of mourning wreaths to place at the foot of the Memorial, together with a portrait of a young woman. She was not an official Martyr at all. She was Zhang Zhixin, a Party member in Liaoning province who had been executed in the Cultural Revolution for remaining loyal to Mao's main rival, Head of State Liu Shaoqi. Before execution her windpipe was cut, without anaesthetic, to prevent her shouting out a last slogan of loyalty to the Party as she died. To display her portrait was still an act of bravery.

By this time Deng Xiaoping had already begun to dismantle both the structures and the values of the Maoist period but it was not yet clear how far this process would go. Many British sympathizers thought I was exaggerating when in December 1978, as the posters went up on Democracy Wall, I reported that the Cultural Revolution as a whole was about to be repudiated. We watched with particular interest, sometimes with alarm, what was happening in education and in rural organization. Maoist policies in both fields had seemed to resonate with our concerns of the 1960s and 70s. In 1980 I visited a so-called 'key school' in Beijing where the intake was selective and the pressure to achieve so great that children who flunked their exams could be expelled. My report that Beijing was abandoning comprehensive education shocked friends of China: some were also perturbed by descriptions of the – still very modest – new consumer values of post-Mao society.

In 1982 I visited Fengyang County, Anhui province, one of the poorest regions notorious in the past, and more recently in the famine years after the Great Leap Forward, as a source of migrant beggars who knocked on city doors. It had now become a model for the new experiment in transferring land-use rights and the responsibility for production (and for paying taxes) to individual households. That evening in the county hotel, I found myself the only guest – except for an 85-year-old scholar for Beijing. To my amazement he was Chen Hanseng, an expert in rural economics who was already well-known before the war for his studies of the commercialization of the Chinese countryside. (He wrote a classic account of how the British–American Tobacco Company had persuaded impoverished peasants to grow their tobacco.) Chen suffered severely from cataracts after having been deprived of medical treatment in the Cultural Revolution, but his mind was as sharp as ever. Did I believe in the Holy Trinity, he asked me, of Communist Party, local government and rural production organized jointly into the single People's Commune? I confessed that in the West many of us had idealized the communes. He replied that many Chinese leaders had done so too – and they had no excuse for it. (I would visit Professor Chen again through the years. In 1997 he celebrated his hundredth birthday, still cheerful though his memory had finally failed him, cared for by a loving sister.)

At this stage many Chinese officials still endorsed the principle of collective endeavour which they said was correct but had become hopelessly distorted in the Cultural Revolution. Within a few years, they claimed on the authority of Deng Xiaoping himself, new, more 'genuine' forms of cooperation would emerge in the countryside. This was a brief illusion. Agriculture became semi-privatized at the basic level: individual family-farmers cultivated their separate strips though the state still held title to the land. The reforms led to initial gains everywhere which continued in the more developed parts of the country. In many villages near the cities and the coast rural incomes were higher than average urban wages. But by the late 1980s the great surge in productivity had eased off in large parts of the interior. The outside world, and most urban Chinese, lost interest in what was happening in the countryside. It would take peasant riots and the massive migration to the cities in the early 1990s to remind them.

By the 1970s the Western world was discovering China as a partner with which it could do business – economic, strategic and over Hong Kong. The prospects for internal political change at the national level also seemed to be promising. Reform-minded party officials and intellectuals, under the patronage of Secretary-General Hu Yaobang – himself the protégé of Deng Xiaoping – discussed schemes for reforming the Communist Party and opening up the media. There were bouts of political reaction, as in the infamous campaign against 'spiritual pollution' in 1983 when foreign hairstyles and platform heels came under attack. Much of this could be attributed to the generation gap. Older Party officials told me how they were distressed by their grown-up children who rejected the revolutionary habit of plain living. But hardliners had more fundamental objections to the process of reform which they feared would eventually undermine the Party's rule. In the winter of 1986 a fresh wave of student protest provoked a new conservative attack on 'bourgeois liberalization': this time it won Deng Xiaoping's support. In February 1987 Hu Yaobang was dismissed, allegedly responsible for having failed to control the students. Friends in Beijing shook their heads over 'His Excellency Deng' whose political conservatism was in sad contrast to his enthusiasm for economic reform, but no one anticipated how it would end in Tiananmen Square two years later.

Western opinion, particularly among governments and business elites, had shown little concern one way or the other for political change in China until now. It was much more interested in the rapid changes in urban China which made the country much more traveller- and business-friendly. There had been no protest at the suppression of Democracy Wall and the savage sentences on Wei Jingsheng and other Chinese dissidents in 1979–81. They attracted none of the support given by Washington and its allies to their counterparts in the Soviet Union: the crucial difference was that Beijing, although ruled by a Communist Party, was ferociously hostile to the Communist leaders in Moscow. Many foreign observers had little sympathy with the ideology of student protest which was still partly based upon socialist values, or with its opposition to foreign 'exploitation' – hardly a welcome theme for Westerners eager to penetrate the new China market. Foreign diplomats swallowed the reassuring explanations given by Mr Deng's entourage: the bottom line was that 'the reforms would continue' and the market would remain open. The students were derided as 'politically naive' – good at writing poems but not much else. When they began to muster again after Hu Yaobang's death in April 1989, British diplomats reported condescendingly to the Foreign Office that this was just the latest bout in the eternal struggle of Chinese political culture between 'left' and 'right': nothing would really change.

Once again we were back in Tiananmen Square. Two weeks before the tragic climax, I followed the biggest popular march of the whole period. Perhaps a million took part, denouncing the declaration of martial law by Premier Li Peng. It was, though no one realized at the time, an unacceptable provocation to the diehard elders around Deng Xiaoping, tipping the balance against Hu's successor (and Li's rival) Zhao Ziyang, who sought a peaceful solution to the student protest. Officials at the Chinese embassy in London had exclaimed to me with great enthusiasm before I left for Beijing: 'Have you heard the news about the student demonstrations? Isn't it tremendous?' Ten years after the Beijing Massacre, the suppression of the students may seem to have been inevitable but hardly anyone expected it to happen at the time – let alone with such ferocity. We underestimated the threat posed to the regime by the true revolutionary spirit expressed in that simple yet powerful cry which I heard on the march from Beijing University: 'Long Live the People.'

Two weeks later, at two in the morning, I was retreating across the Square, in the light of a burning armoured car. The northern side which I was traversing, in front of the Forbidden City, is technically part of *Changanjie*, the Avenue of Everlasting Peace, not of the actual Square. The next day the Chinese authorities were able to assert that 'no one was killed in Tiananmen Square', and their statement was literally true. But the exact designation of a particular stretch of pavement made little difference at the time, as I made for the safety of some trees on the north-east side. The monstrous shapes of troop carriers loomed from the west and there was the sound of shots. Troops on foot then emerged from the Forbidden City and fired at random, intent on securing the whole area and driving back the mixed crowd of demonstrators and spectators. Soon the bodies of the wounded began to be carried past me. I retreated yet again.

It should really be called the Beijing Massacre rather than the Tiananmen Square Massacre – and not just to deal with the narrow topographical point made above. For the participation of the ordinary people of Beijing, the *shimin* or citizens, was the most impressive feature of the whole mass movement; yet their role has been largely overlooked. It was their quiet principled support which made this so much more than another student demonstration. Many of them middleaged, including Party members and former soldiers, the *shimin* emerged from the little lanes of Beijing to set up their barricades, outraged that the People's Army should have been sent to repress the People. This was still the spirit of the original revolution, which they believed had been betrayed by their leaders.

The trauma of 1989 was compounded for me by a brief glimpse of Chinese repression in Tibet and it transformed my approach: I was no longer interested in formulaic interviews with top officials or with textual analysis of the *People's Daily*. Beijing was a gloomy place where dispirited intellectuals, cowed by the repression, wrote 'for the desk' (i.e. themselves only) or not at all. I resolved to get out and explore the hinterland between the coast and the more exotic provinces of the far west: the central region which I called Middle China. There was a convenient North–South railway which had been completed in the 1970s, lying several hundred kilometres to the west of the familiar route from Beijing to Guangzhou. It was slow and circuitous but traversed Middle China from Henan in the north to the southern coast opposite Hainan island. On the way it traversed the uplands of the North Chinese countryside into Hubei, crossing the Yangzi below the Three Gorges, then entered the corrugated landscape of western Hunan, the province of Mao Zedong and many other famous Chinese. The railway then curved into mountainous Guangxi, passing close to an area which suffered appalling violence during the Cultural Revolution. Prosperity was only now beginning to trickle up the main lines of communication to these more remote places. From the final destination of this second North–South railway – the port of Zhanjiang – thousands of hopeful entrepreneurs crossed every month to Hainan to seek their fortune.

Travelling in the provinces of Middle China, far away from the booming coast and Westernized cities, gave a very different sort of insight. The lesson is not just that the centre is less advanced than the eastern provinces (and that the west lags even further behind). Some Western analysts have begun to see this as a threat to Chinese unity, yet the reality is more complicated. This is not pre-war China. Provinces are no longer self-contained as in the time of the 1920s warlords, or even more recently in the Cultural Revolution. We can imagine separatist movements in some of the minority regions – Tibet, Xinjiang and Inner Mongolia – which might seek independence if central rule was weakened. But the heartland of historical China, whether coastal or inland, is meshed together not only by a strong sense of cultural unity but by a rapidly expanding network of new roads, railways and trade links which cross provincial boundaries which were once barriers.

In 1992 Deng Xiaoping kickstarted the economic reform process back into life by staging his famous 'southern expedition' to the economic zones which bordered Hong Kong. Yet development is still very uneven throughout the whole of China as well as between the regions. Today those areas with substantial advantages are likely to move ahead much faster while others will make only superficial progress or may even go backwards. This lesson is beginning to be grasped in Beijing where there is, at last, real concern about the extent of localized disadvantage. Inequality may be felt between provinces, between districts, or between one county and the next – as I discovered when visiting Deng Xiaoping's birthplace in Sichuan. The rich–poor divide may be visible within the same county – or even at opposite ends of the same village. Rich peasants build villas with balconies and iron gates. Poor peasants still live in houses built of packed mud with a squat communal toilet behind a low earthern wall. Many rural towns have their new housing developments, with attractive maisonettes for officials and for managers of state-owned enterprises (which are effectively privatized). New complexes of restaurants, karaoke bars and night-clubs are built, attracting rich people to buy their services and poor people, especially women, to provide them. Outside, beggars wait with outstretched hands or deformed limbs. China is not going to split up, but life in its provinces is changing fast and unevenly, to the better for some, to the worse for others. As Deng Xiaoping said, it is meritorious to 'get rich first'. Some millions will manage to do so, but many more will stay poor to the last. They are the great unseen, unknown quantity in China's future.

These great swathes of inner uncertainty lie a long way behind the external image which China projected in the mid-1990s. The paradox is that today, when travel is relatively so easy, we may actually know less about the country than when any attempt to explore it was tightly restricted. Even the tourist itineraries on offer cover more narrow ground than in the 1980s. Today, the prime requirement is high-quality accommodation which is only available at the main attractions. (Most backpackers stick to the familiar routes too, merely trying to cover them more cheaply.) Visitors are less interested in exploring what used to be regarded as a 'different' society, though they may then be disappointed by the similarities with their own societies of the parts of China which they are shown. The Chinese naturally want to show the outside world how their country has become less 'different' too – as well as persuading the tourists to spend more time in the over-priced gift-shops.

Western (and some Chinese) academic research, often of a very high quality, does penetrate more deeply into the further reaches of society, and as a result there is far more information available in the specialized journals. But very little of this ever percolates into foreign government or media perception, and until recently not much more into official Chinese perception. It took the World Bank – which has invested more in China than anywhere else – more than a decade to recognize the dangers of the widening gap between rich and poor, and the weakness of most of the statistics on which it had relied. Beijing too only began to acknowledge these problems, and that of pervasive corruption, from the mid-1990s onwards.

When Hong Kong was returned to China on 1 July 1997, endless variations were explored around the familiar alternatives: would Hong Kong become more like China, or China more like Hong Kong? The Special Economic Zone of Shenzhen across the border provided the reference point. Did it show that China could duplicate Hong Kong's success on its own territory, or was it still defective by comparison? A new third North–South rail link running from Shenzhen through eastern China to Beijing was formally opened, creating a new axis of development. This one was a high-speed affair, covering the distance in thirty hours. The pace of urban development in China is breath-taking: huge sums are being poured into concrete, tarmac and tinted glass. The old department stores selling Chinese goods are turned into shopping malls with Western-style boutiques. Pedicabs are replaced by taxis, street food stalls by fast food outlets. Yet exploring Guangdong province in the weeks before the Hong Kong handover, not far from that same railway line, I had no difficulty in finding areas of poverty little changed from the early 1980s – as well as the new industrial towns expanding fast with overseas investment. It was also evident that a great deal of Chinese prosperity in Shenzhen and elsewhere along the eastern seaboard, which attracts most investment and provides most of China's exports, was highly dependent upon the external economic climate. If the miracle shattered elsewhere, could China's be indefinitely sustained?

I have called the story of China one of the great epics of the twentieth century: that epic is not over. Till quite recently the dynamic for transformation has been generated internally, but the country is also enmeshed now in world-wide trends which themselves are changing at an ever greater pace. In urban China a new middle class is emerging with values which are at least Asian and increasingly global. China's successes and failures have much in common with those elsewhere – including both the rapid rate of economic growth and its disastrous effect on the environment. Yet China also retains a state apparatus dominated by the Chinese Communist Party which must change, and do so radically, before very long. The mismatch between economic boldness and political timidity cannot be maintained indefinitely. New interest groups have already emerged to press for more widespread change: there is at least an embryonic civil society which is increasingly autonomous of, and indifferent to, the ruling structure. My own view is that the Party has a window of opportunity, probably a decade at the most, in which to correct this imbalance and return to the path of political reform which it abandoned in the late 1980s.

There were encouraging signs, in the spring of 1998, that a more liberal atmosphere was beginning to re-emerge in Beijing as the post-Deng Xiaoping leadership settled down. The new spirit of discussion operated within careful limits: the lessons of 1989 had been learnt on both sides. Yet critical discussion of many of the evils of the new society, including corruption, the rich–poor divide and environmental damage, began to be published more freely. Increasingly outspoken accounts of the critical episodes in the history of the Communist Party, from the 1957 Anti-rightist campaign to the Cultural Revolution – and even some controversial aspects of 1980s politics – appeared in popular magazines. Though couched in historical terms, they had obvious contemporary implications.

The economic picture was also changing. The new premier Zhu Rongji and his team grappled with a set of problems generated by the contradictions of the Asian 'economic miracle' in which China had taken the lead. (Mr Zhu was regarded as much more pragmatic than his predecessor Li Peng: the British Prime Minister Tony Blair welcomed him in March 1998 as a 'fellow-modernizer'.) China appeared relatively insulated from the immediate crisis, in part because its own financial institutions were still protected from outside speculation. But these external pressures placed a premium on the skills of the new leadership in macro-economic management. Domestic pressures were also considerable: the need to reform the state sector clashed with the risk of increasing unemployment if surplus labour was laid off. Mr Zhu also set himself the ambitious target of housing reform: the aim was to move away from public provision to make housing part of the market economy. There was a sense generally that China was embarking upon a new period of transition with many important initiatives on the agenda.

President Bill Clinton visited China at the end of June 1998: in a joint press conference with President Jiang Zemin he criticized the Beijing Massacre and urged China to respect human rights and move towards democracy. Mr Jiang's willingness to allow this debate to be televised caused great excitement, particularly among the US media where it was seen as justifying Mr Clinton's policy of 'constructive engagement' with China. Yet Mr Clinton made no effort to meet any Chinese dissidents (unlike President Bush in 1989) and even as he was travelling to Beijing, local dissidents were being harassed and prevented from talking to foreign journalists, including myself. Here too the signals of change were mixed, though pointing on the whole in a more hopeful direction. But hopes were dimmed in December 1998 when President Jiang launched a new clampdown, with heavy prison sentences for dissidents who sought to register an independent political party.

The magnitude of the tasks which China has already tackled, and of those which have still have to be confronted – however long it may take – makes the Chinese experience over the past thirty years of immense significance to us. This is not only because of the evident geopolitical and economic importance of the country and its people. In spite of its differences, China has confronted questions which are universal to the modern world. Its transition from something which called itself socialism to something which does not yet call itself capitalism raises issues of public versus private benefit, idealism against materialism, which Western societies also undergoing rapid change need to consider too. The unfinished nature of the Chinese transition, and the possibility that it will all go seriously wrong, is a shared danger. Yet if after the epic of its revolution China can find a path which has eluded the post-communist societies of Europe, and learn too from the horrendous errors of the capitalist world, that will be the start of an even greater story. On the verge of a new millennium, and after half a century of hard struggle with mixed results, China is poised between these alternatives. Either way, the consequences will affect us all.

Finally, as we contemplate these large and daunting questions, let us not forget the Chinese people as people, all 1.2 billion of them. The history of these thirty years is not just about political upheavals and economic reforms. It is about an amazingly variegated society – or perhaps a collection of societies – composed of individuals, often fascinating, sometimes maddening but almost never 'inscrutable'. In what can only be an inadequate attempt to make the point, I have concluded this selection of writings with a few sketches of just a small handful of them, and it is to the Chinese people and their future that I offer this book.

December 1998

Note: All the material in this book, with the exception of the introduction and the first chapter, originally appeared as news articles and features based upon my visits to China – nearly all of it in the Guardian. *Most of the material is reproduced without alteration, except where small changes or deletions have been made to establish a common style, e.g. in the spelling of Chinese names, to correct obvious errors which may have arisen in sub-editing or transmission, and to avoid repetition. A few longer articles have been excerpted: these are indicated in the list of sources which appears before the index. Dates given in the text at the start of an article refer to the timing of the events which it describes, not to the date when it appeared. Titles and sub-titles are also new: original titles and dates of publication are given in the list of sources.*

I thank the Far Eastern Economic Review *(Hong Kong) for kind permission to republish the articles in chapter 1, and Guardian Newspapers Ltd for kind permission to use the reports written by me whilst on the staff of the* Guardian. *The materials in question remain their copyright. I would also like to express my gratitude to Derek Davies, editor of the* Review *at the time, and to Ian Wright, foreign editor of the* Guardian *when I started writing for it, for their help and encouragement.*

The same team of friendly critics who helped me to put my last book, Real China, *into shape, has done so again with this one. My deepest thanks to Michael Simmons, Aelfthryth Gittings and Helen Lackner.*

1

Rise and Fall of the Red Guards, 1968–9

In the summer of 1966 the student Red Guards took to the streets to launch the Great Proletarian Cultural Revolution. They took everyone by surprise, including almost all of the Chinese leadership except for Mao Zedong and a small group of radical supporters. (His wife, Jiang Qing – Madame Mao – played a leading part behind the scenes, and her small cabal would eventually be labelled the Gang of Four.) Mao had been brooding over the failure of the Greap Leap Forward (1958–60) and over the rift with the Soviet Union (1963) which he accused of betraying socialism and taking the 'revisionist road'. By now in his eighties he had become wholly intolerant of criticism and could not forgive senior colleagues who had queried his zeal to push ahead with setting up the People's Communes. This had led to chaos in the countryside and famine from which millions died, and Mao was forced to accept a scaling-down of the collective system. But he still maintained that China should speed up the pace of revolutionary change, and keep advancing towards a more fully socialist society.

China had been isolated by the United States since the early 1950s. The split with the Soviet Union widened as Moscow and Washington began to seek détente, intensifying China's isolation. Both superpowers feared the potential threat of a stronger socialist China and its acquisition of nuclear weapons. Mao believed that he was developing a distinctive 'road to socialism' and that China was the only country to stand up against 'US imperialism'. After leaving Beijing and brooding for several months, he and Jiang Qing encouraged their radical supporters to denounce senior Party leaders for 'bourgeois revisionism' and 'taking the capitalist road'.

Recalling how the modern Chinese revolution had originated among the students in the early twentieth century, Mao sought to build a new revolutionary generation from China's youth. The Red Guard movement, covertly inspired by the Maoist radicals, first appeared in Beijing's universities in June 1966.

Manifestos published by the Red Guards compared Mao to the Monkey King of Chinese legend who had breathed life into a swarm of little 'monkeys' and sent them to cause 'chaos across the land'. Millions of Red Guards flocked to Beijing to take part in huge adoring rallies. They denounced their teachers for promoting elitist education: some were driven to suicide. 'Red Rebels' appeared in factories, shops, businesses and government offices and ministries. Encouraged by Mao's ultra-left supporters led by Jiang Qing and Minister of Defence Lin Biao, the rebels then targeted senior leaders with Head of State Liu Shaoqi and Party Secretary-General Deng Xiaoping at the top of the list.

By early 1967, Liu, Deng and the other 'capitalist-roaders' had been toppled and the whole apparatus of the Communist Party torn apart. The Red Guard and rebel movement split into factions, each claiming to be the true defenders of Chairman Mao. Idealism marched with opportunism. There were passionate debates on how to build a new set of socialist values: there was also vicious fighting in which the factions used weapons stolen from the army. Efforts were made to coax the students back to college and the workers back to work, but the ultra-left leaders called on the Red Guards and rebels to 'fight to the end'.

Hong Kong survived serious rioting in the summer of 1967: local radical communists gained some popular support in confronting the 'British imperialists' with street demonstrations and bombs. Sympathetic Red Guards in Beijing sacked the British diplomatic office. Very few foreigners could visit China, and then rarely outside Beijing. Those in Hong Kong trying to understand what was happening in China – the professional 'China Watchers' – searched for clues. Red Guard manifestos and newspapers were smuggled out by Chinese with relatives in Hong Kong (who could sell them for a good price). Every sentence of every editorial in the official Party newspaper, the People's Daily, *was studied and analysed. Provincial radio broadcasts were monitored and translated: they hinted at even worse troubles in the interior. Visitors returning by train from China were intercepted and quizzed at the railway station. There were clues too in Hong Kong's mainland-owned department stores. They sold revolutionary paintings and papercuts illustrating the latest political campaign. There were even children's games with images of heroic struggle.*

Finally in the summer of 1968 violence in several provinces reached a peak which persuaded Mao to intervene. Combined forces of soldiers and workers marched into schools and colleges where no classes had been taught for two years. The students were persuaded – or ordered – to go 'down to the countryside' to live indefinitely in the villages, helping the local peasants in the fields and learning what real life was like. (A smaller number of students was sent to work in factories, and a few were enlisted in the armed forces.) By April 1969, when the Communist Party held its long-delayed Ninth Party Congress, this first radical phase of the Cultural Revolution seemed to have come to an end. Yet the whole of Chinese society had been turned upside down: all the universities remained closed and thousands of intellectuals were in labour camps or undergoing 're-education'. The Party had been shattered; most officials were still suspended from work, and the armed forces – the People's Liberation Army – under Lin Biao now dominated the political scene.

The floods of violence
June 1968, Hong Kong

While Guangdong province struggles to contain the monsoon floods, which are now said to be threatening Guangzhou city itself, the swollen waters of the Pearl river have brought to Hong Kong the grim evidence of an even greater menace: the pent-up floods of bloody factionalism which have burst through the dykes in the last month. One is usually reluctant to accept at face value the lurid stories of violence in Guangdong (and in many other provinces) which find their way to Hong Kong. But the evidence of Red Guard papers, of refugees, and of the more than twenty bodies (some showing signs of violent death) which have been fished out of the waters around Hong Kong in the past week, and of a dozen more off Macao, is now overwhelming.

One report suggests that the bodies originated in some mass grave which was washed away by the rising floods. Other stories in early June spoke of large numbers of bodies floating down the Pearl River from Guangxi province (where violence has also been severe) into Guangdong. The fact that most of the bodies are bound disposes of any wishful thinking that they might be straightforward victims of a natural disaster.

There is abundant evidence of serious factional fighting in Guangzhou and – perhaps more alarming – of disorder in the countryside. But the most ominous indicator of bad trouble may be found in the desperate appeals of Guangdong Radio for people to pull their weight in fighting the rising floods. It is one thing for peasants to slacken their efforts in the normal work of farming, but it is much more disturbing when they fail to rally round in the face of a common emergency. On 25 June, the Guangdong Anti-Flood Headquarters complained that in some places 'insufficient importance has been attached to the flood situation, the ideology of paralysis and dependence on luck still exists, and no practical or effective steps have been taken.' And a week before, the *Southern Daily* commentator condemned those 'class enemies' who 'hide in obscure corners to make trouble, create trouble in water-conservancy projects, incite struggle by force, steal equipment and material for fighting floods, and sabotage the structure of water-conservancy'.

It appears that some villagers are quite prepared to build their own dykes, but will no longer give a helping hand to their neighbours – at least, according to one report, not unless they are given more 'work-points'. Since the essence of flood-fighting is mutual aid – saving the next village upstream in order to protect one's own fields – this lack of solidarity could prove disastrous.

Perhaps the most important cause of slackness in the countryside is the lack of firm leadership by Party cadres, who no longer dare risk criticism by acting decisively. Deprived of proper leadership, the peasants seem to have simply let things slide. Old inter-clan and inter-village rivalries (the two are often synonymous, since many villages are still monopolized by one family surname) have also surfaced in the laxer discipline now prevailing. There have been references to the emergence of 'historical disputes' between production teams, and to the 'feudalist clan concept'.

Meanwhile back in Guangzhou, the gang warfare between the two major Red Guard factions, the 'Red Flags' and 'East Winds', each almost indistinguishable from the other in terms of policy and seemingly only concerned with a struggle for influence on the Revolutionary Committees, has flared up since the end of May. On 22 May, the East Winders bombed a meeting of the Red Flags; many were killed while the People's Liberation Army and Workers' Provost Corps 'stood idly by'. In the next few days, the East Wind kept the initiative, kidnapping or beating up isolated Red Flag members, and attacking their premises.

The Red Flag hit back in a major battle at Zhongshan University which lasted from noon on 3 June to the following day. The Red Flag students used two machine-guns which had earlier been stolen from the PLA. The East Wind students retaliated by showering their enemy with home-made phosphorus incendiary bombs. A number of students were killed and several university buildings were set on fire. One Red Guard pamphlet carries the text of a desperate telegram to Chairman Mao, despatched on 5 June by the beleaguered East Winders who were trapped in the building.

'Now they are laying a big number of mines at the foot of the building and setting fire to the building … In the gymnasium of the university lie our fighters who have been seriously wounded and are dying … Chairman Mao, oh, Chairman Mao, our fighters ask you to save them!'

What is the basic explanation for the crisis in Guangdong? The floods are an unfortunate 'natural disaster', but the difficulties now experienced in coping with them suggest a major erosion of social discipline and cohesion in the past year with – Mao's instructions notwithstanding – 'self-interest' on the ascendant over 'selflessness'. The factional fighting, however, stems directly from the green (or rather

red) light given by Beijing in recent months to 'mass
activism'. As reports of serious trouble in other parts of
China begin to come in, one can only hope that the central
leadership will be quicker than it was last year (1967) to
revert to moderation and stem the floods while there is still
time.

Red Guard ideology
June 1968, Hong Kong

While the Chinese claim that the 'student power' movements throughout the world have been inspired by the Great
Proletarian Cultural Revolution, the sterile arguments of
most of China's Red Guards have little in common with the
imaginative ideals of the students in the Sorbonne. But a few
heretical organizations in China – now officially denounced
by Beijing – do share the same spirit of iconoclastic rebellion.
An analysis of the documents produced by one such
organization, the Shengwulian of Hunan province, suggests
that they may be the real inheritors of Mao Zedong's own
rebellious youth.

What kind of society does the Shengwulian actually
envisage for its brave new China? It takes as its text Mao
Zedong's directive of 7 May 1966, which was the first – and
also by far the most revolutionary – of all the directives which
have since appeared under his name. The essence of this
directive is that there should be no specialization or ex-
clusivity in fields of work; soldiers should also learn politics,
engage in agriculture and run factories; workers, peasants
and students should also diversify their activities, and so
should those working in commerce, service trades, Party and
government. Of course the workers should still work, and the
peasants should still produce – that is their 'primary task'. But
by assuming secondary tasks outside their own field, they
would break down the barriers between town and country,
and between intellectuals and the workers. Everyone should
be developed in 'an all-round way' to become 'a new
communist person with proletarian political consciousness'.

This directive has had a somewhat chequered career.

Although issued in May 1966, it was not publicly revealed until August, and there is little indication that much effort has ever been made to carry it out, except for the basic provisions that everyone should 'study politics'. The first anniversary of the directive was celebrated in a *People's Daily* editorial in 1967, which discussed its revolutionary provisions at some length. But the *Liberation Army Daily*, which greeted its second anniversary last month, completely ignored the theme of diversification of employment, while concentrating solely on the need for universal Mao-study.

The visionary idealism expressed in the 7 May directive has a close affinity with the same spirit which pervaded the early months of the people's communes movement during the Great Leap Forward, and it is not surprising that the Shengwulian should claim that the ultimate goal of the Cultural Revolution is the creation of a 'People's Commune of China'. It is quite possible that Mao had some idea, at the start of the Cultural Revolution, of recreating on the political scene the same commune model which he had inspired in the countryside during the Great Leap, and the example of the Paris Commune was cited with approval in the 16-Point Decision of the August 1966 Central Committee Plenum [which launched the Cultural Revolution].

But in February 1967, when the Shanghai revolutionaries announced the formation of the 'Shanghai Commune', the concept was criticized by Mao himself and soon replaced by the now-standard Revolutionary Committee. Presumably the commune model, with its implied acceptance of mass democracy from below (the 16-Point Decision actually provided that elected officials could be 'recalled by the masses' if they proved incompetent), was felt to be fraught with dangerous implications.

Some of these implications have been spelt out by the Shengwulian students. To bring about the People's Commune of China, they argue, the existing Communist Party must undergo 'revolutionary changes' – and here they frankly concede that the forthcoming Ninth Party Congress (eventually held in April 1969) will not change anything. The reconstituted Party which will emerge at that Congress 'will necessarily be a party of bourgeois reformism that serves the bourgeois usurpers in the revolutionary committees'. The Shengwulian also argues that in the new society of the Paris Commune type the entire class of the bureaucrats 'including 90 per cent of the senior cadres' should be overthrown. This argument runs directly counter to the official view that 90 per cent of the cadres should be rehabilitated.

The Shengwulian is too ultra-revolutionary even for the most radical members of the Cultural Revolution Group in Beijing, but it is from this radical element that the organization seems to draw its inspiration. The Shengwulian claims that a speech by Jiang Qing (Madame Mao) of 12 November 1967 gave them the green light by indicating that a 'new stage' of the Cultural Revolution had begun, and that a directive by Mao's chosen successor Lin Biao on the Hunan question of 24 October confirmed that 'Hunan is the vanguard area of revolutionary struggle of the whole country.' Neither of these claims appear to be justified, but the fact that they are made underlines the confusion which is caused by the proliferation of loosely worded directives from the 'Centre' in Beijing.

The Shengwulian has been denounced as an organization of 'hoodwinked' students who are manipulated by 'capitalist-roaders' for their own evil purposes. But while there may be an element of trouble-making involved, one cannot fail to be impressed by the mood of genuine – if misplaced – idealism which pervades their writings.

In their insistence on the need to smash the old authoritarian society, and to replace it with a new egalitarian system, the students of the Shengwulian have much more in common with the rebellious European students (now so loudly praised in the Chinese press) than do the orthodox and officially approved Red Guards. Like their counterparts in France and elsewhere, they are better at analysing the failures of the past than at predicting successful tactics for the future. They say they are opposed to the 'infantile Leftist' belief that victory can be achieved at one fell swoop; they are equally opposed to the argument that China must now wait for a 'second Cultural Revolution', and accept for the time being the limited gains of the first. They argue instead – claiming that this is Mao's strategy – in favour of a process of permanent revolution, progressing by graduated stages towards their long-term goal: the overthrow of the Revolutionary Committee and the birth of the 'People's Commune of China'.

One should not be carried away by the fine rhetorical style and penetrating criticisms of the Shengwulian. Their policy of continuous revolution would almost certainly prove disastrous for China, exacerbating beyond repair the fissures in its society which have already been exposed by the Cultural Revolution. But it is one of the paradoxes of the Cultural Revolution that these students from Hunan – anathematized by the central leaders who claim to speak for Mao – may well be the real inheritors of the spirit of iconoclastic rebellion which inspired the most famous Hunanese of them all, Chairman Mao himself, to lead the Chinese revolution to victory.

Stifling the students
August 1968

'You have let me down,' said Mao. 'And, what is more, you have disappointed the workers, peasants and armymen of China.' With tears in his eyes (according to one version of the story), Mao harangued a specially convened meeting of the five top student leaders in Beijing with bitter complaints at their failure and at their persistent factional fighting. They had struggled (against Liu Shaoqi and other capitalist-roaders in the leadership), they had criticized (other Party leaders and cadres), but they had not even begun the final stage of the struggle–criticism–transformation (of themselves and society) formula. There were only two solutions: either the student factions should be physically separated, each occupying its own college or school, or they should submit to military control.

Mao's interview with the student leaders was on 28 July, three days before China's Army Day was celebrated with strong demonstrations of support for the PLA. And whether or not he actually had tears in his eyes, he certainly had good reason to. During July, the excesses of the Red Guards and 'proletarian revolutionaries' had inspired a series of increasingly tough directives from Beijing – or 'battle calls' as the *Sichuan Daily* of 12 August described them. Each was concerned with a particular situation; the 3 July directive calling on the Guangxi factions to stop paralysing railway traffic, the 18 July directive in response to persistent fighting in south Zhejiang, and the 24 July directive calling for a return to law and order in Xi'an (Shaanxi province), among others.

The use of teams of workers, peasants and/or soldiers to move physically into colleges and schools and sort out the recalcitrant students has become widespread. The first such team of workers and peasants entered Beijing's Qinghua University immediately after Mao's 28 July interview with the five student leaders. The campus was then surrounded by soldiers, and a long silence ensued, to be broken ten days later by Mao's famous gift of mangoes* to the team, signifying his assent for its action.

Meanwhile attempts are again being made to dissolve unwanted Red Guard organizations, to prevent students roaming around the country on the pretext of doing 'liaison work', and to pack them off to the countryside on 'permanent assignment' to practise integration with the workers and peasants. In a number of cases they have been described as 'high school graduates of 1966' (students who left school at the start of the Cultural Revolution and have been unemployed ever since). One of the by-products of the Cultural Revolution was the return of earlier generations of students from the countryside, claiming that they had been victimized and maltreated, and that the whole policy which had sent them into exile was a wicked plot of Liu Shaoqi.

There is a pronounced anti-intellectual tone in some of the latest criticisms of the once-idolized student. 'We would like to advise those college students,' said the *People's Daily* in an editorial note of 22 July, 'who look down on the workers and peasants and think themselves great, to throw off their conceited airs.'

---

*A present to him from a visiting delegation from Pakistan.

Lessons of the Cultural Revolution
February 1969, Hong Kong

Neither sweet nor sour, the picture of the Chinese people which has now emerged from the Cultural Revolution assumes for the first time since 1949 something of a three-dimensional character. The mixture of idealism and opportunism which it has revealed, the remarkable variety of regional, cultural and occupational differences, the wide range of human activities and emotions, all add up to a much more complex picture which resists pigeon-holing to the last. It has taken the Cultural Revolution, in short, to make the world in general realize that the Chinese people, 'even under communism', are human beings. Not only do the Chinese make love, play cards and have to cope with the problem of 'unemployed youths', they are also more than ready to indulge in passionate argument over the future of their society, and to question the very foundations of the bureaucratic rule on which it is built.

The phenomenon of the generation gap is as real for China as for the other parts of the world where it has also led to revolutions of a less violent but equally profound character in contemporary society. Mao foresaw the problem, even if the Cultural Revolution has been unable to solve it. Two decades after China's liberation, the middle-aged leaders had become old, the young enthusiasts had become bureaucrats, and the infants had become youths with a mere second-hand knowledge of the revolutionary past.

'Of the workers of Guangzhou, the best are seamen,' said Premier Zhou Enlai in one of his speeches to the Red Guards, adding with a touch of nostalgia, 'You who are in your twenties of course do not know the glorious tradition of the seamen of Guangzhou.' And of course he was right.

In human terms, the generation of the revolution had almost played itself out by the time of the Cultural Revolution, and this was just as true in terms of policy. The conventional approach to economic development, which had begun on orthodox lines – a hybrid import both from the modernized West and the modernizing socialist bloc – had proved inadequate for China's purposes, and Mao's attempt to find a different path along the revolutionary lines of the Great Leap Forward had also petered out. In foreign policy as well, both the conventional approach (China's 'people's diplomacy' of the mid-1950s) and the revolutionary alternative (the deliberate break with the Soviet Union) had ceased to pay dividends. But China's domestic social superstructure was still very much at the conventional stage, with a well-defined bureaucratic hierarchy imposing an intricate system of control and response upon the 'broad masses' of the population – again a hybrid mixture, although this time from the traditional Chinese as well as from the 'socialist' matrix of political culture.

The Cultural Revolution has accentuated, rather than alleviated, the conflicts of interest which exist in any society, but had previously been kept in check by the appearance and sometimes the reality of monolithic party power. One of the most striking features of the Red Guard and rebel movement was the speed with which it fragmented into distinct and identifiable interest groups, each with concrete grievances or ambitions of its own. In most places the movement could be roughly divided into the 'Left' and 'Right' wings (although both claimed to be dead centre in the Maoist mainstream of the revolution). The ranks of the 'Left' would typically include casual or temporary workers, students with poor job prospects (who had graduated with low marks), civilian draftees to the countryside, unskilled or semi-skilled factory workers, and disgruntled low-level party cadres. The 'Right' would embrace those with a larger stake in the status quo; better-paid workers in fixed employment (enjoying social security benefits), well-qualified students with good careers ahead of them, more senior party cadres and their children, and reasonably well-off peasants. The forced migration of millions of rebels to the countryside must have shattered their organizations (although some clandestine networks may still be maintained) but it can hardly have wiped their minds clean of the demands and complaints which were so vocally expressed in the past two years.

As with the rebels, so with the Party, Government and

armed forces, none of which can fail to have become much more conscious of the internal stresses and strains within their own ranks during the Cultural Revolution. The Party bureaucracy functioned in the past according to well-defined rules of the game, even if they were not necessarily those enshrined in the Party constitution. Promotion, demotion, career prospects, the routing of paper work, the channelling of decisions, all were mechanisms whose operation was clearly understood by those on the inside. But can they be so sure any longer after three years in which the Party and Government have been pulled apart and put together again (and how do they know they are still on the inside)?

Confidence has also been shaken in the ability of the Party organization to act as a closed forum at which conflicts of interest can be reconciled while maintaining the customary facade of unity. The Cultural Revolution has created a new precedent: the use of the mass media and of extra-Party political lobbies to conduct policy debates. The most famous lobby of them all was the Red Guard and rebel movement, and its various factions were often manipulated (and financed) by rival political pressures. Although the factions have been dissolved, the political pressure group has become an apparently irremovable fixture.

In one province after another, complaints have been voiced about the failure of the new Revolutionary Committees to maintain unity. Individual members go behind one another's backs and drum up support outside the committee, instead of laying all their cards on the table. Some people are 'proud of their ingenuity in devising ways whereby to avoid carrying out central instructions. They have formulated their own regulations . . . they have excluded people who do not agree with them . . .' The provincial committee in Guangdong recently admitted that 'it was no surprise that differences of opinion arose among members of the Revolutionary Committee', and its members pledged themselves to oppose the tendency of 'each going his own way'.

The army is also no longer so sure of its own terms of

reference. Gone are the simple days when its place in the political system was clearly defined, an executor but never a initiator of policies, a political 'model' which was a symbol rather than an actual vehicle of the Thought of Mao Zedong. Once the model was put into actual practice, it soon became tarnished by daily involvement in the rough and tumble of the Cultural Revolution.

All these manifestations of dissent and contradictions – in the Party, the Government apparatus (or at the moment the Revolutionary Committees) and the army, plus the repressed but as yet unsatisfied grievances of the 'rebels' – can be explained in terms of the 'Left' against the 'Right', or the 'radicals' versus the 'moderates'. But the picture which this conjures up of a grand military exercise, conducted across a nationwide battlefield, is much too neat and superficial and it is very doubtful whether those actually in the field can define their own positions so precisely. The Cultural Revolution has certainly brought the factions into being, but it has also breathed life into ideas and aspirations which had lain dormant for the many years of comparative peace which preceded it.

Scarcely a single commune or factory floor in the whole nation can have passed through the Cultural Revolution without its perspective on the rest of society being radically altered. This does not necessarily mean that the violence of the last two years will erupt again, or even that the Cultural Revolution, in its present form, will not lapse into a prolonged lull. It may take another decade or more before the problems of China's future course arise again in such an acute form – perhaps now that the rigid structure of the pre-Cultural Revolution society has been broken apart, the necessary changes may even occur gradually and without any major upheaval. But like many other countries, and for some of the same reasons, China is in a state of transition whose ultimate direction may only become clear to the future historian at the distance of many decades. The Cultural Revolution, whatever else it has failed to do, has broken the ice.

A dissident tune
June 1969, Hong Kong

Shops selling Chinese goods in Hong Kong recently carried an attractive line in Yu Ping bamboo flutes from Guizhou province. Each is inscribed, in traditional manner, with a poem in classical style, but the message is highly contemporary.

The poem which has attracted most attention is by China's most famous writer of the twentieth century, Lu Xun. Itself modelled on a Tang dynasty poem, it laments the Japanese occupation of Manchuria and the threat to Beijing – the ancient 'city of culture'.

> *The people of culture have ridden away with the culture;*
> *Here there is only an empty 'city of culture'.*
> *Once the culture has gone it will never return.*
> *The Ancient City is left forlorn for a thousand years.*
> *Special trains are drawn up in ranks at the Qianmen station.*
> *University students are in trouble again and again.*
> *When they arrive at Shanhaiguan at sunset, how can the students resist?*
> *At the big celebration rallies no one sees the danger.*

Without changing the original, the sense can easily be adapted to present events. The 'people of culture' are the young intellectual standard-bearers of the Cultural Revolution. They have boarded their trains at Qianmen station in Beijing on their way to re-educate themselves in the countryside. Meanwhile the masses are celebrating the victory of the Cultural Revolution, but it is a hollow victory.

Other flutes recently on sale (they have now been withdrawn) carry similar classical couplets or complete poems on the familar theme of the exile's lament: 'Who can see my silent weeping in the darkness?' But one flute is much more ambiguous, for its poem (also by Lu Xun) was singled out by Mao himself in his 1942 Yan'an speech on literature and art as a praiseworthy example for 'intellectuals who want to integrate themselves with the masses'. 'I bow my head,' wrote

Lu Xun, 'and like a willing ox I serve the children.' Perhaps this eminently acceptable sentiment was used by the anonymous calligraphists of Guizhou to cover up for their more critical efforts.

The reaction of the China Watchers in Hong Kong has been as fascinating as the flutes themselves. Authentic examples, originally purchased for a few Hong Kong dollars, are now being offered second-hand for as much as US$20. (No doubt the fakes will soon be on the market.) Lu Xun's 'willing ox' may fetch slightly less, but his 'Qianmen station' is already a collector's item. European China Watchers puzzle over the cursive script in which the poems are inscribed; unaware of its origins, some have interpreted Lu Xun's 'willing ox' as an 'anti-Mao poem'.

The Hong Kong Chinese anti-communist press has plunged into scholarly fray, with all the zeal of a classical historiographer. Were the flutes inscribed by loyal Maoist Red Guards, protesting that the Cultural Revolution had been betrayed? Or, as one right-wing account would have it, are they the product of a working-class flautists' atelier in Guizhou, condemning not just the Cultural Revolution but the whole two decades of Communist rule? One writer regards the flutes as conclusive proof of an imminent collapse on the mainland. All that the flautists are waiting for is for Taiwan to launch the invasion.

2

Mao Zedong's Last Years, 1971–6

The Cultural Revolution had abated by 1971, and select groups of foreigners were allowed to visit on 'study tours'. Our party from the Society for Anglo-Chinese Understanding crossed the railway bridge from Hong Kong by foot, and sank into huge armchairs on the Chinese side to be greeted by our earnest guides. A new society, we were told, was being built in which peasants and workers would go to college, and college students tackle real life in the factories and fields. After supper in the empty dining rooms of gloomy hotels we were shown films of the Revolutionary Operas devised by Madame Mao (Jiang Qing).

We visited schools, factories and people's communes, listened patiently to lengthy 'brief introductions' and took copious notes. Sometimes our hosts seemed nervous: they waved Mao's Little Red Book *uneasily and exchanged glances if our questions were too searching. More often there seemed to be a real sense of enthusiasm, especially among youth and in particular among young women who in their confidence seemed to justify the slogan that 'women hold up half the sky'. We made allowances for the more dogmatic statements, and laughed at the more absurd examples of the cult of Mao – but not out loud.*

Other foreign visitors came back impressed by the spirit of commitment. After the February 1972 visit of President Nixon ended China's diplomatic isolation, they included Americans: even passionate anti-communists found something to admire. Returning home, we followed closely the theoretical debates in the Chinese press. Should those who worked harder get more for their efforts? (The answer was yes, but not too much more.) How much should the peasants consume, and how much should be put aside for investment? How fast should the level of ownership be raised to a higher degree of collective organization?

Though the Red Guards had been packed off to the countryside in 1968, there were outbursts from militant workers who denounced the return of the bureaucrats, and from students who criticized the revival of formal education. Some of this was genuine, but extremist views were encouraged covertly by the ultra-left leadership. Madame Mao and her followers waged a vicious propaganda war against Premier Zhou Enlai, masked as an attack on the ancient philosopher Confucius. By this time, Deng Xiaoping, the number two target of the Red Guards in 1966–7, had been brought back into the leadership. He was regarded by the radicals, with good reason, as a moderate reformer who supported Zhou's efforts to tone down the political struggle and give first place to economic priorities. Deng, pugnacious by nature, soon clashed with the ultra-left, denouncing their lack of competence and empty rhetoric. When Zhou died in January 1976, the scene was set for the final leadership struggle.

The atmosphere in Beijing in April was extremely tense. I arrived with a group of British sinologists on the day after a vast and completely unexpected demonstration in Tiananmen Square had been broken up. The crowd were mourning Premier Zhou who was popular both in his own right and as a symbol of moderation. They laid wreaths, recited poems and chalked slogans on the pavement denouncing 'evil demons' in the leadership – the ultra-leftists now manoeuvring for power as Mao too lay dying. There were scuffles and fighting: a police station was set on fire. The feuding leaders watched the demonstration through binoculars from the Great Hall of the People at one side of the square. Mao was persuaded by the ultra-left to approve the dismissal of Deng Xiaoping, while the sycophantic Hua Guofeng took over as acting Premier. An official counter-demonstration was organized hailing Deng's dismissal and Hua's elevation as a triumph: everyone who took part looked miserable in the spring sunshine.

I borrowed a bike and enjoyed my first exploration of Beijing's back alleys. But I also talked to survivors from the dark side of the Cultural Revolution, and began to understand how the 'masses' had been manipulated for the sake of a vicious power struggle, and how far the vision of a new society was flawed. Events now moved rapidly: Mao died in September, the Gang of Four was arrested a month later, and its closest followers were soon rounded up.

Vision of a new society
April 1971, Beijing – Shanghai – Guangzhou

Schools in revolution

'The world is yours as well as ours,' Chairman Mao told the youth of China in a quotation which became famous during the Cultural Revolution, 'but in the last analysis, it is yours.' And the Cultural Revolution itself must, in the last analysis, be judged by the effect it has had upon the country's education system and upon those to whom the future of China belongs. It is not just a demographic fact that the youth of China outnumber the adults. They are literally everywhere, marching to the fields to do labour or camping exercises, practising gymnastics in the parks, chanting quotations from Chairman Mao at well-known beauty spots (especially if foreigners are around), or standing at street corners to recite road safety slogans.

Of course children in China also do many of the more mundane and unpolitical things which we expect them to do, like skipping and playing tag, but we cannot take refuge in the comforting cliché that children are the same all over the world. These kids are different, and the Cultural Revolution has made them more different. One reason why they are different is that they are taught from the age of seven when they enter primary school that 'learning is not everything' – learning, that is, in the classroom.

At a primary school in Nanjing, the school workshop was turning out oil filters and other car fittings, and the fifth-grade twelve-year-olds spent four weeks a year in these workshops and two more in the countryside. At a 'middle' or secondary school in Beijing, the children spent two months in the year at local factories or in the fields. At a teachers' training college in Canton, the students assembled oscilloscopes and radios, grew experimental rice, and planted sugar cane on waste land. At Qinghua University in Beijing, they turned out trucks, producing most of the parts, engine and suspension included, on the spot. Not all of this work has a vocational purpose. Some of it, especially at the primary school where the children were working punches and stamps in a primitive assembly line, was repetitive and dull. The purpose is not so much to teach a trade as to bring the children to understand that manual work is not degrading and that they should not complain if that is their lot in the future. The goals are explicitly stated: to eliminate the difference between countryside and factory, between workshop and office, and also (by means of military-type exercises) between the army and the people.

This area of productive work is where the biggest changes have taken place since the Cultural Revolution. The content of formal tuition in the schools has changed much less. Chinese language and mathematics are the main subjects, although English is taught in the middle school and experimentally in the top classes of some primary schools. There is a daily session for Mao-study but politics in general only takes three or four periods a week. With large classes of forty to fifty and a tradition of collective learning by rota, teaching methods in the classroom may strike the British visitor, brought up to believe in self-expression, as excessively formal, although a French or German visitor would, perhaps, be more at home. Mao once advised children to fall asleep in class if they were bored by their teachers, but none of those whom I saw would have had a chance. On the other hand, there were student representatives on the revolutionary committee which runs the middle school in Peking speaking up quite freely alongside their teachers.

Discipline seems to be more a matter of group criticism than of punishment. On the walls of each classroom, the children pin their own 'small self-criticisms'. 'At a time when the situation is unprecedentedly good at home and abroad,' said one of these, 'I still fool around in class and I don't run out fast enough for exercise in the play-ground. I must learn from the Liberation Army and improve my working style.' But apart from the productive work there has also been a major change in the length of the school curriculum, now reduced from a total of twelve to nine years, although the new system is still described as 'experimental'. After years of primary school and four years of middle school (although not everyone in the countryside gets even that far) the children become workers – or peasants, or soldiers. Only after two or three years of practical work can those who wish to apply for further education. Their applications must first be approved by their work-mates, and if they go on to college, they are most likely to go back to their place of work after graduation. Under the new system there is even less room for competitiveness and ambitions of 'having a career' than in the past.

We were told that formal examinations, criticized by Mao because they were like 'ambushes' on the student, had been replaced by open-book tests and discussions between students and staff. There was no grading either – 'All read the same standard and none fall behind.' This cannot literally be true, but it does suggest a system where collective study has won over the competitive instinct. Job direction and partici-pation in labour was a feature of Chinese education before the Cultural Revolution, but the new changes have made it more comprehensive, taking in the small minority of bright students who used to go straight from middle school to college without shifting so much as a single load of night soil in between. To compare it with our own system is beside the point. A more relevant comparison can be made with those Third World countries which allow their intellectuals to choose their subjects and withhold their labour, and have in consequence a surplus of unemployable arts graduates while those whose skills are needed emigrate to the United States.

What happens if the Chinese system is allowed to lapse was vividly illustrated during the Cultural Revolution. It is not so much the violence which upsets the Chinese who spoke to us about the Red Guards' movement as its lack of discipline, and the competition which developed between rival factions. The actual fighting, they insisted at Qinghua University, had been much exaggerated. Only 300 students out of 10,000 physically took part. And it lasted only for 100 days. Only two or three were actually killed, they said, laughing hilariously. (The truth may lie somewhere between this bland version and the lurid Red Guard reports of the time.) What was unforgivable was the factionalism. Even after the workers and soldiers were sent by Mao to sort out the university (5,000 came in at the start), the students would kick each other under the table while shaking hands over it.

Higher education is still being sorted out. The Cultural Revolution began in the universities and many leading officials – some of whom are now under criticism – were actively involved in the factional ups and downs. One feels a certain political edginess about the way in which institutions like Qinghua University are put on show for the visitor, with a tendency to stick to interminable set speeches which can be very off-putting. There is, perhaps, a danger that this area of education will be retarded for some time to come by an over-dogmatic and fussy approach to getting it politically right.

Yet the innovations are impressive enough in the class-rooms and workshops. Here, the value of productive work is vocational: students of architecture work on construction sites. (The 'reactionary theory of the big roof', which meant that traditional ceramic-tiled roofs were put on top of otherwise modern buildings, is especially criticized.) The School of Water Conservancy goes to work on a dam: engineering students learn how to make machine tools, and so on. Even when the universities are fully open, the staff–student ratio will be exceptionally high – at one to four in Qinghua University, plus the worker technicians who teach practical skills.

But it is the sense of a collective spirit which is, perhaps, most impressive in education as it is in the rest of Chinese life. And the Thought of Mao Zedong, itself a rather off-putting concept for eclectically minded visiting Western intellectuals, begins to make sense as the cement which holds the whole system together. It is not so much a cult of personality but more a collective way of life, which provides the moral imperatives for the youth of China who will inherit Mao's revolution.

The pace of daily life
One of the most striking features of Communist China today, and yet perhaps the hardest to communicate to people outside, is the relaxed – almost leisurely – pace at which the

country lives. It is only in propaganda films that the Chinese peasants work flat out. In real life, with a working day which starts in the busy season at 5 a.m. and ends only at sunset, the pace is rhythmic but slow. The great set piece scenes of thousands of peasants working side by side, red flags flying, and Mao-posters planted in the ground, are rarely to be seen. Usually they operate in small groups, often just singly, seeming almost immobile to the passer-by, as if they have grown roots.

In the factories the tempo of work is generally faster, but it varies according to the degree of mechanization. It is not uncommon to see a fully automated process established next to one which is still entirely labour-intensive. At a fertilizer plant near Nanjing, completely rebuilt since the liberation, nitrates were sent on their way by conveyor belts and fork-lift trucks, while the phosphates were still being moved by wheelbarrow. Vast steel and concrete girders are trundled on hand-carts through the city streets from the factory to the construction site. A lorry might be quicker, but it might be bringing fresh vegetables to the market. The dividing line between industry and agriculture is blurred, just as the local commune cultivates its fields right up to the factory wall.

The atmosphere also seems relaxed because, on the whole, life is quite good these days. The shops are full of basic consumer products, from children's toys to spare parts for bicycles, not only in the city centres but in the back streets, the workers' settlements and the communes. I saw only one queue here in nearly a month in China. The contrast with the Soviet Union, where shopping queues provide everyday evidence that many goods are in short supply. was remarkable. Most shops are open from 9 a.m. until 9 p.m., seven days a week. Local factories take their working day off in rotation, so that the demand is spread evenly. The only goods subject to rationing are grain and cotton. The grain ration, at nearly 41 lb a month for the non-manual worker and more for the heavy worker, seems adequate. The cotton ration is tighter, but it can be extended by buying synthetics or wool. In Shaanxi province, where temperatures were still wintry, everyone was warmly clothed. There were, to state the obvious, no rags in China (and very few flies, either).

Comparing wages and prices is a complicated business but as far as I could tell, an ordinary family with two wage earners, each receiving a minimum rate of forty *yuan* a month, can get by adequately on a daily diet which should include some fish or cheaper cuts of meat. Higher wage earners – sixty *yuan* is the average – are likely to have money to spare. Factories, housing estates and even Government offices will have their own kindergartens where working mothers can leave their children. Rents are cheap – no more than forty *yuan* a month for a two-room flat. Standards vary considerably in the towns, from modern estates which include schools and shops to higgledy-piggledy timber-frame or mud-wall housing. But slums would be too strong a word for the lower standard accommodation, since the majority have light and water laid on, and – of great importance in a rainy climate – a pavement outside.

Standards of health, diet and clothing seemed only slightly lower in the country than in the town. Housing was perhaps in advance with more land to build on and cheap materials (mostly mud brick) and labour available. Health facilities have greatly improved, with clinics at the brigade level where semi-trained 'barefoot doctors' can treat common ailments, give inoculations and teach hygiene. The tell-tale signs of rural poverty – skin diseases, cataracts and rickety children – were almost non-existent.

Street scenes in China are conventionally described by some Western visitors as 'drab', just as the uniform clothing of baggy trousers, tunic and cap attract the epithet 'sexless'. Certainly the streets are dimly lit, but the natural colour comes from the movement of thousands of people on foot or on bicycle, ebbing and flowing in a leisurely but purposeful way. Vehicular traffic is limited to buses and trolleys, which provide fast and cheap services to the suburbs, some lorries and a handful of official cars with chaste lace curtains in their windows – a curious vestige of the old bureaucracy. As for 'sexless', I must say at the risk of sounding incorrigibly bourgeois, that it is simply not true. With no ornaments except a couple of ribbons to tie on their pigtails, the Chinese girls command attention, and the most stunning of all are those in army uniform. It is not just a question of looks, but of the self-confident and 'liberated' way in which they handle their work, whether they are bus conductresses or air hostesses.

During the Cultural Revolution, or even a year ago, everyday life in China might have appeared to be a good deal more 'tense', to use a favourite Chinese word. But it is a measure of the success with which the revolution has been tempered by practice that the atmosphere now seems so relaxed. Perhaps the very blandness of the atmosphere has an anaesthetizing effect upon the interpersonal relationships which we value so highly in the West, and the high and low emotional peaks may, for most people, have been ironed out by the Cultural Revolution. But these may be luxuries in a collective society; it seems to be a good working atmosphere for a society which must live by its work.

Workers' control in Shanghai

Before the Cultural Revolution, the organizational system in, for example, a factory, looked rather like an inverted pyramid. The management and the Communist Party Committee occupied the two top corners, bearing down on the lowest point where the workers were represented by their trade union. Today the new system centres upon the Revolutionary Committee, a group which contains representatives from the army and Party, from the old management, and from the workers' mass organizations which have replaced the unions. The Party Committee is still the ultimate authority, but most of the management offices such as Production and Welfare are run directly by the Revolutionary Committee. A typical Committee in a fertilizer factory near Nanjing had a total of twenty-seven members, seventeen of whom were workers, seven officials and three from the Army.

One hardly ever came across the kind of nervous bureaucratic fuss usually to be expected when the management brings visitors to the shop floor. The workers carried on unhurriedly with what they were doing, or chipped in with information if it seemed to be needed. And it was painfully obvious on the one occasion where the system was working badly. At a machine tool factory in Shanghai, there was much edgy laughter and harrying of visitors who stepped a few feet off the guided track, with cries of 'Let's go, we are late'. The plant is supposed to be a showcase for the policy of transforming factory floor workers into technicians, but in some shops there were idle machines and workers who did their jobs in sullen slow motion. Posters on the wall denounced the management and Party for bureaucracy, and the leaders of the Revolutionary Committee criticized themselves in front of their visitors. 'If we think we are better than the masses,' they said nervously, 'that is a remnant of [disgraced former Head of State] Liu Shaoqi's revisionism.' As the Chinese would say, this factory still has 'big problems'.

Peasant power in Dazhai

New productive forces, it is claimed, have emerged in China which can move mountains like the foolish old man in the legend made famous by Mao. Most of the mountains are being moved, as they always have been before, on the back of the Chinese peasant with his carrying pole and two buckets. The showpiece communes like Dazhai [brigade] in Shanxi province, where whole ravines have been levelled and mountainsides terraced, are impressive enough. But the point is really driven home by the casual glimpses which one gets from the back of a bus or the window of a train, of feats of labour so commonplace that the guides from the China Travel Service hardly notice them. It is easy enough to straighten a bend in a river and gain two acres of land. All that is needed is the stones from this hill, the earth from that one, and fifty pairs of feet trotting a barefoot path till the sun sets.

Dazhai may be a showpiece, but they are still up against it there. The retaining walls of the new terraces used to burst in the winter floods until they learnt to build them bow-shaped like the coffer of a dam. Brigade leader Jia was much less interested in impressing his foreign guests than in plunging his fist into the soil of every field that we passed, searching for a trace of moisture to help the spring sowing. That new reservoir which they built last year will be needed:

so perhaps will some of the eighteen months' store of reserve grain in the barn.

Most of Dazhai's successes antedate the Cultural Revolution, and it is noticeable that fewer claims were made in the communes that we visited than in industry for the specific success of the Cultural Revolution in promoting new increases in production. The Great Leap Forward (1958-60) had reached a sort of productive plateau by 1964–5, and it was Mao's belief that the peasants were being restrained from greater efforts by bossy and bureaucratic local officials. If he is right we should expect another leap forward in the next few years. But if it happens it will come from below this time.

The army keeps guard in Beijing

It is a truism of China Watching that the army is everywhere after the Cultural Revolution, and one knows that the new party apparatus and the provincial revolutionary committees have a high percentage of military men. The military control committees, set up during the Cultural Revolution to safeguard essential services, still display their signboards in the cities.

Public security is one of the services still under military control, as I discovered in Beijing when I and another colleague inadvertently ended up in the local cophouse. The masses, in the shape of some large and heavy-footed high-school girls, thundering after us down one of the narrow *hutong* alleys, had suspected us of being class enemies. Only too aware of our eccentrically unChinese appearance, we could see their point of view. It was the People's Liberation Army (PLA) officer who checked our story in the police station and sent us on our way, still maintaining the polite fiction that we had been lost and that the masses had only wanted to help us.

And yet, to use a different sort of China Watching argument, the injunction to 'Learn from the PLA' only came seventeenth in the list of May Day slogans this year. One simply does not get the feeling of an oppressive military presence in the country, and propaganda in favour of the PLA does not stand out from the general run of slogans. The

PLA is undeniably around in the urban areas, where most factories, schools and offices have at least one soldier in a position of some authority on their revolutionary committees. In the rural communes, where there was less disorder in the Cultural Revolution and less need for PLA intervention, the army is hardly to be seen.

It is not perhaps a question of straightforward PLA control, but of a less easily definable influence which keeps the country on the straight and narrow revolutionary path. People do not have to submit to PLA discipline, but they should and do learn from its 'working style'. In the factories, workshops are designated as companies and the workers divided into platoons. Each worker takes part in the 'five-good' campaign, copied from the PLA, pinning a personal assessment of his merits and demerits on the noticeboard for everyone to read. Twice a month he and his comrades discuss their progress, with an annual summing-up to decide who has become a 'five-good worker', excelling in the five essential departments: political study, military training, working style, good behaviour, and good conduct in the canteen. The same system is practised in the schools.

There is also a paramilitary aspect to learning from the PLA. Schoolchildren from primary age upwards march out to the countryside for camping exercises like miniature conscripts with bedding packs on their backs, as part of a national campaign to 'prepare against war'. A new drive has been launched to build up the militia, and in some cities workers' auxiliaries have been organized to help keep public order. In Guangzhou, they were armed with black and white striped staves and crash helmets.

Then there are the mounds of earth, about which it is more tactful not to enquire, which obstruct so many urban streets but which provide excellent adventure playgrounds for the local children. New drains and pipelines may account for part of the work, but half-completed shelters are sometimes clearly visible. Preparedness against war obviously includes some form of civil defence against the contingency of a surprise attack which today is more likely to come from the revisionist North than the imperialist West.

An agricultural debate
January 1972

A major debate within the Chinese leadership over the future direction of agricultural policy is now becoming evident. A strong call has been voiced in the Communist Party journal *Red Flag* for a new upsurge of socialism in the countryside and for greater efforts at saving and investment by the Chinese peasants. This basic question of economic and social priorities, affecting 80 per cent of China's population, appears to have been one of the central issues behind the downfall last autumn of Mao's 'chosen successor' (former Minister of Defence) Lin Biao and his followers.

In an economy where growth is essentially based upon the accumulation and investment of agricultural surpluses, it is vitally important to strike a correct balance between what the peasant consumes and retains for himself and what he saves or contributes to the collective enterprise. The Maoist strategy, as it has emerged in recent months, is to promote a boom in the establishment of local industries, in those key sectors – fertilizer, farm machinery and building – which directly affect agricultural productivity. But this boom can be financed only if the Chinese peasants refrain from taking a larger share of the surpluses which they are now producing.

According to the Maoist view, argued at length in the latest issue of *Red Flag*, the Chinese peasants already have a fair share. The causes of poverty have been eliminated, and 'after taking the socialist road they have become rich'. It is only on the basis of the further 'accumulation of funds', argues *Red Flag*, that production can be expanded. There is no contradiction between this process and the interests of the working people, since 'the funds accumulated under the socialist system are used directly or indirectly to improve the welfare of the producers.'

Red Flag accuses those who oppose this argument of preaching a kind of half-baked egalitarianism, in which the short-term interest of the rural population is satisfied by a larger share of the surplus but at the expense of their long-term interests. The magazine claims that (ex-Head of State)

Liu Shaoqi and other swindlers' (a standard phrase to denote the current political opposition) have 'opposed the accumulation of funds under the socialist system', and that they argue instead that 'socialism means to get a little more and distribute a little more'.

Another article in *Red Flag* evokes the spirit of the great collectivization movement in 1955–6, when at Mao's prompting the campaign to establish agricultural cooperatives was speeded up, a process which prepared the ground for the Great Leap Forward in 1958. Chairman Mao's discovery in 1955 of 'the essence of the masses' enthusiasm for socialism' is said to be 'of vital significance today'. Once again the unnamed opposition is criticized for belittling the readiness of the Chinese peasant to push ahead on the socialist road.

Two practical questions arise out of this debate over how, and at what rate, greater agricultural productivity should be financed. First, there is the share-out itself. How much should the State take, how much should the individual keep, and how much should be reinvested in small-scale industry by the 'collective'? This is a very real issue at the present time when every commune in the country is discussing how to distribute the income which has been accumulated in 1971.

Second, under what system of social organization can funds for reinvestment best be accumulated in the countryside? This question has been only hinted at in the Chinese press, but it affects the whole structure of the commune system. The basic counting unit of the commune – where the vital 'share-out' is made – is pegged at the lowest level of the 'team', where such decisions are more likely to favour the individual producer. Should these decisions be taken instead by the higher level 'brigade' or even by the commune itself, which would be more concerned with investment?

Paradoxically the present debate is being conducted not because the economic situation is so poor but because it is so healthy. It is precisely because output has increased so impressively since the Cultural Revolution (by 10 per cent in 1971 according to the latest statistics), because the granaries are full and the shops well stocked, that the question of how to distribute the surplus now arises.

Biking in Beijing
April 1976, Beijing

Some may prefer to go walking on the Great Wall, or explore the pavilions of the Summer Palace. For me the best sensation of all in Beijing is simply to take a ride on a bike. A lot of the pleasure comes from being part of that life-stream flowing by at the rate of a hundred bicycles a minute in the rush-hour. We spend so much time observing it from the pavement or, in a still more alienating form of behaviour, bursting through it in our tourist bus. Today it took a quick push off the kerb, a bit of nerve and we had joined it.

Of course there are some rules to be learnt. 1. Never stop except (sometimes) at a red light. 2. Maintain the same speed as everyone else. 3. Don't take any hooting personally – keep going regardless of trolleybus or taxi. 4. Ring bell all the time. To slow down or stop out of turn is the Chinese equivalent of being caught on the hard shoulder of a busy motorway – you will never get moving again. The contradiction between 3 and 4 is intended: everyone hoots or rings; nobody listens.

To ride through the great Square of Tiananmen itself is the sort of heart-catching experience that makes me ask 'Am I really here?' For a moment I share some of the feeling of those Red Guards who marched one thousand miles to Beijing, toiled up Changan Avenue for several more miles, found themselves in the Square for a minute and a half and then on into the dusty haze, their backs now to the Great Sun of China, perhaps not even quite sure whether they had actually seen him. That was ten years ago when Chinese politics were rather different. Today the main part of the square is still blocked off by militiamen after the 'counter-revolutionary' demonstration at the Spring Festival. We turn right into the Forbidden City, under the vermilion arch. Inside we find more militiamen in lorries ready to be transported to a better sort of demo. No other foreigners are around; the bikes have earned us immunity.

Around to the north side now to visit the antiquities. Rather casually exhibited in an unheated pavilion is the twin to the Chinese exhibition that came to Europe in 1973. Equally magnificent ancient bronzes and pots, gold ornaments and prancing horses, just more of them. And remember the Jade Princess? Well, here is her mate, the Jade Prince. He is distinguished by a large belly and a very princely jade cod piece. We shall never know whether or not it was just feudal flattery.

Beijing's parched miles are annihilated by the bicycle. Now we head west to the Xidan district, a friendly, rather scruffy area good for parking and food. We park our bikes. The Chinese people are honest but we still have to lock our bikes. Otherwise they do tend to get knocked off by the occasional bad element. 'Hooligans' are officially recognized as a social problem these days, and they were blamed for some of the troubles in Tiananmen. They crop their hair very short and have rather fancy footwear. Some of them are school leavers who have refused to go to the countryside, or have come back illegally. But they may also be local lads who have simply been corrupted by the sight of the increasing numbers of foreigners like ourselves. There are never fewer than a couple of dozen youths outside the Beijing Hotel, peering through the hedge at the tourist traffic and at the most famous set of sliding doors in Asia.

South now in search of the Liulichang where one may find such art and antique shops as still remain. We stop for free air at a cycle shop (yes, another service to the community . . .) and then plunge east into the narrow *hutongs* – paved lanes lined by the blank doors of traditional Chinese courtyards which, where they survive, take one instantly back to nineteenth-century Beijing. There is a difference. The courtyards have running water now, though sewage is still collected by night-soil cart and hauled to the countryside. And each courtyard (several families will share one) is organized into a 'socialist courtyard', the 'street committee' translated to a smaller dimension where neighbourly things like sweeping up, looking after children and swapping contraceptive advice, are done.

Even in the narrow *hutongs*, the same rule applies: keep moving. Here we stand out again; loose-kneed foreigners squawking round corners and looking lost. It is easy enough to end up in a neighbourhood factory but on this occasion the maze unravels satisfactorily. The Americans have ruined the market, the old Beijing residents say, and there is nothing much to buy. So we have lunch in the local restaurant which is fortunately too small to have a special room for foreigners. Our table has not been wiped, and will not be till the end of lunchtime when a dozen more people have spilled their bowls on it. One of the realities about Beijing is that things can be very dirty. But the food is excellent and comes to a ridiculous one *yuan* (30p).

So back to the sliding doors of the Beijing Hotel. On the way I discover that a yellow and green light combined means that one can turn left, if one dares, across incoming traffic. Very interesting.

As Mao Zedong lay dying
May 1976, Beijing

To visit China during an acute political crisis clears the mind wonderfully. Mao's death in the near future now seems more likely. The situation is inevitably transitional, giving rise to uncertainties and tensions. These have been exacerbated by the factional struggle which the Cultural Revolution, in spite of its achievements, unhappily brought about. And that struggle is visible. One sight, the Chinese are fond of saying, is worth ten thousand words.

That sight, for me, came on the fifth day after the notorious affair in Beijing's Tiananmen Square in April, when the members of various government departments had supported a pro-Zhou Enlai demonstration. On subsequent days they were obliged to do penance. For two days the Martyrs' Memorial and the Square itself were symbolically washed by municipal watercarts and scrubbed clean by hand. (True, there were chalk marks and even some blood to be erased, but it became an act of purification.) Then came the right sort of demonstration: three days of sponsored enthusiasm for the 'Enlightened Resolutions of the Party Centre'. These included the dismissal of Deng Xiaoping and the appointment of Hua Guofeng as Premier and First Vice-Chairman of the Party.

On the last day, as I stood watching, the marching ranks of the entire staff of the Fourth Ministry of Machine Building appeared out of the dusty haze at the far end of the square. Never have I seen such glum enthusiasm. Just in front of me, by the vermilion gate of Tiananmen, two cameramen from the New China News Agency fussed around with an aluminium stepladder. They were trying to get some good shots of spontaneous joy. They called out to the marchers, but the response was pathetic. The front echelons of the Fourth Ministry of Machine Building limply raised their little red and green flags, mumbling a sacred slogan which should properly have echoed against the walls of the Great Hall of the People.

Not all the marchers who passed through Tiananmen Square (several million according to official statistics) were so dejected. Many of the schoolchildren and factory workers seemed to enjoy the outing. Every column had its activists who were quite keen. The university students who appeared first of all, late on the evening that Deng's dismissal was announced, shattered the cold stillness with their drums and cymbals. They really seemed enthusiastic. But the general opinion, even among friends of China and long-time residents in Beijing, was that the first demonstration, when wreaths were placed in memory of Zhou Enlai, had been a spontaneous one, while the later ones were definitely not. Nor, to judge by the television newsreels I saw in various provincial capitals, with their stony-faced line-ups of the local leadership, were the demonstrations elsewhere any more spontaneous. It was striking that even in edited films an impression of liveliness should be so difficult to convey.

Of course the vast majority of these reluctant marchers are not supporters in any personal sense of Deng Xiaoping. There is no evidence that he enjoyed a mass following. Foreign diplomats who come into contact with the ministries in Beijing have found scant evidence of bureaucratic support for Deng, whose rough style was if anything a liability. A majority of ordinary people are almost certainly in sympathy, not with him, but with the 'radical' view on how to continue the socialist revolution – along the lines developed since the Cultural Revolution – though they may have reservations about how it is working out in practice. But they are worried about who is manipulating the anti-Deng or anti-revisionist campaign for their own purposes. They want to know who else is jumping on the radical bandwagon, and where it is all going to end. The anxieties of ordinary people can be traced quite distinctly, even if one has to read the message back to front, in the attempts now being made by the official press and the provincial radio stations to allay them and to refute the 'counter-revolutionary rumours' which are supposed to be circulating. Quite a number have also been referred to in anti-Deng posters which foreigners are allowed to read.

An obvious question concerns access to power and the use which has been made of it by the trinity of 'radical' figures in the Party Politburo, Jiang Qing (Mao's wife), Vice-Chairman Zhang Chunqiao and the Shanghai intellectual Yao Wenyuan. These three are widely regarded as indivisible although Zhang is sometimes set slightly apart. Both Jiang Qing and Yao were criticized at some provincial demonstrations and in wallposters during the Spring Festival. (The group with which I was travelling saw a 'Down with Jiang Qing' slogan in Nanjing.)

The chief source of the power enjoyed by this radical trinity comes from their access to Mao himself. They gain substantial advantage from bring able to interpret his utterances to the general public – and perhaps to their own political colleagues as well. Chinese officials are noticeably reluctant to mention any of these leaders by name when talking with foreigners. I had several long discussions in various places on the problems of 'socialist transition', for which the most obvious reference points are two long articles written by Zhang and Yao last year. Yet only one Chinese official, in Shanghai, quoted either of the articles to me. Another cause for concern is that the radical takeover has to some extent created its own bureaucratic machine. Many of the younger cadres who have risen since the Cultural Revolution are idealistic and uncorrupt, but others are ambitious and none too scrupulous about how they gain power. This was one of the complaints made by Deng Xiaoping.

'There is a batch of people,' he said, 'who make their name by criticizing other people, and who climb on other people's shoulders to get on the scene of power.' Deng also claimed that some of these young radical stars 'don't know how to get things done, lack enthusiasm for their work, but have a factional spirit'.

And yet another reason for concern is the way that the radical group seems to accept a compromise and then breaks it in order to attack new ground. These same tactics led in 1967–8 to a good deal of the 'ultra-leftism' which disfigured the Cultural Revolution. The initial appointment in early January of Hua Guofeng as Acting Premier was just such a compromise. But several leading members of the Party and Government, dismayed at the way the anti-Deng campaign (with its anti-Zhou Enlai undercurrent) continued to develop, then deliberately withdrew from the scene to cultivate their own gardens. These seem to have included the Minister of Defence Ye Jianying, the veteran Vice-Premier Li Xiannian, and the popular peasant leader Chen Yonggui, himself a genuine 'radical'.

The events in Tiananmen Square at the Spring Festival, however they were engineered, forced the struggle onto a new stage and led to a new compromise. Deng was dismissed; Hua's appointment as Premier was confirmed; and Ye, Li and Chen came back into view as if to offer public reassurance that the campaign would go no further. But by this time many people must have been quite glad to see an end to the uncertainties of the spring, and hoped that the whole business had been finally resolved with Deng's dismissal.

Yet only last week the *People's Daily* returned to the attack, denouncing the 'counter-revolutionaries, desperados and social scums' who had allegedly staged the affair in Tiananmen Square. The paper called for a fresh offensive against the 'ghosts and monsters, demons and clowns who dance to the music from Deng Xiaoping's flute'. This is not the healthy language of a principled struggle on behalf of socialist policies which most Chinese would support. Yet it is important to require that that struggle, in a more genuine form, does indeed go on.

A hero becomes a clown
December 1976

The Chinese student who became a national hero after turning in a blank examination paper is now being called a 'counter-revolutionary clown' and an agent of Jiang Qing (Madame Mao). In July 1973 the case of Zhang Tiesheng, a student in the north-eastern province of Liaoning, set in motion the whole 'anti-Confucius campaign' which sought emphatically to reassert the values of the Cultural Revolution.

Today Zhang stands accused of being an 'opportunist and thug' used by the Gang of Four and particularly by Mao Yuanxin (Mao Zedong's nephew), who was linked with them, to stir up trouble. By implication the whole revolt of youth against authority in the Chinese educational system could be vulnerable to attack.

Zhang was an 'educated youth' – a former high-school student – who had been working in the Liaoning countryside for five years before he sat a college entrance exam in the summer of 1973. Unable to answer the questions, he turned over the paper and on the blank side wrote an open letter to the examiners. Zhang explained that he had no time to prepare for the exam from his old high-school textbooks – he had been too busy in the fields. 'To tell the truth,' he added, 'I have no respect for the bookworms who for many years have been taking it easy and have done nothing useful. I dislike them intensely.'

Zhang's story was published in the local press, and soon appeared in the official *People's Daily*, then controlled by Jiang Qing and the radicals. Priggish though he may sound, Zhang struck a note which many other young Chinese radicals quickly echoed. The old elitism and bureaucracy, they complained, of which the examination system formed an important part, was being reintroduced despite the Cultural Revolution.

The radical press praised Zhang for speaking out and 'going against the tide' of official opinion. A wave of criticism developed in which Party and army officials were exposed for trying to get their children to college 'through the back door'. Wang Hongwen, one of the Gang, persuaded the Party's Tenth Congress which met soon afterwards to record its approval of 'going against the tide'.

Today Zhang Tiesheng has been debunked. He did not leave his examination paper blank, it is now claimed. He made a very poor shot at answering the questions and his mark was only 6 per cent. He then gained a place at a veterinary college 'through the back door' because he had become a protégé of the Gang.

Late in 1975, the radicals launched a fresh offensive against more traditionally minded educationalists led, behind the scenes, by the former Vice-Premier Deng Xiaoping and the Minister of Education Zhou Rongxin. Zhang was paraded around university campuses urging the students to 'struggle' against their teachers. In April this year, when Deng (now rumoured to be on the verge of a come-back) was ousted by the radical group, Zhang Tiesheng 'struggled' against the minister himself for a week on end. Soon afterwards Zhou died, it is believed, of a heart attack.

Clearly the case of Zhang Tiesheng was a special one, and not every Chinese student who 'went against the tide' and criticized his elders need necessarily fear denunciation in the same terms. Zhang's connection with Mao's nephew – a Party secretary in Liaoning who made many enemies (he is now accused of 'enjoying dirty foreign films and smoking foreign cigarettes') – did him no good either. But Zhang still represents a more general spirit of assertiveness among Chinese youth who have been radicalized by the Cultural Revolution and who are now likely to have their wings quite firmly clipped.*

The most common complaint of older Chinese about the

---

* Zhang Tiesheng was sentenced to fifteen years' imprisonment in 1982 for the crime of 'counter-revolutionary propaganda and attempting to subvert the government'.

Gang of Four is that Jiang Qing and her colleagues 'led China's youth astray'. Of course China needs fresh blood for the future, it is now explained, but the young people should be properly 'nurtured' and 'tempered by experience'. They share the complaint voiced last year by Deng Xiaoping that young Chinese radicals were shooting up into the higher ranks of the Party 'like helicopters'.

3

Mr Deng Changes China's Face, 1978–80

China had already become a very different place within two years of Mao's death. The attempt by his immediate successor, Hua Guofeng, to assert that all of Mao's policies remained essentially correct was challenged by Deng Xiaoping, with support from Party officials and intellectuals who regarded him as the only leader capable of restoring normality and promoting economic reform. In Urumqi, capital of Xinjiang in the far North-west, I visited recently reopened mosques in the Muslim quarter with inscriptions in the Arabic script which had been banned during the Cultural Revolution. At the Shengli Oilfield in Shandong on the eastern coast, the talk was all about 'putting production first' – a far cry from Mao's insistence that 'politics is in command'. I visited the first street markets and peered at handwritten advertisements stuck on telephone poles offering job exchanges and foreign language lessons. A new policy had been proclaimed of 'Four Modernizations' in agriculture, industry, science and technology, and national defence. It was a 'magnificent plan' to make the Chinese economy 'one of the most advanced in the world'. Roadside posters showed China's youth looking ahead to the year 2001, across a vista of rockets, speeding express trains and electric pylons.

Democracy Wall in front of a bus station in western Beijing sprang into life in the grey late autumn of 1978. Former Red Guards debated why the Cultural Revolution had become such a disaster, who was responsible, and what sort of society China should strive for. They also aired the cases of peasants and workers who had been victimized. Though it was a spontaneous movement, launched with great courage by these young activists, Deng Xiaoping and his *supporters soon made use of it to criticize Hua Guofeng and other Maoist leaders. I read the wallposters and tightly written essays pasted up on the wall, over the shoulders of young people earnestly copying the texts into notebooks. Even foreigners could subscribe to the mimeographed wall newspapers which were sold for a few cents. Out of the mist a bus pulled up near Tiananmen Square, selling illegal photos and poems from the great demonstration on 5 April 1976 which was still officially regarded as 'counter-revolutionary'. Soon this verdict was reversed as the remaining Maoists lost power to Deng Xiaoping. Hua Guofeng, who had made himself ridiculous by trying to look like Mao in propaganda posters, was allowed to remain: others were evicted.*

Deng consolidated his power, and then turned on the democracy movement which had helped him. Wei Jingsheng, who argued that democracy should become the Fifth Modernization, was sentenced to fifteen years in jail. Deng also put the Gang of Four on trial, and called on China to 'liberate its thoughts'. For the older generation who had suffered in the Cultural Revolution, he remained a hero. The first of many campaigns against corruption was launched. Wages were increased and new consumer demands emerged, modest at first but breath-taking by comparison with the Cultural Revolution.

I visited factories where lists of piece rates and bonuses were displayed instead of quotations from Chairman Mao. Fridges, TVs and new furniture were carried home precariously on three-wheeler pedicabs. People stopped reading the Party journal Red Flag, *and started buying magazines with titles like* World Cinema *and* Modern Living. *The first cans of Coca-Cola and packs of foreign cigarettes were imported – though only available in the hotels, which were still barred to ordinary Chinese. Patriotism began to replace politics: Chinese football teams no longer put 'friendship first; competition second', but played to win.*

A more open China also revealed social tensions which had been concealed, and others which were being created. In Xinjiang I caught a glimpse of the persecution which the Muslim minorities had suffered till recently, and visited schools where the educational system was based on separate development. In Beijing I talked to graduate students whose path was blocked by old cadres resuming the privileges of power. On street corners in Shanghai, I met

*disaffected youth who had returned illegally from the countryside to
live by their wits. China really was changing.*

The rejection of Mao
October 1978, Beijing

The Cultural Revolution has now been denied in all but
name in China two years after Mao Zedong's death, and it
may not be long before it is done openly. As wallposters in
Beijing begin to raise the question of the state of Mao's mind
in his final years, it is extremely hard to find anywhere in
China a convincing defence of the Cultural Revolution
which he started in 1966.

Negating the Cultural Revolution is the means by which
the dominant group in the leadership hopes to get rid of
some Maoist dead wood – perhaps at a new Third Plenum
of the Central Committee early next month. Many ordinary
and especially young Chinese will also see it as the best way
to criticize and expose the middle-ranking bureaucrats and
to achieve both a more efficient society and something
approaching real 'socialist democracy'. Three weeks of
travelling and interviewing widely in China, as these
questions were coming to a head, have convinced me that
the Cultural Revolution as a source of political inspiration is
now dead, and that if people want to return to the issues
which it raised they will choose a very different way.

The immediate conflict within the leading Politburo is
between the modernizers headed by Vice-Premier Deng
Xiaoping – the Gang of Four's chief enemy before Mao's
death – and those whose past is compromised by equivo-
cation when the Gang held power. The main target is Wang
Dongxing, the Communist Party Vice-Chairman, who was
Mao's bodyguard during the Revolution and whose special
troops removed the Gang led by Mao's wife, Jiang Qing, two
years ago. Wang is portrayed in backstreet gossip, no doubt
with encouragement from his enemies, as a rather stupid
fellow who cannot keep up with the times.

Chairman Hua Guofeng himself has been attacked in one
wallposter this week, and a case can be made that he too has

some explaining to do for his rise to power (at Deng Xiaoping's expense) before Mao's death. But his previous political record is clear, and most people probably feel that with his Party connections and support from the armed forces he is a very important part of the new team. The Politburo still includes Wu De, the former Mayor of Beijing, who was compromised by his suppression of the Tiananmen incident in April 1976, when Deng Xiaoping's supporters occupied the main square in Beijing to mourn the death of the late Premier Zhou Enlai. Another Politburo member likely to go is Saifudin, from the far west Muslim region of Xinjiang, where I was told he had 'suppressed the national minorities' during the Cultural Revolution and had closed down the mosques (now open again).

Some criticism is also attached to Chen Yonggui, China's most famous peasant, who led the 'model brigade' of Dazhai – from whom the rest of Chinese agriculture was urged to learn during the Cultural Revolution. He too seems to be unable to move with events. Models in general are not so popular. The industrial twin to Dazhai – the oilfield of Daqing – is still to be emulated, but there is one feature from which one is asked not to learn: Daqing's policy of low wages which conflicts with the nationwide move towards 'more pay for more work' plus bonuses for the deserving workers and deductions for the lazy ones.

Last week's official verdict that the Tiananmen demonstration in April 1976, which led at the time to Deng Xiaoping's removal, was a 'revolutionary action', will obviously further weaken the power of the residual Maoists in the leadership. But it means more than this for many ordinary people who still demand much more radical political changes. Condemning the Gang, or criticizing (obliquely at first) Mao's tolerance of them, is not just an historical issue, but a weapon with which to curb the still considerable power of large numbers of middle-ranking bureaucrats. A marginal note, scribbled by an anonymous 'citizen of Beijing' on a poster which I read in the city centre, made the point clear: 'Every goverment unit,' he wrote, 'still has secret lairs where the minions of the Gang of Four still hide. Unless we dig them out, then their poison will rise again and infect the masses.'

The rule of law is to be restored, though it seems to be taking rather a long time. (During the week I spent in the region of Xinjiang, I was told that fortunately there were 'no cases at all' coming up before the courts, so less fortunately there were none that I could attend.) Significantly the official Party newspaper *People's Daily* has published a long article, which first appeared in *Chinese Youth*, demanding a 'massive development of people's democracy'. More outspoken articles have been appearing in the *Youth Newspaper* but only – it is rumoured – after Chairman Hua himself insisted they should not be censored.

In the cultural world, there is a sense too of more serious questions trying to break through. So far the new spirit of 'a hundred flowers' has mostly meant lots of foreign films (especially those which are shown by invitation only) and the revival of Beijing opera and local plays. But there are essays and stories about the scars left upon China by the Gang of Four, which by implication also say something about the future. Cultural bureaucrats cannot very well object to these 'scars' being exposed, but they would like intellectuals to write rather more about the 'positive' side of what has been achieved since the downfall of the Gang.

I began my visit to China by carefully enquiring, at every school or factory I visited, what advantages had accrued to this particular unit from the Cultural Revolution. The answers were uniformly embarrassing. Some fell back on the official formula that the Cultural Revolution had been a 70 per cent success; most people mumbled something about how it had improved their style of work and brought them closer to the masses. But all the actual mechanisms by which this was supposed to be achieved were described in wholly negative terms. The managers had come too close to the masses, to the point where they did not dare to take decisions. 'People seized power from us,' one factory manager said with unusual frankness. 'The Revolutionary Committee' (which has now been abolished but used to include worker representatives) 'was legal at the time, but we did not want it.'

The return of institutions and practices which one had thought the Cultural Revolution had finally disposed of – particularly in the restoration of material incentives and competitive education – is quite staggering for the naïve foreigner who felt that in these fields at least socialist morality had taken a step forward. Now one is told with a laugh that 'you can't eat socialism'.

Back to the bonus
October 1978, Beijing

Last month was Quality Month all over China. Workers who excel in the course of it can earn a special bonus of anything between thirty and fifty *yuan*. In more normal months they may now get as much as ten *yuan*, about a fifth of the average skilled worker's wage. At this rate the most diligent among them should be able, I reckon, to buy a Swiss watch by the end of 1979. Not perhaps the Longines which I found, improbably, in an Urumqi department store in the far west of China. But a reliable brand for around 200 *yuan* (roughly sixty pounds at the current exchange rate).

If there was one thing of which most observers outside China were thoroughly convinced during the Cultural Revolution, it was that bonuses had died a decisive death. Differences in pay would continue according to the 'eight-grade scale for workers' and the more elaborate scales for other state employees. Where there was room for argument was whether the differential gaps should remain the same. But the Shanghai dockers had surely got it right when, rejecting a proposed bonus scheme in 1974, they proclaimed that 'We shall be masters of the wharf, not of tonnage!'

Now it appears that this was the 'absolute egalitarianism' preached by the Gang of Four, under whose regime things got to such a pass that 'it did not matter if the worker checked in late or not at all'. Last year the higher-paid workers all got a rise, and the new bonus system is just getting under way. There are various kinds of moral incentives, too, carefully listed for me as consisting of public praise, banners and flags, individual certificates, a favourable entry for one's work record, and being awarded the title of 'advanced worker'. These moral incentives should in theory take precedence over those of a material kind.

Mao said so and is still quoted to this effect. But what one sees being emphasized at the moment in every factory are the sort of incentives which produce more cash, with the targets written up on blackboards. Several national conferences have been held to work out a proper 'socialist' basis upon which bonuses should be awarded. The principles are sensible enough; the only problem is that as far as I could tell they were already being eroded in practice. First, the basic wage system should consist of a time rate, plus bonuses. But two important exceptions have already been made, allowing for piece-rate wages to be paid to manual labourers and those working in handicraft industries.

The diggers of ditches and the makers of plastic flowers will be paid entirely on the basis of how much they produce. Is this not retrogressive? No, one is told, because the piece-rates will be carefully fixed to assure a reasonable income.

A second principle is that a basic wage should be guaranteed. This is only more or less true, since the new system also provides for deductions for managers who are inefficient, for workers who damage equipment, produce too many faulty products or use too much raw material. However, one is told that the reduction of wages should never be excessive – perhaps a figure of 10 per cent would be in order. Nor can workers be sacked except for criminal behaviour, though they can be placed in a special category of 'dismissal on retention' where they are nominally sacked but allowed to continue work.

The Chinese accept that there may be a law of diminishing returns with any bonus system, as the economic slack in the system gets gradually taken up and the marginal gains become less. But they feel – and most Western experts who visit their factories agree with them – that a 20 to 30 per cent rise in efficiency, using the same plant and manpower, is quite feasible in most industries.

Any doubts as to the compatibility of a bonus scheme with the socialist system are speedily dismissed by referring to the

Marxian principle 'to each according to his work' or, more bluntly, to the Chinese phrase *duolao duode*: 'the more you work the more you get'.

A banner flies in one of the factories which I visited, with a little jingle on it in praise of Chairman Hua Guofeng and his Four Modernizations. Roughly translated, it says:

> *The heights to which he does aspire*
> *Are what the masses all desire.*

To modernize thoroughly the whole of China by the end of the century is indeed a lofty peak, and it is being scaled by competitive methods which leave the visitor with memories of the Cultural Revolution gasping.

Reopening the mosques
November 1978, Urumqi, Xinjiang

The bearded patriarch, Tuerdi, whose 'workers' home' I am visiting, has only two teeth left, but he can count eighty-two direct descendants down to his great-grandchildren. This is one for every year of his life. The Uighurs, a Turkic 'national minority' in North-west China, evidently have that Central Asian capacity to produce very old men. The last Imam before the present one, at the mosque which Tuerdi attends on Fridays, died at the age of 100.

In Urumqi, capital of the Xinjiang Uighur Autonomous Region, these old men warm themselves in the late autumn sun, some outside the mosque, some outside the new Chinese department store. There is a cold wind from across the Gobi Desert, and they are wearing their high, leather boots and fur-lined caps with the flaps hanging down. The street looks at first glance like a photograph from a missionary's album of China 'before Liberation'. Old women sell raw pepper, bread and glasses of tea on the pavement. Cobblers sit in their dark doorways. The houses are of whitewashed mud – one-storeyed, with thick wooden shutters painted dark brown.

The Muslim minorities in this farthest west corner of

China have had a hard time in recent years. They were 'persecuted by agents of the Gang of Four', I am told by Temur Dawamad, himself a Uighur and a vice-chairman of the ruling Revolutionary Committee. The chief agent, he reveals indiscreetly, was Saifudin, the veteran Communist Party first secretary of the region who was transferred to Beijing last year where he is still a member of the central Party Politburo.

'They closed the mosques, and would not let people wear their caps,' he says. 'We are still trying to eradicate their poisonous influence.' Later I discover that all the local community organizations for the national minorities, including street committees and the religious affairs committee, are only now being 'restored' after having been closed since the Cultural Revolution began. There are now at least twenty mosques open again in the old Uighur quarter of Nanliang. I even saw a woman begging outside one of them, perhaps tolerated because charity is one of the main Islamic virtues.

Xinjiang has only just been 'opened' to foreign tourists, and next year as many as 1,700 are scheduled to visit the region, helping to relieve the pressure on the main tourist routes to and from Beijing. The local officials are often more straightforward and helpful to visitors than those in the more familiar parts of China, but they are slightly at a loss on how to deal with the expected tours from Thomas Cook.

Tuerdi, in his new house outside the old quarter, represents the more acceptable face of 'national minority' development which the Chinese will want to show their visitors. If one enquires closely into the lives of his eight children and their children, it is clear that within certain limits things have greatly improved. Education, as so often, is the key. The first four children only attended 'lower middle' – the first three years of secondary school. (The two eldest daughters have sixteen children between them.) A fifth daughter went to Xinjiang University; a sixth completed the full five years of middle school; the seventh went to a technical school. The path forward for all these young Uighurs has been as skilled technicians, working in the post office, on the railways or in the armed forces. They are proud of one grandson who is now in the airforce.

Xinjiang was first developed after the 1949 Liberation by a Production and Construction Corps, formed out of the Liberation Army forces and the Kuomintang troops who surrendered to them. Then, in the late 1950s, as relations with the Soviet Union across the border worsened, a big influx of civilian settlers from China proper began. These Han Chinese form distinct communities in Urumqi, living mostly in the new part of the city across the river.

Despite the upward social mobility shown by Tuerdi's family, it is still very difficult for a member of a national minority to cross the cultural divide between non-Han and Han. But his last child, a daughter now aged twenty-four, has done so. She studied physics in Wuhan on the Yangzi River for three years, and is now a supervisor in the Urumqi telephone office, earning the standard rate for university graduates of sixty-two *yuan* a month – a third more than a worker's starting wage. She speaks reasonable Chinese, and has her foot on the first step of the officials' salary scale.

By law, all government documents should be published in the four major languages in Xinjiang: Han Chinese (41 per cent of the total population of eleven million), Uighur (45 per cent), Kazakh (6 per cent) and Mongol (1 per cent). Yet the Chinese language is such a strong unifying cultural force that those without full mastery of it suffer a political disadvantage. At the simplest level, a Uighur official in Xinjiang will have to use Chinese to communicate with a Chinese official; the latter will not reciprocate in Uighur, unless it is a formal occasion with a translator present.

The Han Chinese cadres also have a different status. They have been appointed by the State to serve in Xinjiang and may be transferred elsewhere in the future. My own impression, based upon observing the way that Chinese and minority cadres behave together, is that there is an air of deference towards the superior culture. A senior Uighur official does not command the automatic respect a Chinese at the same level of hierarchy would enjoy.

The children of a mixed nationality school finish their morning drill, 1,400 of them in unison on the dusty exercise ground. Then they disperse for five minutes of free play – Han Chinese children to the left, all cropped black hair and round faces, Uighur children to the right, with a hotchpotch of long noses, broad foreheads, even some ginger hair, and earrings for the girls. There are *Hanzuban*, Han classes, and *Weizuban*, Uighur classes, pursuing a common curriculum each in their own language. The Chinese children are supposed to learn some Uighur, but it is not essential to their lives, and recently it has been dropped in favour of English. The Uighur children must learn some Chinese, but how much?

A few minority children, one or two in each Han class, follow the Chinese side of the system. One imagines that their home background and job opportunities will be very different. At Xinjiang University, the separate language streams continue. Minority students do a year of preliminary Chinese, not so that they can join the Chinese language stream, but so they can use original Chinese texts in their subjects.

The language of instruction is Uighur (the lingua franca for the other nationalities too) but the content is mostly Chinese. Only 20 per cent of the textbook material is of Uighur origin, dealing with things like local customs and raising sheep, but at university there is no study of regional history – abolished, I was told, by the Gang of Four. Proper histories of the national minorities have been written but they come into the category of *neibu* (restricted) material. At the main Urumqi bookshop, and at another one in the biggest department store, I found two recent novels in Uighur and one in Mongolian, as well as a handbook of local traditional medicine. Everything else was translated from Chinese, including the great classical novels like the *Dream of the Red Chamber* and the *Water Margin*. There was a good deal of puzzling over titles by Chinese shop assistants who had no idea what the books were.

Towards the three-piece suite
April 1980, Shanghai

The window of a photographer's shop in Shanghai illustrates a new aspect of Chinese life in the 1980s. 'Western garments may be hired here,' says the sign, in response to the popular preference for having one's picture taken in foreign clothes. Some samples of the studio's efforts are on display. They include the picture of a real live foreigner – a rather shaggy North European with a large beard – and another of a sharply dressed Chinese lad wearing shades. Then there are some wedding photographs in traditional bridal white, but propped against one of these is a very Chinese slogan: 'For the sake of the Revolution, only have one child!'

On a lamp-post farther down the street, the other end of the human cycle in Shanghai is dealt with. 'Public cemetery with a view of the hills!' says the flyposter. A passing Chinese student stops to explain it to me. Space at the Shanghai crematorium is apparently so limited that after three years they throw away the ashes unless you come and collect the urn. Enterprising communes in the countryside now augment their income by selling off minute plots of land for sixty *yuan* (eighteen pounds or a month's average wage).

Insights like these into the everyday preoccupations of Chinese life make the Cultural Revolution and our former vision of a new socialist man in China seem more unreal than ever. At least in the cities, the picture is now one familiar to us from the developmental experiences of most other Third World countries. It is the same jumble of traditional (Chinese) and modern (mostly foreign-based) images and aspirations, the same articulation of consumer demands no less real for being posed in a much less advanced economic context than ours. The Chinese say that these demands are all the more intense for having been politically pent up during the Cultural Revolution, when it was wiser not to betray any material aspirations.

Another reason is simply that, in spite of what is said about the 'wasted years' of the Cultural Revolution, there was continued economic progress, even if by fits and starts.

Whereas in the 1960s many people were still saving up for their first bicycle, today in the towns and wealthier rural areas they have the bicycle and the watch and probably the transistor radio too. Add to this the new money released into the economy by recent wage increases and bonuses for industrial workers and we have the familar phenomenon of a lot of money chasing too few goods.

The *shafa*, a word I had never even heard used on previous visits to China, has now become a new measure of purchasing power. There are single *shafas* (armchairs) and double *shafas* (sofas – the word is a Chinese transliteration of our own term). The three-piece suite has appeared on the Shanghai high street at about 400 *yuan* – more than half a year's wages for the average worker – for a rather shoddy set with simulated leather covers. 'But you can get them made much more cheaply by people working on their own, something they were afraid to do in the years of the Gang of Four,' it is explained. Furniture workers are happy to do some moonlighting on their day off from the state-owned factory and build you a single or double *shafa* in your home.

At the local street market one may see, tacked up on a wall, a duplicated sheet of furniture designs which can be bought for a few *fen* (cents). These free markets are themselves a new concession to consumer demand, abhorrent to anyone who still believes in the 'progressive limitation of bourgeois rights', but they are on quite a limited scale and seem very popular. 'It means that you can get eggs when you want them, and more vegetables in the winter.'

The peasants with produce from their small 'private plots' may have travelled through the night to be there at dawn, dozing on their barrows as they wait for the first six o'clock customer. They must pay a small stall fee to the market inspector, who is supposed to check for excessive prices and prohibited items. Prices that I saw were not wildly above those in the state markets. Shopping is a lively collective business in which everyone standing around is quick to denounce the seller of peanuts asking for five *fen* more than the accepted price that day.

Outside the main department stores in Beijing and

Shanghai, the crowds gather to gape at Japanese colour TV sets on sale for 2,000 *yuan* (three years' wages for the average worker) and other bits of expensive electronics. Is this really a common aspiration in the same category as the need for more vegetables and cheaper furniture, or do the displays of Sony, Sanyo, Hitachi and Toshiba serve a more subtle purpose? Though the brand name differs, the marketing approach is the same everywhere. An entire shop window has been filled with the products of the company concerned, in the home setting of a model consumer family – Mum and Dad plus child. Dad looks Eurasian, and is listening to his stereo on a headset. Mum has an apron, blonde hair and nice European legs. She may be doing the ironing, or using one of those new vacuum cleaners which can get into all the corners. The son in the Toshiba display on Xidan (Beijing) is wearing a Snoopy shirt and looking bored. The daughter on Nanjing Road (Shanghai) is wearing shorts and has the looks of a trim nymphet. It is all absolutely amazing for the crowd, rarely less than a hundred strong, pressing its collective nose against the shop-window.

The goods displayed are not entirely for show: I myself saw two purchasers of Hitachi colour TVs manoeuvring their cartons onto the back of a bicycle or into a pedicab. Often a Chinese-made equivalent product is available – including stereo sets and TV – at a lower price. But it can only be purchased with coupons which are allocated in very restricted numbers through one's place of work.

What I found most disturbing was the lack of any clear rational economic argument for these displays, which are backed up by giant ads on the billboards. In the end I had to conclude that the answer most frequently given was the right explanation. 'It will show the masses how hard we must struggle to catch up with the advanced technology of the developed world. It will encourage them to work harder for the Four Modernizations.' This makes sense of a sort. The sustaining myths of the Cultural Revolution, based on an anti-materialistic philosophy which may have been partly bogus but was compelling at the time, have been systematically and scornfully demolished. The gap has been partly filled by the quite reasonable demands of the Chinese people for a higher standard of living, after fifteen years in which nobody got a wage rise and it seemed as if not a single building in the capital city of Beijing had received a lick of new paint.

But the masses do not demand, unprompted, these expensive goodies from abroad. Just as the ads have replaced the quotations from Mao on the billboards, so these inviting displays are an act of official propaganda, a deliberate attempt to substitute the myths of consumer socialism for those of a revolution which went wrong.

The generation gap

April 1980, Beijing

The old men who run China have been offered a nice deal by Vice-Premier Deng Xiaoping, himself in his seventies and pledged to retire before 1985. They can take their well-deserved rest on 120 per cent full pay, the story goes, plus retaining the office car for their personal use. The problem is that most of them still prefer to hang on to power.

A revolution that has aged means inevitably that its leadership has aged with it. In the absence of the job mobility associated with capitalism, where dud ministers can move painlessly into company boardroooms, old cadres never seem to die. China's system of work organization means that the perks of high office go with the 'unit' – *danwei* - to which one belongs, right down to the provision of free cinema tickets. They cannot be bought with a retirement bonus.

'The old cadres in our place may have been fine in the past,' says one impatient Chinese in his late thirties. 'But now they take five hours to read a document you or I could finish in one.'

During the Cultural Revolution, there was a new institution, or at least a new aspiration, called the Three-way Alliance, which was intended to bring together 'the old, the middle-aged and the young' in an equal and harmonious share of power. One used to meet them all together, smiling a bit too emphatically, on the 'revolutionary committees' which took over management in factories, schools and local goverment. Now the managers have come back, and new measures of social and economic stratification – such as restoration of academic titles and selective pay increases to the better qualified – have only helped to widen the generation gaps. The young are impatient with the middle-aged, the middle-aged with the old, and the old, it sometimes seems, with everyone else. One might say that age warfare has replaced class warfare.

'We have seventy teachers in our schools,' a junior member of staff at a university in Tianjin told me, 'but less than a third of them teach. There are fifteen more working on a dictionary of Chinese–German synonyms, and the rest just collect their pay.'

At the other end of the scale, many of the young people living off their wits in Shanghai have escaped from the land, illegal returnees from Xinjiang in the North-west or Heilongjiang in the North-east, without proper papers or ration coupons. Although no numbers are given, enough have come back for this to be officially cited as an important factor in the housing shortage.

The crime and illegal trading generated by these problems is only a symptom of much deeper discontent. Twelve million students went 'down to the countryside' during the years 1968–76, of whom more than a million came from Shanghai, and only a small number have been allowed back. Those who remain, like the ones in the Aksu Reclamation Zone of Western Xinjiang, whose 'illegal organizations' have recently been banned, not only have no future, but have been deprived of the political rationale which partly sustained their exile.

'What did you think at the time?' I asked one student of a foreign language college who spent six years in the countryside.

'Of course, then, I believed it was a good thing. I would learn what manual labour was like and help to bridge the gap between the worker and the peasant. But now I know I have lost six years of my life.' This student belongs to a particularly vulnerable group who returned to higher education at the end of the Cultural Revolution, having earned their ticket as *gongnongbing*: 'worker–peasant–soldiers' in the portmanteau phrase for those who had been 'steeled through labour' in factories, villages or in the army.

This year the class of '76 will graduate all over China, yet so far there is confusion as to how they will be examined and whether they will merit proper graduate status and the same job prospects. At the national level, the intellectuals who have regained control of education and research say with resignation: 'We have lost a whole generation, maybe two.'

It is little wonder if those who are lost, and cannot even fill their rice bowls by legitimate means, should find it necessary to sell mimeographed love stories or Turtle shirts or foreign coins cadged from tourists on street corners.

4

The New Rural Revolution, 1978–87

In autumn 1978 I travelled in Shandong, then and now one of China's most developed provinces. Rural life was still visibly poor and reliant on human or animal labour. Simple courtyard inns – four-sided low buildings around a large empty square – displayed signs saying they catered for 'horses and carts'. Late at night, the peasant carts were still on the move: vast loads of fodder or straw piled ten feet high, with the driver wrapped in sacking and asleep on top. Opposite the Shengli or Victory Oilfield, a showpiece for China as it now embarked upon modernization, there were local villages of squat mud-brick houses huddled together, with a foot of straw stacked on wooden frame roofs to keep off the rain. The peasants defecated into an open cesspit, whipped by the wind blowing across the salt marshes.

The suburban farms on the outskirts of Beijing and Shanghai had long been modernized, with mini-tractors, greenhouses and plastic tunnels. Even during the Cultural Revolution they had done well, supplying the city's state-run shops with vegetables. They used the proceeds to set up small-scale industry, turning out mats and household utensils, and some simple farm machinery. They began to make more money in the free markets which were reopened in the late 1970s. Their industrial enterprises were the forerunners of the Township and Village Enterprises (TVEs) which would become so profitable in the 1980s. But away from the big cities, the countryside remained backward. On any long train journey, the hardships of rural life were easily visible from the carriage window.

Cautiously at first, the post-Mao leadership encouraged rural communities to revive incentives which had been frowned on, and *to parcel out the land for farming by individual households. By 1980 peasant markets were again thriving in rural towns at the county and district level: a journey across the loess plateau from Yan'an to Xi'an revealed bustling activity. In 1982 I visited Anhui province to splash around in the mud of villages where the People's Communes were being dismantled. The land was divided into small strips with complicated contracts allowing families to farm it individually. Peasants could build new houses, sell produce on the free markets, and start their own small enterprises. The one-child family campaign was pushed hard: couples who signed up for it might get a prize, or be given priority to buy a bicycle or a sewing machine. No one wanted to restore the commune system, and they gave a vivid account of what had gone wrong with it. But I noticed that those who were doing best were often relatives of the local cadres who were most enthusiastic about the reforms.*

A year later in Fujian province, I discussed a difficult question with provincial officials: if the collective assets are divided up and some people are allowed to get rich, might they not do so at the expense of the public interest? And how could eager peasants be dissuaded from digging up good farming land to build new houses? They denied that it was a problem, but the local paper was full of complaints that good earth was being stripped off the fields, and orchards were being cut down, to feed the voracious brick kilns.

The spirit of rural reform was moving away from the collective ethos which I and fellow enthusiasts had admired when we first visited China in 1971. Over sixteen years later, I returned to the model brigade of Dazhai to see how it had changed: I already knew that its peasant hero Chen Yonggui – promoted to Vice-Premier in the Cultural Revolution – had died of cancer, his reputation destroyed by allegations that the Dazhai success was a myth. On the spot I discovered the truth: that Dazhai's new leaders were adopting the new policies without repudiating the popular efforts of the past. I also found out just where we had our group photograph taken in 1971: it was a small but humiliating discovery.

Hard life on the plain
April 1980, Tianjin–Shanghai railway

It is time to go home on the North China plain, along the

railway line from Tianjin city into Shandong province. The peasants work in small groups, a dozen shouldering their hoes to walk back along paths of beaten earth.

A shepherd picks himself off the side of a gully where his sheep have grazed. A ploughman stands in front of his ox and wooden plough, urinating. In the course of an hour's journey, as dusk falls, I see two tractors. One is busy around the wigwam-like framework of bamboo poles which means a new well is being sunk. The other is actually ploughing, on an eccentric course to avoid the low mounds of ancestral graves.

The villages, the Chinese would say, are 'neither poor nor rich'. Houses are single-storeyed, with dry mud walls but solid tiled roofs. They have walled courtyards enclosing the 'private plot' where vegetables can be grown or chickens raised – and, since last year, sold in the free market of the nearest town.

I have seen much poorer. There are frequently stacks of new bricks, heaped in a semicircle. And the pigs look comfortable in their mud pens, circular in shape. The ground is dry and, except where recently broken, covered with late frost at the end of the day. All the ditches have been cleared and channels re-dug ready to irrigate the spring wheat.

Some production groups – perhaps one large family – work late to hoe down the rows. Even allowing for a long lunch break they spend ten hours in the fields. A father cycles home on a path snaking across the fields; three children run behind him. In the train I turn on the light with its blue cut-glass stem and chintz lampshade.

I wake to the classic sight of people standing outside their huts and cleaning their teeth (in the towns they do so on the pavement). This is the Yangzi valley, greener, with more water, and wealthier. Some villages have two storeyed houses with balconies and painted balustrades. Every house has its own small haystack kept dry by a thatched lid looking like a tea-cosy.

There are frequent canals with freight barges poled by two men. Some of these are made of concrete but kept afloat on the simple principle of displacement. The Chinese are proud of them. There is much activity hauling mud out of the bottom of ponds and canals and dumping it at the side. It serves as a low-value fertilizer.

Unlike the North, those working in the fields are segregated – all women, or all young men. Perhaps it is the more commercial life close to a big city which draws off the older men. The villages grow rich selling vegetables to Shanghai and there are long strips of plastic sheeting to cover the early crops.

The women carry water on the traditional carrying pole with a bucket at each end, moving with a springy trot in rhythm to the flexing of the bamboo. In 'revolutionary operas' (Gang of Four period) they would frequently burst into song while doing so, or shout cheerful remarks about the new Party secretary.

I have window-gazed for several hundred miles along a strip of countryside which, next to the railway, the Chinese define as highly developed. Almost everyone I have seen is working with a hand implement, often made of wood, to till land which becomes fertile only with immense investments of human labour.

The revival of rural commerce
February 1981, Huangling, Shaanxi province

The dust is just beginning to rise in the main square of Huangling County Town, Shaanxi province, North-west China. The melon-seller is still asleep where he lies guarding his stock. The man at the noodle stall is pumping his bellows for the first customers. Neat children cross the bridge and head for school above the old shrine on the hill.

Rather scruffy but basically well-ordered, this is the pattern of life in small-town China which the visitor rarely gets to see, although it holds the key to the country's future. This month, a long editorial in the official *People's Daily* called for the 'systematic development' of China's small-town economy. There are over 3,200 towns at the 'county' or similar level, and more than 50,000 small market towns in the communes, some of which – the *People's Daily* said – 'are in desolation and utter decline'.

They have suffered from neglect during years of emphasis upon large-scale development in and around the big urban centres. Local commercial enterprise was also restricted during the Cultural Revolution, so that 'the shops closed down and none appeared on the street.' All this is now changing and the commodity economy rules again. Every sort of wheeled vehicle now seems to be on the move in rural China, taking produce to the small town market. A trussed pig wriggles in a wheelbarrow. Chickens hang on bicycle handlebars.

In Huangling the state administration confronts the individual peasant producer face-to-face across the main square. On one side is the post office, now decked with posters to advertise China's new six-figure 'zip code'. Next to it is the bus station, where no service leaves more frequently than twice a day in this still backward region of the Northwest (not far from Yan'an, where Mao led the revolution). The bus timetables are written up according to the ten-day week of the *nongli* – the agricultural calendar still in general use.

The free market on the other side of the square only opened last year. Local officials throughout rural China have been resistant to restoring petty commerce. In the Cultural Revolution they would have been accused of 'restoring capitalism'. Apart from political hesitations, they are biased in favour of the state-run wholesale and distribution network, which is also a source of sideline perks for them.

Spread on towels in the dust, or on tables made out of boxes, there are local apples, cabbage, peppers, tobacco, twisty doughnuts and glasses of pale tea. Someone has produced a stock of sunglasses, to be worn with panache by young men driving lorries and tractors. But the *People's Daily* wants to encourage local enterprises on a larger scale than this.

The small town has historically been the nodal point of the rural economy. Here the peasant producer sells his produce, and the commune still does so collectively. Here is the only hairdresser, bathhouse, watch repair shop and cinema within reach, probably the only secondary school and hospital and whatever light industry the district possesses.

The Chinese now estimate that by the end of the present century there will be more than 100 million surplus labourers in the countryside*, and tens of millions of unemployed urban youth. But the *People's Daily* optimistically argues that if every small town could create 2,000 new jobs in local industry, service trades and commerce, the problem would be solved.

The concentration of industry in large towns cannot be blamed only on the Cultural Revolution, for considerable efforts were made then to develop small-scale industry in the communes. The process grew worse between 1976 and 1979, in the ambitious mood of Hua Guofeng's 'Four Modernizations'.

Outside Huangling, the road from Yan'an through to the provincial capital of Xi'an is being widened: the 200-mile journey at present takes two jolting days. Bulldozers attack the loose red earth from above; locally hired peasants tamp it down below with the ancient device of a stone in a rope sling, hoisted and thumped down.

Changes like these all help to promote the rural market economy which (as Mao Zedong argued twenty-five years ago) is the vital link between agriculture and industry. The question remains whether this can be done without eventually undermining the collective system which Mao also built up in the People's Communes.

Abolishing the people's communes
February 1982, Anhui

> *Who has not heard of Fengyang's fame?*
> *From where the last Ming emperor came?*
> *His folk took all the land, and then*
> *Fengyang had famine, nine years in ten.*

---

* The number of surplus labourers in the countryside by the later 1990s was in excess of 200 million. At least 70 million of these sought employment in the big towns, forming a new category of migrant workers with its own urban communities.

The people of Fengyang County in China's central Anhui province are not fatalistic about their lives (nor, contrary to the stereotype, are the Chinese anywhere else). They blame people for their troubles, not the gods.

The people of Fengyang now talk again about the state of famine to which they came very close – not in the Ming dynasty but in the last twenty years. And once more they refrain from blaming heaven. The poverty trap from which they are only just emerging had specific causes in the unwieldy collectivization policies of the late 1950s onwards and the inability of local officials to do their jobs properly.

It is a story which Western students of China like myself approach at first with some scepticism. Buffeted by political changes since the Cultural Revolution, many of us still cling to the view that whatever else of Mao's great vision proved fallible, the large-scale organization of rural labour in the People's Communes has worked and will or should continue to do so. Eleven years ago on my first visit to China writing for the *Guardian*, at the height of the Cultural Revolution, I watched the peasants of the national model for agriculture, Dazhai Brigade in Shanxi province, marching out to work for the afternoon, hoes shouldered in military style. They looked a little listless, not to say fed up. But I comforted myself with the thought that this reflected 'the natural rhythm of rural life'. It was a good thing it survived – even a credit to the Cultural Revolution – I said, and later wrote.

The people of Fengyang County have their own explicit view of what it was like to march out collectively to the fields: 'We went out to work like a lazy dragon' (in a long shuffling 'tail' or line) 'but we came back from work like a gust of wind!' And while they were out in the fields, 'we did our jobs all raggle-taggle, just as if we were working for a foreign boss' (i.e. they slowed down the moment no one in authority was looking).

Last year the whole of Anhui province completed a new revolution in the countryside, putting into operation a new scheme which allows each peasant household to farm a plot of land, pay the state taxes, fulfil the state quota, contribute to the collective welfare fund, and keep the balance for itself.

No one marches to work. No one is assigned jobs by the village leader. The land has been divided, although the collective 'team' still holds the title and can reassign it. It is called the 'responsibility system', but a better term for it would be the 'contract system' since the peasant producer acquires through it both rights and obligations. On the earthen shelf in every home, along with the family photos and beneath the New Year posters, is the Contract Book, bound like all official documents in China in a shiny red plastic cover.

Anhui started the scheme in early 1979, before anywhere else, and is officially regarded as the national pace-setter. And Fengyang County is the pace-setter within Anhui. The hot issue at the moment is the virtual abolition of one of Fengyang's forty-five People's Communes in an experiment which, if successful, is likely to be copied all over China. The new system has undoubtedly produced surpluses and some prosperity for the first time in years. It is also still feeling its way, and after a week's travel in Anhui I can foresee, more easily than my hosts would admit, some big snags ahead in the next three or five years.

But before discussing the details, should we mourn and deplore what is at least a whittling away of the collective structure imposed on the Chinese countryside since the mid-1950s (and quite possibly a step towards its complete abolition)? Or should we instead put ourselves in the place of the Chinese peasant sloshing around at this time of year in the mud (there are no cement paths in the villages) and consider a rather different historical perspective towards the People's Communes, which is less flattering both to Mao Zedong and to many of our previous assumptions?

The story starts in the early 1950s, when the Chinese were officially bent upon 'Learning from the Soviet Union'. In appearance, the movement for advanced agricultural cooperatives, launched by Mao in 1955 and followed by the Great Leap Forward in 1958, owed nothing to the Soviet model – and the Russians publicly disapproved of the People's Communes. But people in China now argue that these experiments were marred from the start by a fatal but invisible Soviet import. It was assumed that agriculture could and should be organized on a large-scale and uniform collective basis, and that it could be made to work by the authoritarian intervention of the Communist Party in the whole labour process.

It is true that Mao at that time criticized (though only behind closed Party doors) Stalin's approach to collectivization for not 'trusting the peasants'. But Mao himself only trusted them as long as they accepted the formula 'Big in Scale and Common in Ownership' as being necessarily appropriate for Chinese agriculture. For places like Fengyang, already disorganized by the 1955–6 movement to set up advanced co-ops, the People's Communes caused complete confusion. At first there was free food for everyone, handed out from the overflowing public granary. The peasants were not allowed to keep even one catty (half a kilo) of grain at home, creating the illusion of plenty, since no one had ever before seen so much grain gathered together in one place. The grain soon ran out, and before long they were eating dogs. In the three years 1958–61, out of a total population of 380,000 in the county, more than 60,000 died 'in an irregular manner' – the usual euphemism for starvation. This chilling statistic has never been published before.

Throughout China the situation grew so serious that in 1960 the Head of State, Liu Shaoqi, till then uneasily collaborating with Mao, was summoned back to his home town to see it for himself. Horrified, he returned to Beijing, confronted Mao, and for a short year or so the policies eased. In 1961 the flight of people to the cities seeking food was reversed. But then came in quick succession: 1962, Mao's call to 'Never Forget Class Struggle'; 1963, the Four Clean-ups movement against alleged capitalism in the countryside; 1964, the movement to 'Learn from Dazhai' and 'Put Politics in Command'.

At the height of the Cultural Revolution, peasants in Fengyang had to study the Little Red Book during their lunch-time rest, and again in returning from the fields. They had to respond to a mass movement to write poems in their spare time. 'Some households were so poor,' I was told by a

Chinese researcher who has made his own study of the area, 'that they only had one bowl between them for their rice.' As late as 1978, according to one account, beggars still knocked on the doors clutching their official permits (allowing them to travel – the local authorities were glad to see them go) and asking for food.

Local officials are still reluctant to discuss these years in such detail, perhaps partly because many of them not so long ago were either being struggled against as class enemies or leading the struggle teams. They are more inclined to stress that, with or without the Cultural Revolution, the large-scale organization of labour in a backward rural economy is too ambitious an exercise and that early enthusiasm was bound to wane.

How could local cadres organize anything between 60 and 120 or so peasants in a team or brigade to work efficiently day by day, and then to assign 'work-points' which adequately distinguished between those who made more or less effort? Realistic assessment of work-points caused too much strife, so cadres were tempted to narrow the differentials. The hard worker might get ten, the lazy one would still earn seven or eight. Favouritism was also shown towards relatives and friends. The whole business was *bu haoyisi*, 'not nice', liable to cause aggravation and disturb the harmony which a society living close to the margin must in self-preservation maintain.

A well-known scholar in Beijing, who began investigating the modern transformation of Chinese agriculture long before the Communist victory, makes a more fundamental theoretical point. The whole idea of collective labour and reward in agriculture is based on a false analogy with the employment of industrial labour on fixed differentials of pay. Modern industry can quite precisely quantify its tasks and output, and the industrial process allows for the impartial assignment day by day of work and reward. In the country-side this can only be done where agriculture is thriving and already semi-industrialized – for example in the 'suburban communes' near Beijing and Shanghai. Places like these still keep the commune more or less intact, or have introduced less radical forms of the 'responsibility system'.

But in undeveloped agriculture such a process can only be partial and subjective, and the only quantification is provided once a year by the harvest. Placing even the best-intentioned cadres under heavy strain, it opened the door to lethargy and corruption in the People's Communes.

Trouble with tangerines
November 1983, Fujian

The countryside near Fuzhou, capital of the southern province of Fujian, has long been known for its luscious tangerine orchards. In the last two years it has become better known for the piles of brick, stacked everywhere as part of the big new rural construction boom. The new 'responsibility system' in Chinese agriculture, through which the collectively owned land has been parcelled out under contract to individual households, has helped bring wealth to many peasants. And what is more natural than to spend it on a fine new house with concrete floor, tiled roof and solid walls of brick.

But the apparent harmony of brick kilns amid the tangerine orchards overlays a contradiction which is just beginning to be discussed in the local press. Tangerine trees grow best on raised mounds of earth. Over the years this has led to rich soil being heaped up around them. After visiting Luxia Brigade in Chengmen Commune I asked, almost as an afterthought, where they had obtained the raw earth for the bricks which were stacked by the thousand all around. 'From the tangerine orchards which we have cut down,' I was told. It may have been justified in the case of this particular village, close to the provincial capital, which is rapidly becoming a rural-industrial estate. (As well as bricks, it makes wooden furniture, paper boxes, saws, plastic rope and even suitcase keys.)

But a letter published in the *Fujian Daily* on 25 November which I read on the same day of my visit to Luxia Brigade, pointed to a wider problem. 'The evil trend of digging up the fields to make mud bricks,' said the headline, 'must be stopped.' The writer complained that throughout his county the peasants were helping themselves to good earth for brick-making, in some places baring the soil till they reached bedrock. When reproached for doing so, they would reply that, 'Now the land has been contracted out to us peasants, you can mind your own business. What's the harm anyhow in taking a bit of earth to make bricks?' But some more perceptive peasants, according to the letter-writer, understood very well what was at stake. 'This is killing the chicken to get the eggs,' they lamented. 'If it does not stop, we shall be smashing the rice-bowl of our children and grand-children.'

While some food-producing communes have thinned out their fruit trees, others have been planting new orchards. Perhaps this illustrates the trend towards specialized cultivation which the 'responsibility system' is supposed to encourage. In one such orchard near Fuzhou, the work-force told a revealing story. It was only since 1977 that the orchard had been planted, and only since 1982 that it had begun to show a profit. Yet how had the land been cleared in the first place (it was previously barren) and when? The answer was readily but uncomprehensively supplied. The work had begun in 1972, with the use of volunteer labour to open up the barren soil and plant it with mulberries as a first crop. Was volunteer labour a good thing then, and was it still in practice? Of course not, came the answer amid much laughter. In those days people just came to work for the food. Nowadays under the responsibility system everyone had enough food of their own.

Officials in charge of the Fuzhou area are becoming aware of the problems which will arise if the habit of collective labour is lost. One of the five basic principles of the new system, they say, is that there should be collective labour before and after production (*chanqian chanhou defuwu*). Paddy rice is supposed to be planted and more waterworks to be maintained by joint effort; and the spraying of fields and other pest prevention also done jointly. But a circular issued in November by the Communist Party Central Committee's Rural Policy Research Office suggested that in some areas the problem is still the reverse –

that demands for collective labour are felt to be too heavy. The circular specified that a ceiling should be set on voluntary labour, which should generally be kept within twenty days a year. The maximum was thirty days, after which peasants should be paid. The answer may be that in poorer parts of rural China collective efforts are still generally perceived to be essential, but that in the better-off areas the peasants now wish to go it alone.

The other four principles outlined by Fuzhou officials are:

- To put into full effect the responsibility system, with production fully contracted out to the household. Less than 5 per cent of Fuzhou's production teams – mostly specialized vegetable growers – still function as the basic accounting unit.
- To discard the 1970s policy of 'taking grain as the key link' and to diversify production, with particular attention in the mountainous and seaboard zones to the encouragement of forestry and fishery. Ten per cent of the hillsides has been parcelled out to peasant households to hold 'from generation to generation' (i.e. on the same basis as the 'private plots' of arable land).
- To encourage 'specialized' households and groups which will develop skills in commerce, service, transport, building, repair work, etc. These will provide a substitute for (and, it is claimed, an improvement on) the services formerly provided by the collective.
- To develop flourishing markets and to allow goods to circulate freely for sale. Private shops may be opened and produce may be transported beyond the provincial boundaries without bureaucratic delay – for example, fish to the markets in Shanghai.

In contrast to my last visit to the Chinese countryside – Anhui province in February 1982 – officials will now admit, though with some reluctance, to what are called 'certain problems arising from the new situation'. These were listed in Fuzhou as follows:

1. A falling-off of peasants' enthusiasm for education, with children being kept back to work in the fields. To counter this, more schools were being built, and minimum standards

of education were now demanded for employment in rural enterprises.

2. A revival of feudal superstitions. 'When the masses have money, some of them spend it on making Buddhas and building temples.' This was described as a form of 'spiritual pollution' and I was told in Beijing that the current urban campaign against this unhealthy tendency would in due course shift to the countryside. However it has since been stressed that the countryside will be left alone.

3. Excessive expense on weddings. This is a familiar complaint since the Cultural Revolution.

4. The problem of unregulated building as described above.

5. The burden of collective taxation is still too heavy. Subtractions for the brigade budget should not exceed 8 per cent of peasant income. There were still 'too many cadres' being supported by collective funds, and most teams should be able to manage with just one accountant to keep the books.

It does not take much perception to become aware of the tension between the collective and the individual interest which both the 'achievements' and the 'problems' described to me in Fuzhou reveal. On the one hand the need for collective labour is stressed, while on the other hand the burden of collective taxation is said to be too heavy. One has the impression of an effort to square the theoretical circle behind which must lie substantial differences of opinion which only rarely break the surface.

When pressed hard on this fundamental contradiction between what used to be called 'public versus private interest', one official explained how it is well understood in Beijing that the present system will not, as it stands, provide the necessary incentives for future 'capital construction' in the countryside – the investment of labour and resources in new projects for the benefit of the community.

'Deng Xiaoping has made it clear,' I was told, 'that the new forms of organization contained in the responsibility system are only satisfactory for the present time. As for the future, we still have to investigate how it can be developed. We have only just made a beginning – it is not clear where we shall go next, but we do know that we cannot return to the old system. We also know that we have to create a new spirit of enthusiasm and a new form of collective.'

This commitment to seek the establishment of new – and, it is said, 'more genuine' – forms of collective enterprise is expressed seriously. It also ties in with recent reminders that the post-Mao leadership of the Chinese Communist Party has not abandoned the goal of proceeding along the path of socialist transition in the direction of a communist society. But however serious the theory, it is not at all clear that it is seriously reflected in practice. The most recent innovations to the responsibility system, set out in the Party Central Committee's Document No. 1 of 1984, can only point in the other direction.

Document No. 1, it has been explained, has been drawn up with the aim of 'doing everything to make the peasants get rich', though it is acknowledged that it has faced opposition due to 'remnants of Leftist influence'. Its most important provisions are (1) to allow peasants to hold contracted land for a period of at least fifteen years (until now land has only been contracted out for between two and five years), and (2) to allow contracted land to be transferred from one household to another.

The purpose of these reforms is clear enough. The longer lease for contracted land will encourage peasant lessees to invest more labour and capital in developing its productivity, rather than milking the soil dry of its fertility for short-term gains. And the provision for transfer of holdings will encourage the concentration of land in the hands of those best able to farm it efficiently – while other peasants will give up cultivation altogether and work in the expanding sector of rural industry and commerce. The fact that these reforms are necessary also indicates the inadequacies of the responsibility system in its original form. It is an open admission that the system can lead to a reduction in investment (and therefore a loss of fertility) and to inefficient cultivation – problems which on my first visit in early 1982 were blamed upon the previous system of collectively organized production.

But what will be the effect of these latest reforms upon

production relations in the countryside? Long-term leases must further encourage peasant households to regard the land as individually owned – even though the title still belongs to the surviving rump of the collective system. And the transfer of holdings will be accompanied by the payment of 'proper compensation' on the basis of the original land price 'appraised according to its grade'. Money will change hands, even though the transaction is supposed to be handled by the collective, and land will once again after nearly three decades have a cash value. With reforms such as these, the struggle between public and private interest can only grow more acute.

Revisiting the past
August 1987, Dazhai, Shanxi province

Returning to the former model village of Dazhai in North China, sixteen years after a visit made mid-Cultural Revolution, I faced two problems. The first was how to find the place where we – the Society for Anglo-Chinese Understanding 1971 study tour – had posed for our group picture wearing Mao caps and badges.

My sense of geography was disorientated by the vast 200-bed hotel built in Dazhai, and now dustily empty since the village was 'demodelized' in the late 1970s. But I found the spot eventually. It was right in front of the village public lavatory – a detail we had overlooked when we assembled in 1971 – and next to a large hoarding with a quotation written by Lin Biao (Mao's chosen successor but shortly to die, after an attempt on his life).

The other problem had to do with the relativity of historical truth. It was not just the discrepancies in statistics between then and now, but whether Dazhai's peasant leaders had falsified the record and there had been no model at all.

Fortunately the photograph, now peered at warily by the current village leaders, helped me to find Mrs Song Liying. She had been active in 1971 in the women's branch which worked so hard to terrace Dazhai's rocky slopes, and was still a Communist Party member today, though retired.

The political dramas which had affected Dazhai since I last visited included the fall of the peasant leader Chen Yonggui, made a Chinese Vice-Premier by Mao Zedong but buried without a memorial service when he died in 1981. (His son was also accused of committing rapes.) Dazhai officials were said to have inflated their production figures and relied on special subsidies. Jiang Qing was supposed to have been visiting Dazhai while Chairman Mao was dying – and dawdled on her way back to Peking.

For Mrs Song all of this seems remote and on a different plane from the realities of what she and her husband (the local Party Secretary before Chen Yonggui) and the people of Dazhai actually did. 'We laid the foundation then for all the good things of today,' she says firmly. 'Now the village has six cars, seven motorbikes and eight tractors. But that is only possible because we built the dam, levelled the land, and recovered from the great flood of 1963 by adhering to Self-Reliance and Hard Struggle.'

Yes, she adds, Dazhai had been declared 'ultra-Leftist', and it was probably a mistake to concentrate so much on growing grain instead of diversifying. Yes, she used to go to a lot of conferences in Peking till Chairman Hua Guofeng (Mao's immediate successor and a Dazhai enthusiast) was demoted. But the important thing was that they had made Dazhai what it is today.

There is a poster of Chairman Mao meeting Premier Zhou Enlai on Mrs Song's wall, a modest black and white TV, lots of pictures of grown-up children and their families, and a well-scrubbed earthen floor. Outside they have a patch with ripening tomatoes which would not have been allowed in 1971. Other changes in the village are a private shop – the owner nets 1000 *yuan* (160 pounds) a year – and a private shoe-mender in a building still labelled 'library'.

There are also private vegetable plots at the start of the track which goes up the hill to the reservoir, through terraces of maize and past poplars which were young saplings when I last came. It was once a political nature trail for thousands of Chinese as well as foreign groups every year. (They had to go clockwise round the valley to ease the traffic flow.)

This time there is one old man sucking his pipe and guarding a new orchard where fifty of the villagers work. This is diversification, but it is watered by the sweat of the sixties. Higher up the hill, some of the less fertile terraces have been planted with timber.

There is an evident generation gap between Mrs Song and Mr Gao, the new Dazhai Party Secretary, who does not like talking very much about the years when 'Learn from Dazhai' was picked out in stones on 10,000 Chinese hillsides. History for Mr Gao begins at the end of 1978 when the Deng Xiaoping economic reforms began to take hold. He explains that there was considerable resistance in Dazhai to the new policy of parcelling out the land to individual households, rather than working it collectively and sharing out the proceeds in roughly equal proportions on the basis of 'work-points'.

'Some of our old people remembered the bad old days,' he says. 'There were fears of polarization – that the rich would get rich and the poor poorer. We had to be educated by the party and the state to overcome the spirit of egalitarianism.'

Dazhai edged into the new system slowly, first splitting the 'brigade' into three production teams, and then into six working groups, still organized collectively. It only made the great leap into the household 'responsibility system' in January 1983, probably the last village in the whole of North China to do so.

It was with Mr Gao that I had my problem with statistics. His version has the people earning less than 160 *yuan* (twenty-seven pounds) in 1978. I had been told in 1971 that the figure was already 300 *yuan* (fifty pounds). But Mr Gao was loyal to his predecessors, refusing to admit that anyone had falsified anything. Chen Yonggui, he said, 'made some good contributions – and this is the opinion of the Party's Central Committee.'

Why, I wondered, had I been told in 1971 that Dazhai 'produced more food in one year than it can eat in three'? Well, said Mr Gao, they were probably talking about maize. 'Nowadays we sell our maize to the state for animal fodder and eat wheat three times a day.'

A broad highway to Dazhai from the city of Yangquan was the last reward of the Chen Yonggui days. Now Dazhai is waiting for a more vital rail link to be completed from the same city to the nearby county town of Xiyang. Dazhai, like many other communities in the eastern hills of Shanxi Province, is sitting on coal and it opened its first mine last year.

Yangquan takes its visitors to the new model village of Xiao Gu Cun, where the men have stopped working on the land altogether. That is women's work, says the Party Secretary there, 'for growing vegetables'. The village has a new primary school, an open-air auditorium for local opera performances, and a Daoist shrine (though I noticed that the Party Secretary kept the key to it). The average income is said to be 1,700 *yuan* (280 pounds) a year, and most people are well ahead of Mrs Song in Dazhai. The televisions in Xiao Gu Cun are colour, not black and white.

5

The World Discovers China, 1984–6

Richard Nixon broke the mould when in February 1972 he stood on the Great Wall and proclaimed that it was truly great. US network commentators filmed live from department stores in Beijing, asking bemused shop assistants whether they were 'dating' anyone. China, whose 'foreign friends' had been restricted to Albania and a few others during the Cultural Revolution, was admitted to the UN and welcomed leaders from around the globe. More foreign correspondents were based in Beijing or visited regularly, although still subject to tight restriction. In 1979 Deng Xiaoping visited the US where he wore a Stetson at a Texas rodeo and completed the 'normalization' of Sino-US relations. Five years later Ronald Reagan paid his presidential visit to China where he tried, too openly for Chinese liking, to present the two countries as allied partners against the Soviet Union.

As a British journalist, I was excluded from the events but found them more interesting watched from the Beijing street corner. The crowds were becoming irritated by a succession of international leaders who caused traffic jams. In the huge Soviet embassy, diplomats from Moscow talked hopefully about restoring historic relations, but China preferred to leave the 'Soviet card' on the table. For all the stiffness towards Mr Reagan, it was Western technology and investment which it sought.

This was also the time of shuttle diplomacy over the future of Hong Kong. In September 1984, after two difficult years of negotiation, Britain concluded a deal to hand Hong Kong over when the lease expired in 1997. Margaret Thatcher's illusions that China could be browbeaten into extending the lease had been dashed. The Hong Kong people were told to make the best of it by the British Foreign Secretary Geoffrey Howe and Governor Edward Youde. The negotiations had been conducted in absolute secrecy broken only by the Chinese when they wished to remind Britain of the bottom line that, one way or another, they were going to take back Hong Kong. By procrastinating, Mrs Thatcher nurtured Chinese suspicions of duplicity – not forgotten in later years. Many Hong Kongers wept at the deal, which was confirmed after a bogus exercise in public consultation, and began making plans either to leave, or to come to terms with Beijing.

The pace of democratic reform quickly emerged as an issue. Senior Hong Kong officials who had scoffed at local pro-democracy voices (and kept them under surveillance by the Special Branch) now discussed plans for the election of some Legislative Councillors. At the New China News Agency, Chinese officials made quietly cautious noises.

Britain's diplomatic 'success' too was sealed with a visit. The Queen had long wanted to visit China: in 1986 she seized her chance, with a less enthusiastic Duke of Edinburgh in tow. Popular Chinese magazines carried pictures of the royal family and translated chunks of biography by former royal nannies, but ordinary people were often confused, mistaking the Queen for Mrs Thatcher – much admired, now that the Hong Kong deal had been signed, as a qiang nuren *or 'strong woman' (the Chinese equivalent of Iron Lady). The visit will always be remembered for the Duke's casual question to a British student studying in Xi'an: how did he enjoy working alongside people with 'slitty eyes'? Beijing pretended not to have heard, but the tabloid press back home did not let him forget it.*

A President meets the warriors
27 April 1984, Beijing

After only one full day of the Reagan visit to China, Sino-American differences in style and content on such an occasion have already become as plain as the difference between beancurd and pumpkin pie.

Mr Reagan is always smiling broadly, and seems slightly larger than life – though some American correspondents thought he might be wearing a bullet-proof vest. The Chinese leaders are smaller in the flesh, a bit withdrawn and smile rather tightly. The Chinese convey a precise indication of how the visit rates in their larger political context by the speeches, the amount of press coverage, and even by the number of flags in the streets. The effect Mr Reagan intends to produce is much less clear. In a speech yesterday to Chinese community leaders he led his audience on a moralizing excursion from God to free enterprise by way of the founding fathers. The purpose was perhaps to congratulate the Chinese for becoming, in his eyes, so much more like the Americans. He said that 'China's economy crackles with the dynamics of change.' The American people were not surprised to see 'the fresh breezes of incentive sweeping . . . across China'.

The Chinese like to be told that they are on the track, but not so fulsomely. The embarrassment could be political, too, since Mr Reagan singled out Premier Zhao Ziyang for praise which might provide useful ammunition one day to his detractors. And who could have advised Mr Reagan to boast, in a land of scarcity, that the US is the leading economic nation and 'the bread basket of the world'?

Mr Reagan got a 21-gun salute, just two more than Premier Nakasone, but the Chinese used the same rather tatty bunting down the main street that they would have used for the President of the Seychelles. The *People's Daily* had Mr Reagan's arrival top-right on the front page, but definitely not the lead, which went to a report on party rectification in Hebei Province. However China's hopes for economic gains in access to US technology and investment have been well-displayed for days.

The old myth that the Chinese are inscrutable is disproved once again. Yesterday they communicated very clear messages about where they disagreed on international affairs, in sentences which might have been carved on stone slabs in the Temple of Confucius. Here one should add that the temple in the north of Beijing has a gripping exhibition about US wartime support for the Kuomintang Secret Service, complete with instruments of torture. No one saw any reason to close it during the Reagan visit – the past is never entirely forgotten.

The diffuse image projected by the Americans hints at an ambiguity of content as well as a clumsy style. In the Kissinger days, and again with the normalization of relations under Mr Carter, effects were calculated more precisely because they were well-defined. Is the US still trying to nudge China into shared alignment against the Soviet Union? White House sources said defensively last night that they had no wish for 'strategic cooperation' with China. Is the US really committed to maximize the China market? There is a surprising lack of agreement among Americans. Some businessmen already working in Beijing say that the potential is enormous. Others deride the doctrine of 'lamps for China' and doubt whether China will ever absorb large quantities of US technology.

The Chinese style and strategy is clearer, although not necessarily bound to succeed. Zeng Guofan, the great advocate of 'self-strengthening' in the 1860s, once wrote some advice on how to handle 'barbarian affairs', which might still be the text today. 'In your association with foreigners,' he observed, 'your manner and deportment should not be too lofty, and you should have a slightly vague casual appearance.' He even counselled that if the barbarians were rude or tactless, the right response was 'to look slightly stupid'. But the main thrust of self-strengthening was that China should 'carefully watch and learn their superior techniques – but also observe their shortcomings'. China's strategy today still assumes that a modernizing country can absorb foreign techniques while maintaining the 'Chinese essence', which is no longer Confucianism but socialism led by the Communist Party.

One of the nicest touches yesterday was a picture caption in the *China Daily* which identified Ronald Reagan as the man with a dark tie and his wife Nancy as the woman holding flowers, as if not everyone might recognize them. Chinese enthusiasm goes so far but no further. The modest crowd at the welcoming ceremony on Thursday surged forward at the end, much to the excitement of the White House pool of reporters. They reported that it was 'a spectacular flood of humanity' hoping to see the president. Some may have so hoped. But I was there on the pavement with the impatient crowd and I know that many others wanted to catch a bus or just go shopping after waiting for ages to cross the road.

30 April, Xi'an

Today, Mr Reagan was finally allowed his triumph in China, after two days when things had not gone quite right. Arriving at China's most famous archaeological site, near the North-west city of Xi'an, he could forget about the long list of Chinese complaints on US foreign policy which had been voiced very publicly. Entering the great, roofed excavation, he could overlook the sharp words about Taiwan addressed to the Secretary of State, Mr Shultz, in the morning.

Accompanied by the provincial governor of Shaanxi province, he walked right down into the excavation vaults and among the terracotta army of life-sized horses and soldiers made in honour of China's first emperor over 2,000 years ago. 'You are the first foreign head of state,' said Governor Li Qingwei, 'who has been given the honour of going so close to them.' 'Thank you so much,' replied Mr Reagan and, turning to a terracotta horse, he asked: 'May I touch it? I know it can't kick me.' With a final gesture as he left the vault, Mr Reagan looked around and ordered the soldiers and horses to 'disperse'.

But, back in Beijing, the *People's Daily* found space for less than a fifth of Mr Reagan's banquet speech on Saturday. It cut out with great care a line about cooperation against 'world aggressive forces', just as similar references to the Soviet Union were censored from Mr Reagan's speeches on television and radio.

Tonight, Mr Reagan returned from Xi'an, and Mrs Reagan came back with five little handmade toys from a free market near the tomb of the first Chinese emperor. Mr Reagan himself had paid five *yuan* (one pound) for the toys – a lot of money in China, and perhaps comforting proof of the entrepreneurial ethic. Speeding back along the Avenue of Everlasting Peace, with the traffic as before bottled up and every side street blocked off, he passed through Tiananmen Square. While he was away visiting, four enormous portraits of Marx, Engels, Lenin and Stalin had gone up. It is all part of the refurbishing for May Day, but it may have provoked some thought in the presidential mind.

Hong Kong hears its future
26 September 1984

The Governor of Hong Kong gave a schoolmasterly look at the assembled Legislative Council last night and explained in a precise voice why the agreement initialled earlier in the day is an offer they cannot refuse.

Behind him was the familiar royal coat of arms, on which the motto *Honi Soit Qui Mal y Pense* might on this occasion be translated as 'We did our best – and you'd better believe it'.

Sir Edward Youde made up for the omission of the negotiators at their ceremony in Beijing, who in their mutual congratulations had ignored the role of the people of Hong Kong. He paid tribute instead to the 'resilience and forbearance' which they had shown during two years of being kept mostly in the dark.

The governor softened a little the blunt message of the White Paper as conveyed in paragraph 29: 'There is no possibility of an amended agreement,' says Her Majesty's Government. 'The alternative to acceptance of the present agreement is to have no agreement.'

Down past the old colonial cathedral, with its enormous electric fans hanging from the ceiling, at the foot of Battery Path, young Hong Kong Chinese on their way home lined up to collect copies of the text. It was a mild rush but not a stampede, and it prompted the thought that in Beijing a much smaller number would never have formed such an orderly queue. How much the Brits have achieved!

Getting home, they could watch a Sino-British joint declaration special on television unless they chose a Cantonese pop opera on the other Chinese channel. But in a devastating display of over kill Sir Geoffrey Howe's press conference in New York was shown on all four channels simultaneously.

An enterprising manufacturer of fancy neon signs has captured the mood of Hong Kong at its most determinedly optimistic by a well-timed display in the glass-domed Landmark Centre. First, we see two stars – one larger than the other (surely it must be Beijing) – behind the green peaks of Victoria Island, and then the office tower blocks of Central District light up. The harbour comes alive and a junk sails past. But next there is a flash of lightning (last year's collapse of the dollar?). Fortunately, the storm is soon followed by a rainbow and the rising red sun.

This is probably the most widespread view. It is not a bad document, so why not make the best of it? After HMG's warning that disagreement can harm Hong Kong's health, people do not expect a great rush of contrary opinions to be delivered to the Assessment Office which is going to report on the territory's state of mind.

There is also, quite reasonably, a move by people in public life – those who do not intend to buy a Fiji passport or to avail themselves of the notorious 'OBE clause' in the British Nationalities Act (which granted citizenship to those who had performed good works for the Crown) – to soften any critical remarks they may have.

After the Chinese liberation of the mainland, Mao Zedong welcomed with open arms anyone describing himself as a patriotic capitalist. It prompted the saying, 'Better a late revolutionary than an early one, and best of all someone who is not a revolutionary at all.' The same remark is being applied to some new friends of Beijing in Hong Kong.

Meanwhile, the rain starts as Sir Edward continues his lecture. He has always seemed to chafe a bit, ever since the Chinese slapped him down for claiming to represent the people of Hong Kong on the negotiations.

Sir Edward says, in a slightly waspish phrase, that it is a fact of geography that Hong Kong needs 'a sound relationship with its great mainland neighbour'. Neighbour? In less happy times Beijing would be protesting against that, too.

For a moment it seems as if the Legislative Council is

going to discuss the Marine Fish Culture Ordinance and the Fixed Penalty (Traffic Contravention) Amendment as well as the Hong Kong agreement.

But they are only tabled to remind us that the Hong Kong Government still has to go on running the territory in every detail. The unelected Legislative Council members who protested so loudly not many months ago now sit silently as they are praised for the sincere way in which they have expressed their views. Then they bow and follow Sir Edward out of the chamber, looking slightly diminished.

Over at the New China News Agency, the unofficial diplomatic headquarters of Beijing, there were soft drinks only at a briefing for the Western journalists, which must be a good sign for the future. The men from Beijing are easy to spot in the shopping arcades of Central District, with their white shirts and short back and sides and slightly hesitant air. But people feel that it is soon they who will be walking taller.

Tallest of all will be the new building to replace the present Bank of China, for which plans were recently announced. Designed by the patriotic Chinese–American Mr I. M. Pei, it will have seventy storeys and, says Mr Pei, 'the best view in Hong Kong'.

The new democratic agenda
3 October 1984, Hong Kong

The Chinese posters in the Hong Kong metro urge people to register as voters so that they can express 'the voice from your hearts'. Suddenly, after 140 years, democracy is a public issue and will become more so in the build up to 1997.

Could it lead to heart-to-heart speeches from election platforms in Statue Square, which would surely disturb the colonial spirits of long-dead judges of the Supreme Court and directors of the Hong Kong and Shanghai Bank?

Or in spite of the growing call for untrammelled direct elections and full democracy by 1997 from articulate pressure groups – taking Beijing's slogan of Hong Kongers ruling Hong Kong at face value – will it be a rather more subtle process?

'Whatever you call the new system,' says someone who may become active in it, 'the Chinese will be the elders. You can't get too far out of line. But it's up to the people of Hong Kong to arrange things intelligently so that they don't have to go up to the New China News Agency for everything.'

The Sino-British agreement states simply that 'the legislatures of the Hong Kong Special Administrative Region shall be constituted by elections,' which is a good deal clearer than many had expected. But the route to this destination still has to be worked out.

In July this year the Hong Kong government, which for years had claimed that its consultative processes were the summit of democracy, produced a Green Paper on representative reform. It was largely a holding operation, which helped ensure that the government will have a stake in the necessary process of change towards 1997. It proposes a cautious shift to indirect elections for part of the at present wholly appointed Legislative Council, with a review of the political system fixed for 1989. A White Paper on the same subject, promised for mid-November, is unlikely to yield much to the growing demand for an element of direct elections, but may hint at greater post-1989 change.

The Governor of Hong Kong, Sir Edward Youde, said yesterday that changes to the system of government should not be introduced too hastily as to 'endanger Hong Kong's stability at this crucial time'. He gave no support to public calls, expressed since the Green Paper on representative government was published in July, for direct elections. In his speech to the new session of the Legislative Council he did hold out the possibility of advancing the date for a review of the process by two years to 1987.

Zhao Ziyang, the Chinese premier, has publicly supported the principle of democratization in Hong Kong. Chinese officials are avoiding comment on the Green Paper, saying that they do not intend to interfere, but they appear to share Sir Edward's insistence on the need to proceed cautiously.

Yet the real constitutional authority for the administrative structure after 1997 must derive from the Basic Law to be drawn up over the next few years in Beijing. Interim reforms in Hong Kong may be discussed by the joint Sino-British Liaison Group, which is empowered to consider all matters 'relating to the smooth transfer of government in 1997'. It is not clear how these different strands of decision-making will mesh together.

District Board elections next March will help pave the way for an electoral college to choose the first non-appointed Legislative Council members. The registration campaign for it has been quite successful, with the left-wing trade unions for the first time encouraging their members to sign up. Over 600,000 new voters are enrolled, making a total of about one and a half million, or 50 per cent of the number of eligible voters.

Young Hong Kong professionals – doctors, academics, lawyers and business people – are begining to weigh their careers against a political plunge. Many of them first found their voice when the Sino-British negotiations began two years ago, with the Hong Kong Observers Group in the lead.

A number of the younger and more recently appointed members of the Legislative Council may also submit to the democratic test, and a shake-out of the council could occur in September next year when the two-year appointed terms of all its members expire. But the lawyers and other professionals who are often cynical about China and the agreement, and the 'Legco' members who praise Beijing's sincerity and the 'fine print' in the agreement agree on one thing.

'We just don't know what they really want,' said one of the latter group, 'but we somehow have to evolve a system of administration which will dovetail into Chinese strategy.' At the moment Hong Kong's democratic reforms are in a holding pattern, circling until the pilot gets the right signals from Beijing airport.

The pressure groups who are calling for direct elections, with their broader social base among church and welfare organizations, are more optimistic about Chinese tolerance or are more determined to pre-empt any objections at the New China News Agency.

In the more optimistic view, the Chinese are playing it by

ear. 'How much they allow,' says a leading pressure group figure, 'depends on how much the Hong Kong people want to get.'

It would be nice to believe that China supports an untrammelled system of a directly elected legislature and government. But its reservation about the number one job is already written into the joint agreement. The post-1997 Chief Executive will be 'selected by election or through consultations held locally' – a distinct echo of China's own consultative process.

Some local politicians claiming to be in tune with Beijing are more in favour of indirect elections and the 'functional constituencies' (business and other professional bodies) proposed by the Green Paper for the Legislative Council.

Britain's motives for encouraging democracy in Hong Kong after so many years are not very flattering to China, nor to the people of Hong Kong who have no illusions about it. We had a good system going, say the British, with Hong Kong ruled by Letters Patent from the Crown, and by the 'constraint of custom'. But one cannot transfer unwritten rules to China, and so one encourages reforms some of which were spoken of not so long ago with amused contempt by Hong Kong government officials.

If in the next few years Beijing leans too heavily on Hong Kong's hesitant democrats, or the British behave too cynically, it would be a fatal start. It will be hard enough anyhow to find real potential leaders for the future in sufficient number. 'We have to look for people,' says one pressure group leader, 'who have retained an independent way of thinking under a colonial administration which has so often repressed ability.'

Business leaders and Government supporters look warily on the whole prospect, in some cases fearing the emergence of radical ideas with a primitive horror. In fact there is no chance of it. Those who are concerned about the polarization of wealth, the gaping holes in Hong Kong's social security net, the high rents and sometimes dreadful working conditions, know that they must put their case with care.

No one wants to give the impression of advocating what is

often called a 'free lunch' society. It is noted by Hong Kong visitors to China that some welfare provisions – particularly pensions in the large state sector of industry and commerce – are way ahead of Hong Kong. Chinese wages may be low, but so are rents and medical fees. Beijing's own visitors to Hong Kong have endorsed the need for reform but cautiously. Perhaps it is balanced by their concern for the continued health of entrepreneurial capitalism.

A Queen walks on the wall
12 October 1986, Beijing

The Queen arrived in Beijing yesterday at the start of her seven-day visit to China to an airport reception committee including the Chinese Foreign Minister, Mr Wu Xueqian, a beaming Chinese ambassador from London, and a little boy who gave her a stiff Young Pioneer's salute. Then, like every other first-time visitor to Beijing, it was down the road into town, trying to glimpse something with a Chinese flavour out of the window.

It is not so easy these days. The route to the Diaoyutai Guesthouse goes through the city's north-east district of multi-storey blocks and embassies, before taking the Avenue of Everlasting Peace, which runs for nine miles. Marco Polo wrote that Beijing's 'wide and straight streets' were laid out 'in a manner so perfect and masterly that it is impossible to do it justice'. The Avenue of Everlasting Peace is certainly wide and straight, but the old network of courtyards and lanes on both sides has mostly been replaced by government offices and foreigners' flats.

Racing down the centre lane – where the old French-run trams used to go – the Queen could at least see some of the cycling masses held up by police. She passed six giant billboards still bearing politically appropriate slogans – the only ones left in Beijing. 'Persist in internationalism, support all oppressed peoples and nationalities to oppose imperialism, colonialism and hegemonism', the one just before Tiananmen Square declares. Did she ask Mr Wu for a translation, and how would he explain this fossilized survival from the age of big-character posters?

Turning right through the western district, the motorcade of twenty-eight Mercedes came to the gate of the Diaoyutai Guesthouse, where a second reception committee was waiting. It included eleven-year-old boys from the Hepingmen primary school, waving paper flowers, whose last public appearance on the same spot had been to warmly welcome Prince Norodom Sihanouk of the rebel Kampuchean government. It also included a hundred or so local people waving British and Chinese flags. They had been drawn from the Xuanwu District Services Company, which provides the community with miscellaneous services such as house-cleaning, removals, haircuts at home and maids. It is a product of Mr Deng Xiaoping's reforms. The Queen swept by in about six and a half seconds. Again, like most visitors being warmly welcomed, she gave a wave and a slightly tentative smile, and disappeared. The real China, she may be hoping, starts tomorrow.

Last night Chinese television showed a special film on the life of the Queen, including shots of Speakers' Corner, where, it said, even the Queen could be criticized. The film, interrupted by a US soap commercial, was followed by a programme about a visit of President Li Xiannian to North Korea, where they stage much more lavish receptions. She meets him tomorrow in the Great Hall of the People.

14 October 1986, Beijing

The Queen spent a happy afternoon yesterday on the Great Wall of China, climbing almost twice as far as planned. It was the sort of occasion when one escapes from one's Mercedes and breathes fresh air. The Queen probably did not notice the horde of Chinese security men climbing after her, far less the carefully arranged presence of a 'representative' crowd. Chinese onlookers – and they were not just being polite – said that the Queen looked much younger and 'more beautiful' than she had appeared on television. By doubling the distance she climbed – from tower No. 2 to tower No. 3 – the Queen covered, according to a careful calculation, about one 17,000th of the wall's entire length.

But for her press secretary, Mr Michael Shea, life was not so easy – and not for the first time either. A rather slovenly gang of plain-clothes Chinese security men flocked up the wall behind her, and then swarmed down it in front of her. It was intrusive and unnecessary, as well as getting in the way of the British photographers. 'Can't you control these people?' Mr Shea called despairingly as a Chinese official who should have been responsible walked straight past him.

The palace had been led to understand that, subject to security considerations, the Chinese public would be allowed free access to the wall. But in the hour before the Queen's arrival, the very large throng which is habitually on the wall was carefully thinned out. Those left were mostly employees of the state-run *danwei* or 'unit' which looks after the wall. They included several employees of the environmental section, ordinary workers, office staff and the two charming girls who run their internal broadcasting network. With a nice sense of historical timing, the authorities had also ensured that although virtually all the foreign tourists had left the wall, there was a cheerful party of Hong Kongers to greet the Queen. Mr Shea had already been in difficulties on Monday when some Chinese journalists infiltrated the hall where the Queen was resting in the Imperial Palace while he was outside looking for someone in authority.

Never mind. It was a lovely day on the wall. And the satellite dish, lowered at great personal risk and installed by a Chinese helicopter pilot and ITN technicians, onto a tower on the other side, seemed to work perfectly. I don't know whether any of the royal party are steam engine buffs, but there was a very fine one on the line to the Badaling Pass. There were also several authentic country sights, including a large flock of donkeys and a man with a dead pig on his bicycle.

17 October, Xi'an

If the Duke of Edinburgh does not realize that the term 'slitty eyes' is offensive to the Chinese (and neither, apparently, does the Queen's press secretary), one can only wonder what other gaffes may have been committed by His

Royal Highness. Did he perhaps lean across the lunch table towards Mr Deng Xiaoping, and tell some cheerful anecdote about a little chink?

The serious background to this storm which has blown across the Queen's visit to China is that in several important areas Buckingham Palace appears either not to have been sufficiently briefed or not to have accepted advice on how best to deal with the Chinese. One important omission is the lack of a personal interpreter for the Queen, although it was at one stage proposed that she should have one. Instead she relied on the interpreter provided by the Chinese who in formal meetings with the top leaders translated both ways. This places the Queen, who seems ill at ease anyhow in these armchair situations, at an extra disadvantage. However good the interpreter, the conversation was bound to be dominated by the Chinese side.

Nor is there any evidence that the Queen was ever briefed on what to say. She is not here to negotiate about anything, but the Chinese do expect heads of state to make a few serious remarks. Even a brief polite reference to the 'Four Modernizations' would have carried her banal exchange with Party Secretary-General Mr Hu Yaobang to a different level. When Premier Zhao Ziyang was greeted by the Queen in her guesthouse in Beijing, she shook hands and there was then an awkward silence. There were many things she could have been coached to say. Instead she simply murmured, 'Please come this way.'

The Palace's response to criticisms of this kind is to say that it is all beside the point. What the Press should really be doing, it argues, is to acknowledge the tremendous reception which the Queen and the Duke have received and the historically significant nature of the visit. It is certainly true that the Chinese leadership places a very high value on this visit, seeing it as setting the seal on relations which have peaked on the Hong Kong agreement. But it remains a visit which somehow feels the lack of a central message – and it remains to be seen if the Queen will be able to speak more clearly to the people of Hong Kong, who certainly need one.

6

The Renewal of Urban China, 1980–7

Urban China was transformed in the first decade after Mao, slowly at first but irrevocably. The broad modern avenues, empty except for public transport and private bicycles, filled up with taxis and cars. The red-character slogans came down from the billboards to be replaced by advertisements for foreign TV sets and Chinese patent medicines. Wages were raised, savings were unblocked, and millions of urban Chinese started to do serious shopping. Private restaurants began to appear in the back streets, though they still only served meals at the usual Chinese times. Anything after 6 p.m. was too late for supper. Chinese opera had a brief revival in the old theatres with bare wooden seats and noisy audience participation – before a younger generation lost interest in it. Overseas Chinese from Hong Kong and Taiwan, visiting for tourism or investment, were easily recognizable for their better quality clothing, though South China produced inferior copies of the Hong Kong fashions to be sold on northern street barrows.

Urban renewal proceeded slowly in the working-class areas, but the Beijing lanes were beginning to be threatened by office development. Tianjin, where thousands had lost their homes in the 1976 Tangshan earthquake, was still a city of 'temporary dwellings' when I visited four years later. They were not completely cleared for another two. For millions of urban Chinese, life in the winter still centred around cabbage and coal – the two commodities stockpiled in courtyards everywhere. Cooking – and eating – was often done outside. Real improvements in living standards only became generally visible in the mid-1980s.

Re-visiting Beijing in 1984, I took the commercial pulse in my favourite shopping centre on Xidan Street, where traditional tea-shops and seal-cutters now coexisted with new stores selling the latest 'white goods'. (Ten years later the little shops had given way to new department stores and supermarkets, and the street could no longer be crossed on foot.)

As the economic reforms got under way, a number of coastal towns gained the right to seek foreign investment subject to Beijing's approval, and began to make ambitious plans. They became known and admired for their entrepreneurial talents. I decided to visit Wenzhou – which had become famous as the 'button capital' (it had cornered the national market) – on the Zhejiang coast. The best approach was by local bus over the hills from the nearest railway 250 kilometres away. In the main square of Jinhua, waiting for the bus, I watched a troupe of qigong *(martial arts) performers smashing bricks on one another's chests. A story-teller narrated episodes from the* Dream of the Red Chamber *for a small fee. A notice promised a 'public execution rally' later that week. Arriving in Wenzhou at dark, my eye was first caught by the neon cross of a recently reopened church. Traditional shops with wooden shutters sold imported electronic goods. China was certainly on the move.*

The inland cities of Middle China had to struggle much harder to overcome their isolation and dependence on outdated industries. The strategy of building up the interior for strategic reasons – in case of war with the US or the Soviet Union – had been abandoned. Local Party officials, 'leftist' in their ideological outlook but 'conservative' in their economic policies, at first also held back change. Taiyuan in 1987, capital of Shanxi province, was far behind the coastal cities, though the officials I met there were eager to break out of their isolation. A pall of pollution from outdated coal-burning industry hung in the air: at night several thousand young people flocked to a pop concert in the Workers' Stadium.

Recovering from an earthquake
June 1980, Tianjin

Opposite the public library in Tianjin, China's third largest city, there used to be a pleasant little park with a statue of the famous writer Lu Xun looking wisely down. Lu Xun is still there but he is hemmed in by intruders. The park has been completely obliterated. Small brick huts – earthquake shelters – have filled the space. Smoke from their coal brickette stoves fills the hazy morning air.

It will soon be exactly four years since the great earthquake of 28 July 1976 hit North China, destroying Tangshan and causing great damage in Tianjin. Thousands of *linjian* – literally 'temporary dwellings' – still line the streets and riverside under what looks like fairly permanent occupation. There must be eight or nine hundred along one side of the Huai river waterfront, opposite Central Square. The bricks which are used, loosely piled up with a bit of mortar here and there, were salvaged from houses brought down by the earthquake, so that they look elderly already. Where there is a lamp-post or a roadside tree, the *linjian* is simply built around it. Roofing felt keeps the hut dry, anchored down by loose bricks, windows are filled with paper or chicken-wire at best.

It is a measure of China's human condition and the magnitude of the economic tasks facing the post-Mao leadership that the country's third largest city should still be struggling with this problem. Earlier this year Chairman Hua Guofeng visited Tianjin and even in the sanitized words of the New China News Agency had something critical to say. 'He said Tianjin was an affected area of the Tangshan earthquake,' the Agency reported. 'The damage was fairly heavy. It was necessary to make conscientious efforts to rebuild houses for the residents.' He had been preceded by Vice-Premier Deng Xiaoping whose much sharper words had not been reported at all by the official media.

Incongruously still standing and mostly in good repair are the Doric, Corinthian and Ionic façades of the foreign banks and businesses which once dominated the city. A walk down Liberation (ex 'Victoria') Road to the Liberation (ex 'French') Bridge across the river takes one straight back to semi-colonial China when Tianjin (Tientsin) was divided into nine separate foreign concessions. But there is something wrong with the scale. Liberation or Victoria Road was always too narrow for the pretensions of its expatriate bankers and traders, perhaps pining for the more spacious

Bund of the waterfront in Shanghai. The colonnades are out of proportion to the very ordinary street below. All squeezed up together, it is the architectural Legoland of mercantile capitalism.

The silver cutlery in the Edwardian depths of the Tianjin Hotel bears the original name: Astor House Hotel. I don't believe the official guide's claim that there was once a notice on the park opposite (Middle Gardens) which read 'Chinese and Dogs do not Enter'. But I can believe that there was once, in the words of a European ex-resident, 'a splendid brothel at the hotel'. The rooms are discreetly panelled and the baths are three foot wide. Traffic is sparse and mostly official – buses, jeeps and taxis – on Liberation Road. A hundred yards to the north, and running parallel but winding away to the People's Park is the much more popular Dagu Road. Brick shelters have filled its narrow pavements. At the seven o'clock morning rush hour it is clogged with bicycles, for it is a Chinese street just as Liberation Road, in spite of the new name, still belongs to a foreign past.

Tianjin, together with Beijing and Shanghai, forms a separate category of 'directly administered cities' which are on the same level as Chinese provinces. In recent years Tianjin has absorbed several neighbourhood country districts, and half the population of more than 7 million work on the land. The city's authority extends to the Dagang Oilfield sixty miles away. There are three main harbours and under new regulations Tianjin, like its two sister cities, will be able to transact foreign trade directly with the outside world, bypassing the central government ministries in Beijing.

Textiles are a major export, and there is a wide range of light industry products going abroad, plus the usual oddments – local handicrafts, musical instruments, medicine and ginseng extract. I even discovered a local version of chocolate 'Smarties'. Japanese tourists are beginning to arrive by chartered liner, and new hotels are being built but Tianjin, in spite of its status, is still much more typical of urban life elsewhere in China than Beijing or Shanghai, and so far less exposed to glossy foreign adverts and electronic goods in the shops. Half-way up Liberation Road stands the impressive building, once the offices of the British-owned Kailuan Mining Company, of the Municipal Communist Party Committee. As the trolley goes round the back, I glimpse over the wall a good number of black Mercedes and other superior cars, with the usual chintz curtains to preserve the passenger from public gaze.

What are the real obstacles to the sort of total transformation of the environment needed by Tianjin and by hundreds of smaller Chinese cities? The 'leadership' points quite reasonably to the size of the problem and the lack of spare funds. The people – and this is partly a general mood in a more cynical post-Mao atmosphere – point to the 'leadership' and its privileges.

Last year Tianjin set a target for house construction of 3 million square metres. They achieved 2 million and called it a victory. A cartoon in the local newspaper shows the Chinese character for Happiness, each stroke forming a block in a new housing estate. But the municipality never admitted failure to complete the original target.

The *Tianjin Daily* reports that there are three campaigns under way. One is to eliminate the Three Wastes of effluent, smoke and unwanted by-products which are acknowledged to cause serious pollution. Another records fresh successes in the struggle to reduce the rate of population increase. The annual natural growth rate has come down, fairly marginally, from 9.16 to 8.66 per thousand. Six hundred representatives of Advanced Units (family planning is organized at the place of work) have received silk pennants from the municipal Party.

The other campaign is to elect local delegates to city district People's Councils – the first election of any kind for fifteen years. Each local residents' section is divided into a number of 'slices'. The candidates are supposed to go around and introduce themselves to each slice, and there is an elaborate law to ensure that there are more candidates than places.

But across the river by two-cent ferry in the old Russian Concession, street posters warn of more practical concerns.

No one must build any new temporary building (each bears a licence plate and has been inspected by the housing department). And the temporary dwellers are warned by a graphic picture to keep their stove pipes clean and avoid asphyxiation.

New trousers in Beijing
October 1984, Xidan market

A well-established clock shop in the Beijing shopping street of Xidan, which has everything from cheap Shanghai watches to grandfathers in lacquered wood, has since my last visit started selling refrigerators as well. The 'Snow Flower' brand costs 630 *yuan* (about 200 pounds and equivalent to ten months of an office worker's wage).

The fridge can only be purchased with foreign exchange certificates* (referred to by foreign residents as 'funny money') – worth about 60 per cent more on the black market – but there are plenty of interested customers. With the same currency one can buy Japanese fishing rods in the clock shop, and even Japanese hooks at five cents each. On the pavement outside, the barrow-boys are selling gaberdine trousers at twenty-eight *yuan* (eight pounds) a pair. They affect a brushed-back hairstyle and wear black baseball caps, looking altogether sharper and more successful at avoiding the police than the itinerant salesmen of patent needle-threaders and magic stain-removers. Young women out shopping try on the trousers, over the pair they are already wearing, for a very approximate size.

Can this really be capitalism, as forecast recently in the foreign press when Deng Xiaoping announced his plans for urban economic reform? Whatever it is, trousers are no trivial matter. The old Chinese concept that trousers should be 'worn for three years as new, for three more as old, and then another three as patched-up' is completely out of date. Now a taxi-driver proudly tells me, when I ask what is new,

---

*A special kind of Chinese currency which foreigners used and which had a black market value.

that 'there are no patched trousers in Beijing'.

It is still a modest enough advance for China's capital city, but the change in lifestyle has acquired an irreversible confidence in the past year or so. Beijing's northern austerity (so forbidding to some foreign visitors although probably more Chinese than the softness of the southern provinces) has begun to fray. The native visitors from the interior Chinese provinces, who now go shopping not just for little parcels of shoes and sweets but for big items like TV sets, also take home the contagious impression that it is right to spend (although of course no longer right to make revolution).

In the words of the recent Central Committee resolution on economic reform, they are helping 'to smash blockades and open doors' between the more and the less developed areas and between the cities and the countryside. Young intellectuals who grew up during the Cultural Revolution may have mixed feelings about the new mood of acquisitiveness, and there are some fears that it may provoke a repressive backlash. But they recognize that the aim of the reforms in planning and management is not to demolish a set of socialist relations of production (which have never existed in Chinese industry) but to weaken a system of bureaucratic patronage and influence which creates enormous delays and has much more in common with feudalism than socialism.

'I sit in the office and see people from factories all over China pleading for permission to import machine tools,' says one young cadre. 'Next year they will be able to make their own contracts directly.'

Ideas and stimuli from the outside world already circulate much more widely at all levels, including that of the shoppers in Xidan. Democracy Wall, at the corner with the Avenue of Everlasting Peace, has been turned into a set of glass display cases which at the moment contain a series of models illustrating advanced computer technology.

In a theatre on the opposite corner, the amateur drama group of the China Mining Corporation is staging *The Mousetrap* in translation. And an expanding range of popular magazines with titles like *Healthy Life* and *Young People*, on sale at the nearby bookstall conveys a mass of new information. The 'white revolution' has just started to reach China, says an article in the bimonthly *Knowledge and Living*. More than sixty domestic electrical appliances are now produced by Chinese industry, though this is nothing compared to Japan or the US.

The *People's Daily* has devoted a lot of space recently to meet internal party criticisms of the open door policy. Like the Central Committee's resolution on urban reform, the argument is presented as a defence of real socialism against obscurantist opposition, and although it is a one-sided case it does merit serious reading. When the two superpowers locked the doors to China from the outside, it argues, the Chinese were forced in desperation to rely on their own resources. But socialism should be an open society, not a closed one. Nor should socialism be afraid to learn from capitalism, whose 'highly developed social production is precisely the necessary material condition for a socialist society'.

To fear the outside world, say the Party reformers, is not only narrow-minded nationalism but has a strong flavour of feudalism, which has always shunned new ideas and commodities that might break open its spiritual and material domain. Of course some harmful things will be blown through the open door, but one can always install air filters, and it is better to have to wash one's face occasionally than to live in an airtight vacuum.

A visit to the China Art Gallery in Beijing to see the 1984 exhibition of national art reveals just how far the atmosphere has already been transformed. Suddenly and excitingly young Chinese artists have discovered a new idiom which matches the new times – and without official censorship. There are no more vacuous oils of labour models, or black-and-white woodcuts of long-clichéd revolutionary themes. Even when the subject is a familiar one – peasants setting out for the fields – the treatment is quite different. Their figures are slightly grotesque, their hilltop village perched at a crazy angle. A building site is seen through a window, but the workers are remote and a huge vase of flowers dominates the window-sill. The new art has a strong sense of bright colour and bold technique. Lacquer is the most popular medium for painting. There are tiles, mosaics, wall pictures, stone reliefs and some sculpture which has somehow shaken free of the public park idiom.

Meanwhile the unofficial 'Spark' group of artists, once linked to the Democracy Movement, exhibit their pictures in a public park. Five years ago they did this as a political protest. Now the pictures are all for sale at very healthy prices. It is unlikely that anyone will object – has not the Party resolution said that intellectuals should place a higher value on their services?

Back on Xidan, the Edgware Road of Beijing (it is a mile and a half west of Wangfujing which is often compared with Oxford Street), it is 11 o'clock and already time for lunch. I am reminded that apart from the get-rich-quick operators in the new economic zones, and the officials who have always had their privileges, and now hope for more, most people enjoy very simple pleasures. While we continue our very necessary discussion on which sorts of economic policies are compatible with a transitional socialist society, we should perhaps not be too hard on them for wanting some of the goodies we take for granted.

The Hunan restaurant, which specializes in the province's spicy southern cuisine, is already crowded. With shopping packages piled high on the table, people drink beer and wait patiently for very slow service, cigarette smoke rising in the sun's rays which shine down from a central skylight.

It is a very long way from the *prix fixe* at Maxim's, where top cadres now like to be taken by foreign businessmen, although ordinary people are spending more on their food and eating more meat. Small sums of money still mean a lot, and there is a complicated system of twenty cents deposit on the beer bottle in case you walk off with it. But the open door policy has produced an expensive new air-conditioner for the restaurant. It is sitting in its niche on the wall, just waiting to be wired up.

Button capital of China

September 1985, Wenzhou, Zhejiang province

In the shadow of a banyan tree and next to a tower from the Song dynasty, the old British Consulate at Wenzhou awaits another foreign invasion. For Wenzhou is one of China's fourteen new 'open ports'. The present plan is to build an international tourist village, with cabins in various national styles, on the island of Jiangxin – just opposite Wenzhou, where the British once enjoyed the fresh air and supervised the collection of the Imperial Maritime Customs. There will also be a cable car and an amusement park with video games. The customs duties were mostly mortgaged to foreign bankers when Wenzhou was a Treaty Port – first conceded in 1858 during the Second Opium War. Now Wenzhou is again in the market for foreign funds, and a British company – Cluff Investment and Trading Ltd – has become its exclusive trading and investment agent. The central government in Beijing now counts for much more than it did in the treaty port days. The initiative to throw open Wenzhou came from Beijing in April 1984, after thirty-five years of isolation. The port had been deprived of investment before because it was in the strategic 'frontline' facing Taiwan, and had been largely closed to foreigners.

But the other face of being backed by 'The Centre' (as everyone calls Beijing) is that Wenzhou now depends on the government line remaining constant. 'The foreigners' biggest worry,' admits a local intermediary, 'is that the policies may change.' Recent official concern and confusion over the size of this year's trade deficit, the re-assertion of central controls over all foreign contracts, and new restrictions on television and other consumer imports, do not help the climate. Earlier this year the state councillor Mr Gu Mu, who oversees the open port policy, cut back plans for all except four of the fourteen, just as Wenzhou was getting under way.

Wenzhou officials insist that nothing has changed. But in spite of the fish and the timber and the rare minerals (who has heard of alunite?) and the tourist potential, the city is eleventh in the league table of existing development out of the fourteen. It is a real test for the open door. 'Completely virginal but ludicrously inaccessible,' was one foreign businessman's recent description of Wenzhou. The place buzzes with buying and selling but the goods are mostly Chinese and there is still an air of innocence. No one asks for foreign exchange certificates and the rickshaw cyclists are puzzled to be paid in them.

The shops on Liberation Street have wooden boarded fronts with lattice carving above, and offer a chronological jumble of commerce. Many kinds of dried fish in enormous baskets, bamboo carrying poles and furniture, carpenters' tools, Chinese medicine in porcelain jars . . . But also rows of blue jeans, many shoe shops (platform heels for men are the thing), stylish hairdressers, racks of T-shirts stencilled with messages their wearers cannot understand (including 'British Airways' and 'Hello – good sailing'). Noodle and dumpling stalls until late at night, fruit-sellers who will peel your own Tianjin pear, and at least one dog-meat restaurant.

Mr Gu Mu's second thoughts meant that ten out of the fourteen ports were told to concentrate on building a better infrastructure, particularly in energy and transport communications, before plunging into new technology and industry. Beijing also took back its authority to approve or disallow any foreign investments over 5 million *yuan* in value. Higher limits were allowed only for Shanghai, Tianjin, Dalian and Guangzhou.

It is a leisurely day and night journey by steamer from Shanghai to Wenzhou, or a hard day's drive from Fuzhou in the south or Hangzhou to the north. But local officials recall how Dr Sun Yat-Sen, father of the Chinese republic, once designated Wenzhou as 'The Great Harbour of the East'. They echo Dr Sun's grandiose railway schemes with their own plan to link Wenzhou to the nearest line inland. It looks nothing on the map – a mere 250 kilometres – but it must be engineered along steep river banks and will include thirteen kilometres of bridges. Beijing should pay for one third, the province may pay for another third, and the rest will be funded locally. Peasant communities along the line will be urged to contribute cheap labour, in return for shares in the railway's future success.

The new airport sounds further ahead, and is officially scheduled for completion by the end of next year. Wenzhou will pay for three-quarters and Beijing for the rest (the province again sounds doubtful). It will take everything, they say proudly, except the jumbo jet. There will be many meetings and bargaining, from the rural township through Wenzhou to its inland neighbours, on to the province and finally Beijing. According to one account Beijing has set a ceiling of 30 million US dollars a year for the next three years, which is clearly not enough. Wenzhou is still arguing with the national airline over who will run services from the new airport. Dividing up costs along the railway line is also contentious. Wenzhou's exclusive foreign agent is Cluff Investment and Trading Ltd, a subsidiary of Cluff Oil PLC, which has so far concentrated without much success on offshore exploration for Chinese oil. Its director, Mr David Tang, says now that the way to do business in China is 'not to think big, but to think small'.

Someone who thinks big in Wenzhou is an officially approved rich peasant, Mr Zheng Shize, who has invested 5,250 pounds in a scheme to purchase a Chinese-made airship for carrying tourists to the mountain resort of Wandangshan. Tourist villages are planned here, too, in an area described as famous for its 'queer peaks and singular crags'. The less exotic hills closer to Wenzhou, upstream on both sides of the Wenzhou river, are beautiful enough. Felled timber from their slopes is lashed together in vast formations like the backbone of a long narrow fish and floated downstream.

On a wall on the outskirts of Wenzhou, a different sort of quotation says, simply, 'Time is money'. Wenzhou's most successful business is based on lots of people thinking small but all the time about buying and selling. One quarter of the working population is self-employed, dealing in food, clothing and household goods from all over China. Everyone coming off the ferries from the Ou river brings something to sell in town. National leaders have come visiting to look at the 'Wenzhou Model' of economic activity (a wholesale button market is especially praised).

But buttons by themselves will not generate the volume of economic activity which would justify the ambitious plans of Wenzhou's new city-funded development corporation. The airport will be embarrassingly empty, the new port under-used, and the railway will fail to pay dividends to the peasants who have given their labour, unless China can afford a second stage of industrial development, or foreign capital can be persuaded to take the risk. Only tourism will easily succeed at first, with the danger that – as has already happened further south in Xiamen – a peaceful and uncorrupted environment will be destroyed.

Breaking out of the interior
August 1987, Taiyuan, Shanxi province

The Chinese cadre at the banquet table does not respond when I mention the name of Tony Benn, MP for Chester-field – which happens to be twinned with one of the biggest coal-mining towns in Shanxi province. I am making one of those elaborate statements which foreigners in China always make and which always misfire. My point is that Shanxi may have socialism in common with its British twins (the provincial capital of Taiyuan is also twinned with Newcastle and the province as a whole with Derbyshire) as well as coal.

Socialism could actually be a very interesting topic of conversation in Shanxi, but people want to talk instead about 'opening up', modernizing, this month's symposium in Taiyuan on international economic cooperation, and generally on how to escape from the trap of being a resource-rich but landlocked province in Middle China. Middle China belongs neither to the fast developing coastal regions nor to the exotic but visibly backward provinces of the far west. It is a north–south wedge, starting from Shanxi, which roughly follows a secondary rail system from Taiyuan down to Nanning near the Vietnamese border in the south. It is in the middle as in 'Middle Kingdom' (still the Chinese name for China – *Zhongguo*).

Shanxi was where the Emperor Yu is supposed to have tamed the floods which created its fertile alluvial plain – really a plateau bounded to the north by desert, to the east by mountains and to the south and west by the Yellow river. History easily becomes para-history in China. The Emperor Yu is assigned an exact date (2205 BC), just as a cypress tree in the Jinci Temple grounds near Taiyuan is said to be 3,000 years old. Shanxi is indeed a very ancient province. It contains 70 per cent of all buildings surviving in China from the Song Dynasty (tenth to thirteenth centuries AD), and before. It has mountainside monasteries, pagodas and dagobas, wooden towers and pavilions, Buddhist stone carvings and frescoes, to match anywhere else in China. Yet Shanxi attracts only about 30,000 tourists a year – less than Tibet. Half of those only visit the northern city of Datong, famous for the Yungang stone grottoes and a factory which builds steam engines. Most of the 800,000 tourists to China bypass Middle China.

Shanxi's coal industry illustrates both the potential and the basic problem of a region which still largely walks in the Maoist style on two legs – one stepping far ahead of the other. Roughly a quarter of this year's expected 220 million tons of coal comes from seven large nationally owned mines, where coal extraction is 80 per cent mechanized. Another quarter is produced in local state mines, at the province, city or prefecture level. The rest is mined by collective units – small-scale county or village operations – and these days even by individual private enterprise. On a hillside road coated with mud near Yangquan (the city which is twinned with Chesterfield) I counted four coal lorries and trailers which evidently in the last hour of heavy rain had either jack-knifed or slid into the ditch. Provincial officials duck questions about accident rates. 'Our coal reserves are widely scattered,' says Mr Ma Chaoliang of the Shanxi Mining Bureau. 'We cannot afford much new equipment, so we encourage farmers to open coal mines.'

Meanwhile an entirely separate operation is being financed by Mr Armand Hammer, the American entrepreneur who has diversified from the Soviet Union to

China. His Occidental Petroleum Company is a leading investor in the Pingshuo open-cast mine which starts production soon with an annual capacity of 15 million tons and plans eventually to triple its size. But at the Shanxi Mining Bureau they know nothing about Pingshuo. 'It is handled entirely from Beijing.'

It is a safe assumption that Shanxi is hampered by political as well as economic backwardness. It is one of the few places in China where one sees official slogans about combating 'bourgeois liberalism'. The national vogue for economic decentralization can easily be subverted by bureaucrats who build their own separate kingdoms. The provincial capital seems powerless to deal with the Chemical Fertilizer Company, where the surrounding streams are blue with effluent and which on a sunny summer day is masked by nauseous smog.

Some of the most important conservative figures nationally active in trying to throttle back the demand for political reform belong to the 'Shanxi clique', headed by 84-year-old Politburo member Peng Zhen. Bo Yibo, seventy-nine, has recently been co-opted by Deng Xiaoping into the new moderate reformist leadership which emerged this summer after the resignation of Hu Yaobang as Party Secretary-General. Mr Bo is Shanxi's patron in Beijing, and has secured national investment to build new railways and diversify heavy industry. The goal is to make Shanxi a 'multi-energy base', processing more of its coal before export, and expanding steel and electricity production. But reform for Mr Bo seems mostly limited to the economic side.

On a billboard in the centre of Taiyuan, the citizens are instructed on how to behave: 'Talk of ideals, love the motherland, warmly love Taiyuan, build up Taiyuan, create Taiyuan man of a new age, but do nothing to harm our national character.' Everyday Shanxi life is on a much lower plane. Young people with a chance to do so dream of going abroad to study. For others, there is modern dancing on the top floor of the biggest hotel, with revolving lights and a heavy but restrained rhythm.

Three thousand people recently packed into a concert at

the Workers' Stadium. There was some slinky dancing and Hong Kong-style sentimental songs. The usherettes were police, to ensure that New Taiyuan Man behaved himself. For older people, there is the revival of the local Shanxi opera, with open-air stages in most villages. Young performers in their twenties, trained by the Cultural Bureau, have re-learnt the art of expressing emotion through shaking sleeves, stroking beards and waggling amazingly long feathers in their head-dresses.

7

Hardliners against Reformers, 1983–9

As Chinese society began to open up, for better or for worse, under Deng Xiaoping's economic reforms, the Party faithful in high places became alarmed at the crumbling of old 'socialist' standards. A generation taught by Mao to beware of the 'sugar-coated bullets of the bourgeoisie' found that its own children enjoyed the taste of Western imports – both the goods and the ideas. The veterans were suspicious of the younger leaders around Secretary-General Hu Yaobang who encouraged reform-minded scholars to explore the possibilities of democratizing the Party itself. They discussed the alienation of the people from the ruling elite, suggesting that many of China's problems arose from the persistence of a feudal and autocratic style of government.

The conservative backlash came in two waves, in the winters of 1983 and 1986. The first was a campaign against 'spiritual pollution' which was endorsed by Deng but only under pressure from his veteran colleagues. It gave many intellectuals a scare but was undermined by its own excesses. Women were told not to let their hair grow long, soldiers were ordered to hand over photographs of their girlfriends, the Beijing Party Committee posted a notice banning high-heeled shoes and long hair, and young people had their sunglasses (the new symbol of modernity) confiscated in the streets.

These absurdities were widely ridiculed. 'I'll have a spot of spiritual pollution,' I heard a young woman joking as she bought a tube of face cream in a Beijing department store. Deng was persuaded that the campaign would do great harm to the unfinished economic reforms. Though his attitude towards political *reform remained ambiguous, the debate resumed with Hu's encouragement. In September 1984 he gave heart to the reformists (and outraged the conservatives) by saying that 'the writings of Marx and Lenin [cannot] . . . provide solutions to our current problems.'*

Summer 1986 saw the most lively and varied intellectual discussion since the Communist victory in 1949. Older Party scholars joined forces with a new generation of critical intellectuals to hold seminars and 'salons', crossing forbidden frontiers of thought. Not only did this present a more serious threat to the Party conservatives, but it became associated with a new wave of student protests. These covered a variety of issues: high-level corruption, Japanese economic penetration, police brutality and their own poor living conditions. By the winter of 1986 the demonstrations acquired a sharper political edge, and the Party old guard seized the chance again. They felt threatened by the informal alliance now beginning to emerge between the students and the scholars.

This time Deng Xiaoping supported fully the campaign against 'bourgeois liberalization', sacked Hu Yaobang and expelled the leading dissidents from the Party. And this time Beijing intellectuals were less sanguine: the atmosphere was too reminiscent of past purges when Mao was alive – including the 'anti-Rightist' campaign of 1957 in which Deng had taken the lead. Beijing was enjoying fine weather beneath a clear winter sky, but the air was thick and gloomy. I spent several weeks in a small courtyard hotel in the old lanes north of the Forbidden City, listening to tales of cynicism and disillusion from Deng's previous supporters.

The short-lived farce of the 1983 backlash had turned into more persistent reaction in 1987, as contradictions multiplied in society and among the high-level leaders. There was a fresh lull while Hu's successor Zhao Ziyang established himself and the reformers watched warily. An attempt was made to set a unifying course at the traditional summer gathering of Deng and his colleagues at the seaside resort of Beidaihe. Zhao gained more room for maneouvre, at least on the economic front, but within a year the contradictions had re-emerged. The Party die-hards complained about Zhao as they had about Hu. Ordinary citizens complained about corruption and foreign influence. Disillusioned Party intellectuals raised the issue of the political prisoners from the earlier Democracy

Movement – *a very sensitive spot for Deng who had sent them to jail. As students joined forces with intellectuals, the scene was being prepared for the tragedy of 1989.*

Sartre and spiritual pollution
November 1983, Beijing

Jean-Paul Sartre made a very good stand in the Spanish Civil War, said the Chinese cadre reflectively across the dinner table. 'But we cannot accept his existentialism – it does not reflect socialist reality, and we do not approve of alienation or bourgeois humanitarianism either!'

Other less philosophical concepts, Chinese officials say, as they try to explain their campaign against 'spiritual pollution', have also slipped in through the open door from the West. Tapes, books and magazines of nude photos have been smuggled in, and the *People's Daily* has warned that criminal charges would be brought against peddlers of pornography.

Such things no doubt exist, and have genuinely shocked the survivors of the revolution who still lead China. But in the cold wind which is blowing sand from Siberia through the streets of Beijing, some people are muffling up against a campaign which they fear will have much wider targets. On 16 November they collected the *People's Daily* to find a familiar reminder of previous political campaigns. Two-thirds of the front page was taken up with an editorial blast against spiritual pollution, calling for a new 'ideological struggle'. With practised eyes, they skimmed through the verbiage for the punch line, which was buried somewhere around the two-thousandth character. It said that this would be a long struggle, that opinions opposed to socialism cannot be vanquished overnight, and that a protracted battle must be waged.

In another alarming sentence, it said that 'bourgeois humanitarianism' had already been criticized in the 1960s – a reference to the Cultural Revolution. Although it said that the Cultural Revolution had gone too far because it also attacked Socialist humanitarianism, this is still a disturbingly ambiguous thought. People thought that the campaign might have peaked two weeks ago when Zhou Yang, the aged Party cultural hack who has veered with the wind for decades, criticized himself for getting the concept of alienation wrong. But the word is out that his self-criticism was not sufficient, and there has been the dismissal of two senior members of the *People's Daily* editorial board.

No one is quite sure what this all means. But a teacher of foreign literature quietly cancels a public lecture that he was going to give. Video recorders – a potent indicator of possible pollution – are disposed of. Chinese television shows a meeting of aged intellectuals, denouncing pollution with wooden voices around the conference table as if they have been there before. It then shows happy workers playing football and painting posters which exemplify spiritual culture.

In the official view, the fears are groundless. It may be a struggle, it is explained, but it is not a 'movement' of the type which swept China in the Cultural Revolution. 'You can be sure that it will not be another Cultural Revolution, because it is the present leaders of China who suffered most of all.' The social ills which allegedly require the new campaign are depicted frankly.

The need to re-establish a centralized grip over economic policy reinforces the leadership's concern at the loosening of political control which followed the Cultural Revolution. The most common complaint about local Communist Party officials is that they just do not do what they are told. Meanwhile outside the Party, the spread of foreign ideas, laxer moral standards among the young, growing rank and file cynicism among the work-force, and a straightforward law and order problem, all add to the concern of the old men in Beijing.

'Uphold and improve Party leadership,' said the *People's Daily* recently in a remarkable admission that for a section of society the Communist Party has forfeited its mandate to rule. In 1978–9, it says, 'a handful of people in society advocated so-called democracy by discarding Party committees.' And although these ideas were firmly rebuffed, there are still 'a small number of people who ... deny that Party leadership is a necessity for socialist construction'. Yet others argue that, although the Party should lead, it has disqualified itself by the serious mistakes which were made in the Cultural Revolution.

One way of restoring faith in the Party is through the current anti-crime campaign and the holding of mass executions. These seem to be generally welcomed (though a minority are further alienated by them). But the campaign also undermines the spirit of legal reform which has picked up since 1979.

Foreign ideas, says the leadership, should be judged on the basic principle of whether or not they 'serve China's purpose'. This is essentially a return to the 'self-strengthening' concept of the late nineteenth century when the modernizers of the Qing Dynasty sought to import Western techniques while preserving the 'essence' of Chinese civilization. It may have some value in making the Chinese more cautious about copying foreign models, or importing technological processes that only work on the basis of capitalist relations of production. But the most likely result is that the trivia of Western society – particularly the leisure pursuits associated with the tourist industry and entertainment – will continue to be admitted, while serious and critical ideas are now excluded.

How to come to terms with the outside world remains at the heart of the Chinese dilemma as it has for a century and a half. One young Chinese in Beijing, himself a former student abroad, sums up how he sees the contradiction between the present leadership's attempt to restore the old values and the impact of the new world. 'I remind myself constantly,' he says, 'that China has two distinct kinds of tradition. One is that of Chinese bureaucratic civilization from Confucius onwards, and the other is the Russian political model. It is no coincidence that the two are combining together very nicely. That is what makes China great.

'However,' he continues hopefully, 'there are young people who are making a serious study of Marxism and other political and economic theories. Those who have been and who are now abroad will have a tremendous influence over China's future.' It is an optimistic view of a society still facing enormous economic tasks, run by an elite for whom 'liberation of thought' (another reformist concept which is now rarely mentioned) has very definite limits.

The struggle for reform
October 1984, Beijing

The Central Committee of China's Communist Party, which is now discussing drastic urban reforms, represents a triumph for Deng Xiaoping. But he has had to struggle for it, and opposition to his policies may not yet be over. Ever since National Day, when Deng reviewed the troops in Tiananmen Square, he has been at pains to identify himself personally with the reforms. Last week, as the Party plenum was beginning to assemble, he told a Japanese Komeito Party delegation – which he would not normally meet – that China was determined to transform the economy.

The plenum will formally approve, on a national level, some reforms which have already been tested quite widely, in particular those which decentralize and reduce planning powers, and which give individual factories more control over production and prices. It goes into new territory in seeking to curtail the central regulation of prices. This reform has been delayed over the past year, with the name of Chen Yun – one of the six Politburo standing committee members and with long experience of economic planning from the 1950s – linked to the critics.

But the really intriguing puzzle about this plenum is the missing item on its agenda. The rectification of the Communist Party, which Deng's people have been pushing to the displeasure of some army leaders, is likely to be mentioned only cursorily as part of the political background to the economic reforms. A year ago the last Central Committee plenum agreed to hold a new session soon on ideological matters. It was promised for the winter, postponed until spring, downgraded to a 'representative conference', and now deferred again.

The rectification campaign first ran into trouble with the short-lived but disturbing counter-campaign against 'spiritual pollution', apparently encouraged by the same left bureaucrat forces who might themselves be the targets for rectification. Then the armed forces emerged in the late spring as a focus for discontent. Army officers who had acted on Mao Zedong's instructions during the Cultural Revolution failed to see why they should have to 'completely repudiate' the past.

Opposition to the economic reforms from within the Party (of which the army cadres only form one special interest group) has a variety of sources. There are no doubt some senior leaders who are morally offended by the new get-rich-quick mentality. This weekend the *People's Daily* admitted that some local officials are cashing in on the reforms, 'mixing public and personal business' and using state funds to invest in private enterprise. But it would not be Marxist, said the *People's Daily*, to use these 'side currents' as an excuse for pouring cold water on the whole reform package, or to try to pin 'personal responsibility' for them. One catches here the echo of serious argument within the leadership.

There is also room for real and varied argument about the consequences of the proposed price reforms, as Mr Deng has half-conceded, saying that the policy must be carried out step by step, with caution. In theory, China will still have a socialist-planned economy, and market forces will be restrained by guidelines from Beijing from going too far. The pricing structure belongs to an earlier period when it was used to subsidize a low standard of living, ration goods in short supply and stimulate heavy industry. Price deregulation, although necessary, could lead to inflation and a lopsided production of profitable items.

New laws to attract more foreign technology reflect both sides of the coin. From January next year, local governments and businesses will be able to negotiate more easily abroad, bypassing the Ministry for Foreign Trade. The real question is whether the guidelines from the Ministry in Beijing will be strong enough to prevent local excesses, without negating the object of the reforms.

The dismissal of Hu Yaobang
February 1987, Beijing

The left-wing theologians of the Chinese Communist Party have captured the high ground again, and scholars and artists are taking cover from the righteous 'struggle against bourgeois liberalism'. One option is to travel abroad and write essays on essentially touristic themes. Another is to head for the south of China and 'rest.' When asked to join the struggle, one can try saying 'I am not in very good health, and I'm afraid that my level of understanding is still comparatively low.' That may work, or it may not. There is talk of lists being compiled by the zealous left-wingers in and around the Party's theoretical journal, *Red Flag*. Intellectuals who are Party members must observe Party discipline. In or outside the Party, no one is going to take chances. Even if the struggle fizzles out, everyone agrees, the deep breath of intellectual courage taken last year has expired. There will be nothing very interesting written or performed for a long time.

Last year's intellectual challenge, which led to such a devastating coalition between Party conservatives and left-wingers against Mr Hu Yaobang's reformers, did not come primarily from the older literati who have seen so much before. It was itself the product of a coalition – between progressive Marxist scholars operating from well within the Party establishment and an entirely new phenomenon of scholar-activists like the scientist Professor Fang Lizhi and the journalist Liu Binyan, who have dared to challenge old Party tigers.

The activists reject Chinese intellectual chauvinism and believe that the Party's still semi-feudal bureaucracy must be challenged head-on. Subtle arguments by allegory are no longer enough. Even friends of Mr Liu warned that he had gone too far at a conference last November in Shanghai, where he spoke openly before foreign academic visitors about the need for greater courage. From the 1950s through to the 1970s, he said, Chinese politics had been not just on a mistaken but on a reactionary path. Yet even now writers shied away from tackling the real injustices. Mr Liu also touched on a sensitive nerve when he reproached fellow writers with 'just seeking a reputation abroad ... I think there's a problem when good writers are only concerned with trying to win a Nobel Prize.' The vanguard of the reform movement last year, said Liu correctly but woundingly to his audience, were younger political and natural scientists who had dared to enter the forbidden areas. Their experience abroad has been a liberating one.

The Hefei University of Science and Technology, where the student demonstrations began, has sent more than 100 research graduates abroad since the 'open door' policy began. Professor Fang Lizhi, vice-president of the university until his dismissal last month, seemed recently to spend half his time commuting to Princeton and New York for conferences on astrophysics. Chinese scholars still have problems not usually encountered by Western academic jet-setters. Professor Fang first offended the left-wingers a year ago when he openly criticized a deputy mayor of Beijing – a former 'Worker Hero' – for taking a free trip to the United States to attend a conference on nuclear accelerators about which he knew nothing. Professor Fang was asked to apologize by the Academy of Sciences but refused. He was then criticized by the conservative leader, Bo Yibo, as 'going too far', by the left-wing ideologue, Hu Qiaomu, for 'belonging to the wrong headquarters' (a sinister phrase from the days of the Cultural Revolution) – and by Mr Hu's wife who works at the academy. He was also denied a passport for his next visit to the US.

It is an involved tale, but an essential one for an understanding of the complex web of factional and personal relationships which underlies every 'theoretical struggle'. The tale ended happily with the intervention of Hu Qili, a protégé of Mr Hu Yaobang. But this week Hu Qili's close colleague, the Party propaganda chief, Zhu Houze, formally lost his job, leaving Mr Hu increasingly exposed as an alleged patron of 'bourgeois liberalism'. Professor Fang, a hero to the Chinese student demonstrators, is now a compulsory target for criticism at Party meetings all over China.

High-profile activists like Liu and Fang play for high

stakes, and are criticized by more cautious reformers working from within for risking all at once. It is hard to believe now that an interview with Fang in which he argued that intellectuals were the 'advanced class' of modern society, was published only six weeks ago in China's main English-language journal, the *Beijing Review*. 'Intellectuals,' he said dangerously, 'who own and create information and knowledge are the most dynamic component of the productive forces: this is what determines their social status.'

Meanwhile, last year a much larger group of political scientists were seeking – with Hu Yaobang's encouragement – to argue the case for political accountability and reform in a coded and less provocative way. They began, at a conference sponsored by the Academy of Social Sciences in April, by producing a quote from Deng Xiaoping which legitimized – but only just – their new inquiry. 'Comprehensive economic restructuring,' Mr Deng had said, 'will affect every field in politics, education, science, etc.' They interpreted this to mean that economic reform (which Deng has always championed) must be accompanied by political reform (about which he is very wary). More tactfully than Professor Fang they, too, began to chip away at Marxist class theory: 'The Socialist state,' said some of them, 'should mark the transition from a state based on class to one based on society.'

It is a measure of the seriousness of today's left-wing counter-offensive that I hesitate now to name the leading neo-Marxist reformers who last year breathed new life into Chinese political theory. The more often they are named as potential targets in the foreign press, the more vulnerable they will be. Certainly they are not answering phone calls, and it is rather thoughtless even to try calling.

China is a highly anniversary-conscious culture, and this year is a particularly unhappy anniversary – thirty years since the anti-Rightist movement with which Mao Zedong, vigorously supported by Deng Xiaoping, nipped the Hundred Flowers* in their first hesitant bloom. Can one

---

* The 1956–7 movement in which intellectuals were encouraged to criticize the Party.

blame the literati today for being hesitant about blooming at all? The sociologist Fei Xiaotong published a famous open letter in 1957, asking Mao whether the early spring would lead to real warmth. A month ago Professor Fei spoke out against the reformers and was praised for it by Deng Xiaoping.

The writer Wang Meng suffered for twenty years as a 'Rightist', most of them spent in a village in remote Xinjiang. Finally rehabilitated, he published some mild satires on bureaucracy, and was then lured to become Minister of Culture. Last month he, too, spoke out against the reformers – though perhaps not fiercely enough to satisfy the Red Flaggers. Fei and Wang are both sad figures, still fulfilling a debt to the Party which owes them a much larger one.

But the future, as Chairman Mao might have said, lies not with them but with the youth – both the cynical young men and women of the post-Mao generation and a growing minority who have new experiences, in many cases gained abroad, and a new and assertive view of their role in society.

Down by the seaside
August 1987, Hebei province

Deng Xiaoping's summer politicking by the seaside at the Beidaihe resort in North China is going fairly well – apart from a plague of poisonous jellyfish which have to be kept at bay by fine-meshed nets.

The issues to be thrashed out at this traditional 'summer court' (the term is borrowed from Imperial China) include an outline programme for political reform and an entire name-list for the leadership which will emerge in October out of the Thirteenth Congress of the Communist Party. Hovering in the background, rather like the jellyfish, is the latest unwelcome news of rising inflation. Mr Deng's economic reformers believe they must push ahead to make the Chinese economy more 'entrepreneurial' – the new vogue word. But the figures do give ammunition to lurking conservative critics.

None of these issues are likely to be thrashed out at formal

Politburo meetings on Beidaihe's Middle Beach. The leaders will be relaxing in their *fin-de-siècle* villas (Beidaihe was 'discovered' by British engineers building the railway in the 1890s). Mr Deng will send out for cream cakes from Kiessling Bakery and enjoy another rubber of bridge. The real work will be done by the private secretaries, in discreet coded discussion. 'The Chairman is concerned for the health of his colleagues,' the message goes out. 'He hopes they will not have to work so hard after October.' It is a delicately Chinese version of *Yes, Minister*.

Every so often a signal from Beidaihe reaches Beijing. Last week the *People's Daily* published a commentary reproaching the Party's 'theoretical workers' for failing to keep up with the times. 'The value of theory depends on whether it can satisfy the demands of reform,' it said. It was not very helpful to stick to old ideas or spend time arguing over 'who is right and who is wrong'.

The obvious message is another reproach to the conservative left-wing ideologues who briefly made the running early this year in the campaign against 'bourgeois liberalism'. Has the chief ideologue, Deng Liqun, perhaps been obliged to make a self-criticism?

But things are never quite so simple. One hears simultaneously that two of the most prominent names on the blacklist of bourgeois liberal intellectuals – compiled last February by the theoretical thugs of Deng Liqun – have been asked to leave the Party. One of them is the controversial Party theoretician, Wang Ruoshui, whose argument about the persistence of 'alienation' in a socialist society helped to provoke the last conservative counter-attack in 1983 against 'spiritual pollution'. 'It's only two out of twenty,' one is told reassuringly. 'And a price has to be paid for getting all those old men to step down.'

Everyone agrees that Mr Deng has jockeyed his old colleagues, President Li Xiannian, and Politburo members Chen Yun and Peng Zhen, to move back with him a few paces in October. As to who will fill these and other vacant slots created by the forced resignation last January of Hu Yaobang, there are as many different scenarios as there are

1. *Dazhai, April 1971. A delegation from the Society for Anglo-Chinese Understanding poses with Chinese guides at the model agricultural brigade. John Gittings is sixth from left in the back row.*

2. *Beijing, April 1976. Apathetic citizens are mobilised by 'ultra-left' leaders to demonstrate against Deng Xiaoping in the power struggle while Mao Zedong is dying.*

3. *Beijing, 1980. One of the first tourist shops occupies a pavilion in the Temple of Heaven, as China opens to the outside world.*

4-5. Fengyang County, Anhui, 1982. Contrasting scenes of rural poverty and enterprise as the people's communes are abolished. An older peasant in the doorway of his mud house and an ex-soldier with new wife and new house.

6-7. Beijing, May 1989-90. Office workers march in support of the students in Tiananmen Square. The white banner says 'Long live democracy!' A year later, a silent crowd watches as police cordon off the square to prevent any demonstrations on the anniversary.

8. *Lhasa, October 1989. A Chinese officer and his wife pose outside the Potala Palace while the city is under martial law.*
9. *Wuxuan, Guangxi, 1993. The peaceful Qian river, where victims were massacred during the Cultural Revolution.*

10. *Zhengzhou, 1993. Tired young peasants sleep outside the railway station, on their way to seek work in the south.*

11. *Anyang, 1991. Popular magazines on sale in the city's new shopping centre.*

12. Shenzhen, 1992. The Special Economic Zone across the border from Hong Kong leads a new economic boom.

13. Guangan, 1995. A 13-year old girl begs in Deng Xiaoping's birthplace, a written plea for help hanging from her neck.

14. Nanchang, 1998. Firecrackers are lit and incense is on sale at a busy Buddhist temple, as millions of Chinese turn to new and old religions.

Hong Kong magazines publishing 'Letters from Beijing'.

'Don't believe what you read there,' warns a Chinese journalist in touch with the Hong Kong scene. 'They may be right, or it may just be someone in Beidaihe floating an idea out on the waves.' One idea refloated last week was the notion that the Party's ruling Standing Committee of the Politburo might be abolished altogether in October. It has a certain attraction. If it is so difficult to fill the vacancies created by Mr Deng Xiaoping, Mr Li, Mr Chen and Mr Hu (who is till technically a Standing Committee member) that could leave a committee composed of one – Mr Hu's successor as secretary-general, Premier Zhao Ziyang.

It will be hard finding a replacement for Mr Zhao as premier – currently there are at least four names in the air. The problem is that the Chinese political style still requires some sort of Gang of Five (or Six or Seven as in the old days of the Standing Committee). Any threat to abolish may simply be designed to speed up agreement on a new list.

Any new list should contain at least one spokesman for the People's Liberation Army, probably the deputy chairman of the Party's Military Affairs Commission, General Yang Shangkun. He is reassuringly close to Mr Deng, yet here too Mr Deng may have to pay a price. The Minister of Defence, General Zhang Aiping has criticized 'some people' (the usual phrase for dissenting colleagues) who say that China now enjoys a peaceful international environment and can afford to 'put the weapons back in the arsenal and graze our war-horses on the hillside'.

Even more preposterous, said General Zhang in a speech on the 1 August Army Day, is the view expressed by such people that China impoverished itself in the past in its struggle to develop a nuclear capability. There is a strong whiff in army propaganda today of the McNamara doctrine of limited war translated to China in the 1980s. National defence, it is said, in the age of superpower deadlock, requires more attention to the dangers of regional conflict. Strategic frontiers, explained the army newspaper recently, may have to differ from geographical frontiers.

Ever since the Hu Yaobang affair, it has been widely

believed that somehow or other the PLA – politically on the decline ever since it lost its dominating role after the Cultural Revolution – must somehow profit. It may not be necessary, some observers believe, for the PLA to feature too obtrusively in the October name-list. What it is really asking for, and what Mr Deng can hardly refuse, is to move defence much higher up in the list of the Four Modernizations.

Meanwhile, the reformers led by Zhao Ziyang remain back on track. Their definition of political reform is more limited than the radical explorations of last year which brought about Hu Yaobang's downfall. But the main thrust for greater efficiency and real measures against bureaucracy are designed to deal with the Party's dangerously low reputation in the public eye.

A lower political profile also allows a sharper cutting edge for economic reform. The *Economic Daily*, which has regained its leading role in sparking new ideas, last week called for 'large numbers of entrepreneurs, in the real sense of the word' to run China's industrial and commercial enterprises. The point is – and the *Economic Daily* did not conceal it – that they would replace thousands upon thousands of government officials who, it argued, merely carry out plans made by superiors and do not answer for taking risks or making profits. Things were managed much better, it said, in the 'developed' (i.e. capitalist) world.

A name-list of many thousands, reaching down into the provincial and local bastions of bureaucratic self-interest, will prove at least as difficult to draw up as the more exalted list at the Central Committee level. Nor can it be simply fixed by early morning conversations at the seaside.

Dissident voices unite
March 1989

A Red Guard poet who used to compose secretly in a photographic darkroom; a former director of the Institute of Mao Zedong Thought; a journalist threatened with libel cases by two Chinese provinces; and an astrophysicist who was sacked from the Communist Party.

These and other dissenting voices in China, of very different generations and outlook, have come together recently to present the first united challenge to the Chinese leadership. This new working alliance, in a political culture which is habitually weakened by the divisions of age and elite connections, proves that dissent in China has finally come of age.

The barring of the astrophysicist Professor Fang Lizhi, last weekend, from President Bush's Texan barbecue at the Great Wall Hotel has now forced a largely reluctant audience outside China to pay attention. Western governments have ducked the issue of human rights in China because – unlike the same cause in the Soviet Union or Eastern Europe – there is no political advantage to be gained. But after ten years of uncoordinated actions, starting with the 1979 Democracy Movement, China's dissenting voices can no longer be ignored so easily.

It was Professor Fang who took the initiative last month with a letter to Deng Xiaoping appealing for the release of the 1979 dissident activist, Wei Jingsheng. Ten days ago, thirty-three intellectuals, young and old, joined to send a second open letter. Mr Wei, a young Beijing electrician, belongs to that generation of former Red Guards who were radicalized by being 'sent down to the countryside'.

Mr Wei is still serving a fifteen-year jail sentence, no one knows exactly where. But last week the poet, Bei Dao, another prominent signatory of the open letter, said that he heard he had 'gone mad' in solitary confinement. During the Cultural Revolution, Bei Dao took advantage of his job as a building works photographer to start his first novel, using a darkroom where no one would disturb him. 'Let me tell you, world,' he declared in his most famous poem published on Democracy Wall, 'I do not believe!'

But the defiant shout of the Democracy Movement was suppressed by the early 1980s, and found at that time no overt support among older intellectual critics of the regime. These include Professor Su Shaozhi, who is also a signatory of the appeal. Unlike Professor Fang, he, together with the playwright and cosignatory Wu Zuguang, was allowed to pass the police cordon to enter the Great Wall Hotel. As a young political scientist after the 1949 revolution, Professor Su had loyally charted the reefs of Mao's shifting thoughts on political economy until the Cultural Revolution. After Mao's death he played a leading part in the think-tank set up by Mr Deng to redefine socialism in terms of the struggle to improve China rather than the class struggle.

As head of the Institute for Marxism–Leninism–Mao Zedong Thought (a compromise concept to appease surviving Maoists) Professor Su argued mostly from within. But in 1986 he became prominent among Communist Party scholars who – encouraged by the then Secretary-General Hu Yaobang – queried Marx's relevance to China's problems.

'Without a spirit of democracy,' he argued, 'there can be no spirit of science,' calling for a fresh study of advanced capitalist society. Professor Su lost his post following the enforced resignation of Mr Hu in the 1987 conservative backlash. Surviving in silence, he spent much of last year at St Antony's College, Oxford, researching for a new book called *Re-interpreting Socialism*. But he returned to China to speak out on the tenth anniversary of the reforms. 'China is in a crisis,' he said last month, 'a spiritual, economic and cultural crisis.'

From the leadership's perspective this is clerical treason in dangerous reverse by China's most distinguished neo-Marxist scholar. Professor Su now argues that other schools of thought should be encouraged by the Party, and warns openly against a recurrence of 'the personality cult and despotism'. The editor of the radical *Shanghai Economic Herald*, who published Professor Su's speech, has been sacked. Professor Su has also described corruption in the Party as the worst for forty years – that is, since the dying months of Chiang Kai-shek's Kuomintang, which has always been the benchmark for corruption.

The unprecedented unity of old and young dissenting intellectuals now makes it possible for the first time to envisage the development of a dissident movement in China comparable to the Soviet or Czech examples. The catalyst appears to have been the gloomy collapse of all the fresh hopes attached to Mr Hu's successor, Zhao Ziyang, whose own political future is now being questioned.

Signs of a renewed counter-offensive by the Party conservatives (who overlap politically with the remnants of Mao's leftist leadership) have prompted the dissenters to speak out first, defying official warnings, in the phrase so familiar from the past, not to 'go too far'.

Chinese students and scholars who increasingly travel abroad have also become impatient of the tacit rules of the game which allowed passports to be issued against the implied obligation of good behaviour. The open letter appealing for an amnesty was also signed by Liu Binyan, the crusading journalist who has written nothing since he was forced out of the Communist Party in 1987, but has been allowed to take a fellowship at Harvard. Mr Liu's exposés of official oppression had provoked bureaucrats in two provinces to threaten libel action against him, with the complaint that 'wherever he writes something, chaos ensues'. He caused particular offence by drawing attention to many cases of injustice.

Chen Jun, who distributed the petition to foreign journalists in Beijing, typifies the breaking down of national barriers. Mr Chen studied in the US but now runs a private bar in Beijing and has a British wife. A colleague of the poet, Bei Dao, he has named the new grouping Amnesty 89. But Professor Fang remains the voice who has gone the furthest.

8

The Beijing Massacre, May–June 1989

Beijing in May 1989 was a city transformed. The death of the reformist ex-leader Hu Yaobang brought the students back into the streets. It coincided with the seventieth anniversary of the great 4 May Movement of 1919, when China was governed by warlords and manipulated by foreign powers. Then, as now, students from Beijing University had marched in support of the person they called 'Mr Democracy'. The rapid growth now of high-level corruption, and the rich concessions given to foreign interests in the new Special Economic Zones, seemed to demonstrate how little China had advanced since then. The writer Lu Xun had described China before the 4 May Movement as a nation suffocating in an iron room without windows. Today's students were determined to smash a hole in the wall.

Tiananmen Square became an encampment with banners flying over the students' tent city. A sit-down blocked the gate to the exclusive Zhongnanhai park next to the Imperial City where the leadership lived. In the streets there was a sense of comradeship mixed with excitement that so many people – workers and ordinary citizens as well as students – had found their voices. Even when confronting the armed units which hung around uncertainly in the suburbs, people were good humoured, offering the soldiers food and drink. Everyone noticed that the usual Beijing rudeness had faded away.

After martial law was declared on 19 May, there was a night of nervousness, but the troops stayed out of the city centre. On the impromptu barricades there were lively discussions in the evening. Dissidents from the early eighties emerged on college campuses to debate the future of the Chinese state and the mass movement.

Hundreds of mimeographed leaflets were produced and handed out in the Square, written in a traditional mixture of invective, satire and serious argument.

The road in from Beijing's Capital Airport was barred by citizens' checkposts, staffed night and day by the local residents. 'Only the old people and children are in bed,' they said cheerfully. Foreign journalists were welcomed everywhere, and exhorted to 'tell the world' about the students' demands and the refusal of the Party leadership to engage in dialogue. In the business centres of the new international hotels, the staff copied faxes of articles from the Hong Kong newspapers reporting what was happening in the capital. These were then pasted up on lamp-posts along the Avenue of Everlasting Peace. News of the democratic movement was published in regular editions of the China Youth Daily, *while staff at the Party's flagship newspaper, the* People's Daily, *produced an unofficial 'extra edition'.*

The leadership seemed to be paralysed and the streets belonged to the masses. Very few believed that a military assault would be ordered: at most they feared that the regime might stage some small incident in which one or two people were killed. Zhao Ziyang, successor to Hu Yaobang, argued that the students were not a threat to the regime. On the day that his rival Li Peng declared martial law, he paid an emotional visit to the student hunger strikers in the Square, apologizing for not visiting them before. It was a futile gesture: he was outnumbered in the leadership and stepped down.

The demonstrations continued and thousands of students arrived from the provinces, marching up from the railway station in columns. They brought news of protests in many of the provincial capitals. The student leadership in the Square rejoiced at the apparent leadership vacuum in the Zhongnanhai. To keep the momentum going, they raised the statue of the Goddess of Democracy in front of Mao's portrait. This may have been the final provocation. Deng and the Party elders decided 'not to give ground': they believed that otherwise 'everything would collapse'. By everything, they meant the Party's domination. After a false lull while preparations were being made, the army moved in on the night of 3 June with orders to occupy Tiananmen Square no matter who was in the way. Hundreds were in the way, and hundreds died.

The students take to the streets

4 May 1989, Beijing University

The 'Internationale' was a wise choice for a marching song today in Beijing. Apart from being a good tune, it cannot offend the authorities and everyone has known it by heart since primary school. The band was a ghetto-blaster, strapped to the front of a bicycle.

Each of the forty colleges started from its own campus. Beijing University (*Beida*) is one of the farthest away, but it was the right place on a day which celebrated the great 4 May demonstration by *Beida* students in 1919. Do we have to wait another seventy years, asked several of the slogans marshalled at 8 a.m. under the acacia trees inside the gates. There were other echoes of 1919: 'Hello, Mr Democracy' and 'Save our country'. There was also a simple but very effective marching chant, agreed on by all the colleges: 'Dialogue! Dialogue! We must have dialogue! But if they are not sincere, it is a rubbish dialogue!'

The stylized confrontation with the police, on the pattern established last week, took place near the zoo. They had formed up looking very grim in a legionary square. 'You've got more police here than students,' screamed one of the girls at a very young policeman. It was so evidently not true that both burst out laughing, and the square collapsed soon afterwards.

Without the police, the traffic chaos was terrible. Bicycles crashed to the ground. Lorries and buses were stranded, and then requisitioned as platforms for photography and handing out leaflets. Very unusually their drivers did not mind and didn't curse anyone's mother. Many of the watchers lining the route clapped the slogans and raised two fingers in a victory salute. Workers ran out of their factories or waved out of the windows.

'Long live the students!' they shouted somewhere near the Yuetan Park. And 'Long live the people!' shouted back the students. It was one of those moments which makes everything clear – and brings a lump to the throat. Long live the people! What an obvious slogan, yet I doubt if it has been heard in China since the revolution. 'Long live the People's Communes', of course, plus many other things including Chairman Mao which have come and gone. Even today there is 'Long live the Communist Party of China'. But 'Long live the people' (*Renmin wansui*) is as subversive as it is splendid.

By now there was the usual discussion about 'Is this demo as big as the last one?' The answer seems to be no, but there are many more delegations this time from the provincial universities. This leads on to stories about what has been happening elsewhere. Someone has heard that at least one person was killed in the provincial city of Xi'an the Saturday before last. She was aged twenty-four, a waitress at a foreigners' hotel. At Wuhan in Hubei province last week, they used teargas. And there were supposed to be 30,000 soldiers at Shenyang in the north-east.

Under a very hot sun we reach Tiananmen Square. The colleges read one another's slogans and sit down, still in very good order, drinking bottles of lemonade and eating buns and sunflower seeds. A teacher asks if we knew that last evening there was a reception for a Japanese firm at the Beijing Hotel? It cost 1,000 *yuan* (160 pounds) a head, a million in all. An eighteen-year-old student tries to explain what he means by democracy. This is a people's country, he says, and yet we don't even know who the president is going to be until it is announced.

But I then rejoin another section as it marches home. A worker emerges from the crowd with a large bag of iced lollies to distribute to the leading column of linked-hand marchers. Everyone laughs and claps, including the passengers stuck on the number one bus.

Resisting martial law
22 May, in the streets

If the army has been held at bay in the Chinese capital, most of the credit can be claimed by the sturdy and plain-speaking citizens of Beijing who have gathered on street corners to stop them. 'We'll never let them in,' they were saying during the tense hours on Sunday night. 'Only the old people and children are asleep. The rest of us are in the streets.'

The *shimin*, city people, expressed their determination to 'defend the students' in terms which echoed the simpler politics of the past. 'How can the government be so lacking in proper virtue?' a worker in Tiananmen Square exclaimed, thrusting his jaw forward angrily. 'The people's army belongs to the people!' The citizens standing nearby, he pointed out, were individuals who had decided to come along because they no longer believed the government was 'sincere'.

None of the citizens I spoke to had the slightest thought of offering a political alternative to the present system. They just wanted two people to go. Premier Li Peng was loudly condemned as a bastard; Mr Deng Xiaoping's name often had to be inferred from a grimace. Whatever came after that would be tested when it happened. No complicated name-lists here: 'Whoever represents the people, we will support them.'

Several citizens were concerned that the foreigner might get into trouble for breaking one of the martial law regulations which forbids journalists getting involved in 'law-breaking actitivies' or 'instigating propaganda'. But they enjoyed my answer: 'This is not a formal interview, we are just having a chat among friends.'

And they would go on chatting, about serious matters. 'Do people abroad really support the students?' 'Has your government protested?' It was galling to have to explain that the American President had spoken out before the British Prime Minister. 'Why has the International Red Cross not intervened?' The answer – that it could only do so at the invitation of the Chinese Red Cross – provoked a lively pavement debate. In the end, they patriotically agreed. Yes, it was entirely proper that the Chinese people should them-selves decide whether or not an international organization became involved.

The citizens' actions – bringing water and towels, offering ice-creams, 'comforting' demonstrators with praise and applause – echoed the civic values of an earlier generation. 'Everyone's a soldier now!' joked a middle-aged technician, who had been in the Square for two nights, standing guard.

He must have remembered from his youth the famous militia campaign of the Great Leap Forward. But then participation was compulsory.

'They can't get in,' repeated the citizens reassuringly. 'They can't get in as long as we're here.'

23 May, march to the Square
Everyone was shouting the same thing today in Beijing: 'Down with Li Peng' – meaning down with Deng Xiaoping as well. 'It's better tactics not to say it out loud,' the demonstrators explain. But on the noticeboards around the Square, and in leaflets thrust hastily into our hands, both leaders are being attacked in open polemics.

This demonstration is the most overtly political of those held so far: perhaps Beijing senses that the inner-Party struggle just needs one sharp shove. Even when a thunderstorm drives spectators to huddle against the walls of the Forbidden City, the marchers carry on. *Li Peng xia tai*, they chant, and the spectators give an answering cry of *xia tai* – resign!

Mr Deng is the subject of a poem, five characters to the line. It sums up the people's loss of faith in the man who seemed to offer such hope ten years ago:

> *When cult is added to power, even the chairman makes mistakes.*
> *Xiaoping suffered criticism (in the Cultural Revolution),*
> *   and the people raised him up.*
> *Now he represents bureaucracy and official corruption.*
> *The country does not want him, the people do not want him.*

The poem then expresses the simple levelling philosophy much heard these days:

> *The officials eat the food, the common people labour all year;*
> *A small handful get fat, a billion are poor.*

It ends with a statement of political aims which is as principled but lacking in detail as the opinions of the vast majority of the marchers:

*To overthrow the old system, the people must become the real
    masters;*
They should elect the good, and dismiss the bad!

On a less elevated level, a handbill asks 'What sort of person
is Li Peng?' It answers: he is head of China's biggest corrupt
family. He is also accused of using army funds to build a
private restroom for himself behind a swimming pool
which he uses. This makes him, the handbill says, with
pamphleteering licence, 'more corrupt than the Empress
Dowager'.

Yesterday afternoon, he was also being blamed for having
sent the provocateurs who defaced Chairman Mao's portrait.
The most convincing charge is that it is Mr Li, not the
students, who has caused 'disorder' by bringing in the troops.
The slogan which gets the loudest applause is simple:
'Beijing does not wish to live in front of the muzzle of a gun'.

Massacre by night and day
3–4 June, Tiananmen Square and surrounding streets

A two-pronged attack from east and west shattered all
illusions in Beijing on Saturday. Dozens of citizens and
students who only hours before had repeated their pledge to
risk death for democracy, had it brutally confirmed.

The main thrust of President Yang Shangkun's loyal and
murderous troops came from the west, just after midnight,
when hundreds of trucks moved up the main avenue. The
tactics were brutally simple. Armoured personnel carriers
formed the spearhead, while soldiers on foot shot to kill from
both sides.

Meanwhile, the first of the night's armoured cars and
tanks smashed its way through the citizens' barricades to the
east. It showed all the ruthlessness which must be contained
in the army's orders to smash the 'turmoil' allegedly created
by the mass movement. Several cyclists who could not get
out of the way in time were crushed or tossed aside.

At top speed the armoured car scattered a crowd of several
thousands at Dongdan. Enraged citizens, still not aware of

the full scale of the attack, headed for Tiananmen Square, cursing the government as 'fascist' and 'heartless dogs'. I was grabbed by people urging me to 'report it all'. 'None of the people will give in,' they said, insisting that I write it down.

But by 1.30 a.m., close to Tiananmen Square, the grey shapes of the personnel carriers could be seen approaching from the west. The first armoured car was burning less than forty yards from Mao's portrait. With curses and laughter, the crowd milled around the Square. There were distant explosions and tracer bullets in the sky.

At 1.50 a.m. a crackle of gunfire sounded on the far side. 'Don't be afraid, don't run!' many cried out, believing that it must be the sound of exploding tear-gas canisters. The official loudspeaker soothingly repeated its message: 'The Beijing government is the People's government.' Police from the Beijing public security headquarters peered curiously out of their gate, evidently unaware of what was happening. At intervals, fresh bouts of gunfire echoed closer. Then came a lull, and many in the crowd walked closer to the army.

Meanwhile the army sharpshooters appear to have worked their way close to the wall of the Forbidden City. Others emerged from inside, and at 2.10 a.m. the shooting restarted alarmingly close. The first casualty in the Square was rushed away – a girl with her face smashed and bloody, carried spread-eagled towards the trees. Another followed – a youth with a bloody mess around his chest.

Ambulances began to press with urgent sirens through the crowd. Other casualties were carried off on pedicarts with a dozen cyclists in escort. Within twenty minutes the same number of casualties were evacuated. A commandeered jeep had one wounded man on the roof, and two or three sprawled inside.

At 2.40 a.m., another lull. People streamed back towards the Square as ambulances pleaded for a clear path. Had the army stopped on the eastern side, its mission completed?

From under the acacia trees on the dark pavement near the Beijing Hotel, or perhaps over a wall from the Workers' Palace, the sound of semi-automatic fire spat out. The crowd fled around the corner, stumbling in panic, tripping over parked bikes. 'Who's afraid? It's nothing,' scoffed one who reached shelter. 'I've just seen a man with his skull blown away,' reported another.

Within the next hour, squads of military police who had been lurking in the shadows around the Square now appear to have started to take control. By 4.30 a.m. new columns of tanks were smashing their way in from east and west, eventually to form two north–south lines across the Square. Witnesses later reported that the army had been a bit less savage in the square: it had mostly shot at the students' legs or above their heads.

But when they retreated after 6 a.m., there were reports that at least a dozen students were crushed by tanks. There were many bodies outside the Xinhuamen Gate.

New lines were formed in the morning. Two buses were set on fire outside the Beijing Hotel, and fresh crowds piled up behind them. Their numbers diminished closer to the Square. A witness went forward with some forty workers to plead with the soldiers. After taking sixty steps forward, they were shot down. Eight died immediately and the others crept back.

Machine-gun fire also seemed to come from the roofs of the museums in the Square. Near the Kentucky Fried Chicken restaurant, the body of an old man was lying in the road.

Wherever they were not faced with gunfire, the Beijing people continued to show spirit. Troops believed especially loyal to President Yang were stranded near the diplomatic quarter. Bicycles thrown in their way lay smashed, and truck tyres had been let down. It looked like a repeat of the last two weeks, but this time everyone knew that at any moment the soldiers could get ready to fire.

4 June, Avenue of Everlasting Peace

'I feel as though we are being hanged by the government,' said the man standing on the traffic island outside my hotel today, one hand briefly clutching his throat. 'There is no way out.' The street-corner mood was angry, but mixed with the dull despondency which comes from seeing tanks come crashing through. 'We have no machine-guns, nothing,' said the informal group leader in a small evening discussion around the deserted area outside the hotel.

Over on the pavement there was a more forceful speaker of the kind who has dominated the evening citizens' chat sessions since martial law was declared. Several of the more articulate neighbours have disappeared in the last twenty-four hours. No one quite knows why.

But this survivor, too, started with the tanks. 'The students were sitting down in the Square,' he told a silent audience. 'The tanks went criss-cross among them, and scattered the bodies everywhere.'

Life and death continues to extend itself along the east–west meridian of the now grotesquely misnamed Avenue of Everlasting Peace. The central zone around Tiananmen Square is a no-go area, except for the army and the bravest citizens.

From a distance it has an uncanny neatness about it. Just at the entrance to the square from the east, there is a thin line of the ordinary people. Then, some forty yards ahead, two thicker lines of sitting soldiers with their officers standing behind them. Another gap, and then a line of stubby tanks. The crews are standing on and around each turret as if ready to leap into action – which they probably are.

Behind them, a phalanx of armoured personnel carriers, also swarming with soldiers, apparently at the ready. Far away at the western entrance to the Square, another double line of soldiers, and another rank of brave citizens.

Anyone who has pedalled up to the Square and returns safely to tell his tale deserves a good audience at the street corner. 'This worker was waving the flag of the Workers' Autonomous Union,' one returnee explained. The union is now labelled an illegal organization. 'The soldiers just sprayed him with machine-gun fire.'

No one, including most foreign journalists, could be blamed for caution yesterday. A visiting Swedish teacher was dragged cheerfully up to the front line by two of his Chinese students. As he raised his camera to record the soldiers, they opened fire. Everyone ran and no one could say how many bodies were left.

A few postal vans still hesitantly cross the avenue well away from the Square. There are burnt buses outside the Beijing Hotel, an unburnt barrier east at Dongdan.

The bold speaker on my local corner can still laugh with that special brand of Beijing contempt when asked whether people may follow the students' call for a workers' strike. 'Why should we work for this sort of government? Those cadres could buy up a whole street in the United States if they wished to. How couldn't we strike!'

When a government uses tanks to declare war on its people, anything is possible and the people now know it.

The army versus the people

5 June, central Beijing

After two days of military occupation, most Beijingers are getting used to the sight of squadrons of tanks and troop carriers performing inexplicable manoeuvres on their streets. Yesterday's entry of over fifty trucks of soldiers with weapons at the ready added a new mystery. Why were the last dozen crudely camouflaged with tree branches?

The code which determines if pedestrians get shot or not is also clarified. The soldiers' code apparently includes a pledge: 'We shall not oppose those who do not oppose us.' So anyone who shouts something abusive like 'animals' can expect to be shot for opposing the provisions of martial law. But well-behaved citizens are probably safe to stand on the corner and watch the soldiers go by – at least during daytime.

But these basic ground rules do not help in the slightest to understand the strategy which has filled the centre of Beijing with enough firepower to fight a small war. Over a long period of time forces from two military regions, Beijing and Shenyang (the north-east), had been moved in what the experts regard as the sort of massive logistical operation which the People's Liberation Army does very well. But since the declaration of martial law, nothing has really made sense.

On the first night after martial law was declared, the

troops appeared in the suburbs often as if they had been woken up from bed. Some had no arms, others no uniforms, and many lacked food and water. Then came the strange attempt on Friday, 2 June – the day before the massacre – to infiltrate Beijing, mostly with young soldiers who had jogged fifteen miles and seemed to be without any officers. For a few hours on Saturday the general opinion was that the army had tried – perhaps deliberately not very hard – and had failed. No one believed that the tanks, just two to three hours' drive from Beijing, were being readied for action.

Was this really a sharp reaction to the army's second humiliation, or had stage three been planned all along? And if so, what sort of military rationale brings tanks and armoured personnel carriers in massive strength into Beijing, instead of forces trained in crowd control and bulldozers to clear the barricades? These types of armoured vehicles are quite unsuitable for operation on city streets, slithering on the tarmac, unable to stop or start smoothly.

The simplest theory is that a contingency plan for the defence of Beijing against an enemy attack from outside has been clumsily adapted to the needs of internal repression. But there was surely enough time to work out a different plan in the six weeks of military build up. A more plausible theory takes the official broadcasts at their word: This army is in hostile territory. Whoever controls the Communist Party believes it is facing a 'revolt' – the word used in yesterday's statement. Before too long the armoured personnel carriers will fan out into alleys and 'pacify' what it must now regard as a lumpenproletariat.

Numerous stories are now circulating about alleged intra-army hostilities. It is likely the move to martial law was not popular with some senior generals, but there is no reliable evidence to support stories that tanks and carriers have been immobilized or set on fire by dissident troops. Nor does the disposition of troops and tanks so far suggest deployment with hostile intent against other units.

The most likely explanation of all these ambiguities is to be found in the more fundamental political ambiguity which means that no national leader – even the president who presumably ordered the troops in – has spoken since Tiananmen Square was occupied. There is still a large, ugly piece of the puzzle missing and everyone has the grim feeling that in the next few days we may be even more unpleasantly surprised.

7 June, outside International Hotel

The massive army convoy came out from Tiananmen Square yesterday morning like a triumphal procession, though it was not clear what it had to celebrate. First came the tanks. Then two companies of foot soldiers with patrols marching in front and behind, carrying their weapons proudly. And then a stream of troop trucks and armoured personnel carriers, snaking through the remnants of the barricades they smashed down four days ago.

Only three hours beforehand, a unit of this same army had sprayed machine-gun fire on innocent spectators, striking down five or six. Now, as the parade passed the same spot, many of the same spectators were applauding it. The contrast was as stunning as it was hard to fathom.

It had been 6.45 a.m. when the machine-gun fire began to echo against the curved wall of the International Hotel. Rolling out of bed, I reached the window to look down at the crossroads below in time to see the last truck of the convoy heading toward the Square – and the citizens of Beijing scattering like sparrows.

They quickly regrouped into little knots of agitation. The victims' inert bodies were scooped up onto pedicarts and rushed into the maze of little lanes behind the hotel within a minute.

The 10 a.m. convoy, heading out of the Square, managed to communicate to the public that it was going to be completely different. Instead of aiming AK-47s at them, some units of soldiers were shouting sympathetic slogans. 'Down with official corruption,' they cried – one of the demands of the democracy movement. 'Protect the people of Beijing,' they shouted, as if that was what they had been doing since Saturday.

Some soldiers bent over the side and waved. The crowd at

the crossroads swept forward – a reaction which denied all logic – and it soon seemed as if they would be cruelly deceived again. Two-thirds down the triumphal column of nearly a hundred vehicles, the firing began. Volleys of semi-automatic fire rattled off the hotel walls, shattering windows and echoing through the open fire-escape doors. The noise undermined the commonsense view that huddling against an inner wall should be sufficient protection. Chinese staff laughed and cried at the same time.

The volleys lasted well over five minutes. The last truck having passed, the terrified citizens emerged to count their new losses. Not a single body lay on the ground; it had just been high spirits – otherwise known as hooliganism – by troops who were, perhaps, going home.

Three hours before it had been very different. The ruthless arc of the tailtruck machine-gunner had began with a student on his bike. His satchel of books was still hanging on the saddle. Within ten minutes a rough message had been scribbled on cardboard and propped against the handlebars: 'This student was shot by the heartless soldiers.'

Traversing, the machine-gunner's arc scythed a line of pedestrians crossing the road. 'I was halfway over when they fired,' said one. 'He dropped at my side. He came from Qiqihaer . . .' As I moved from one group to another, this witness followed me, repeating as if it was the most significant detail of the whole affair: 'He came from Qiqihaer . . . He came from Qiqihaer . . .'

Two more victims fell on the pavement and one more on the hotel's grass verge. Little circles of stones were erected around the blood. One patch was so abundant that death must have been very quick. My grim tour ended in front of a small shop at the end of the arc. I saw the bullet holes in the door. My gaze was then drawn to the fragments of flesh sticking to the wall.

State television presents the army as a disciplined force that respects the people; yesterday it claimed that a bad element fired first upon the troops. I had asked whether anyone even cursed the soldiers – enough to merit one shot.

'No, we were just crossing the road.' A foreign tourist, one of those who step out of the railway station these days and find themselves caught up in tragedy, gave confirmation. They were just innocent passers-by.

8 June, Avenue of Everlasting Peace

Propaganda was delivered at the barrel of a gun yesterday along the Avenue of Everlasting Peace, as the Chinese army started sweeping up the mess it had created. To be exact, the loudspeakers were at the front of the army lorry labelled 'propaganda van', while the soldier with the AK-47 was peering over the tailgate.

In much the same way, the troops, who had been issued with brooms to clear up the debris, had their weapons slung over their backs. Just in case any counter-revolutionary elements should make a criminal assault on these Selfless Soldiers protecting the people of Beijing, armed guards were at the ready.

To be able to cycle freely – although warily – across the foot of Tiananmen Square was an indication of the slight, but significant, relaxation which has brought more people out into the streets. They just have to get used to the sight of armed soldiers at street corners with red bands indicating that they are on martial law duty. Everyone cycles at a careful speed and is especially wary at road junctions, where loudspeakers urge them to hurry – or to stop when a military convoy approaches.

The Square looks deceptively peaceful from the southern side. There are only half a dozen tanks, guarding well over a hundred troop trucks lined alongside Chairman Mao's mausoleum. All the other tanks are at the other end near the Imperial City. Chinese television has been showing film of soldiers in the Square receiving a delivery of biscuits by helicopter. This may be designed to counteract the rumour that the choppers are used to carry away bodies.

The soldiers do not look particularly threatening. They are young, chat and wave to each other, and people have been told that they are from the 38th army. This is supposed to be an improvement on the hated 27th army, which learnt its killing skills on the Vietnam front. But there are an awful lot of them. The stream of cyclists veers out into the middle of the road every so often to circumnavigate a large group with their transport. One encampment flanks the entire length of what used to be Democracy Wall ten years ago.

The propaganda vehicle was delivering a familiar message as it cruised down the avenue near the Nationalities Hotel: 'We have achieved initial success in dealing with the counter-revolutionary revolt. But we must be on our guard against the gangsters who still try to disturb the peace.'

The debris ranges from trolley buses, erected by the Beijing people (now called gangsters) to stop the army coming in last week, to piles of tarmac scraped off the surface of the avenue by tanks. More than twenty burnt-out buses have been shifted off the road near the hotel.

A convoy of trucks bringing supplies for the troops heads in to the square. It, too, is more relaxed. There are only four armed soldiers in the guard truck – instead of fifteen – with their weapons aimed. Each food truck just has one soldier, usually lying on the roof with his gun balanced on the canopy. It still seems prudent to pull into the pavement and watch the convoy pass from behind a parked lorry. 'Don't bother to look at them,' says an old man sitting comfortably on a low wall. 'They do what they do, and you do what you do.'

It is the authentic voice of the independent-minded Beijinger. But everyone has to take heed of new regulations issued yesterday requiring cooperation with the army clear-up. Anyone who disturbs the operation may be 'handled' by any means.

Bitter lessons of bloodshed

12 June, Liubukou junction

When the true history of the 3–4 June weekend in Beijing is written, the road junction at Liubukou, half a mile west of Tiananmen Square, will have a chapter to itself. This week the tanks and armoured personnel carriers are still there: some on the north-west corner with bivouac tents behind, others tucked sinisterly into an alley on the south-east which no one may enter. Cyclists flow by with sidelong glances, two pickets of soldiers with semi-automatic weapons guard the pavement. Nowhere else in Beijing still receives such heavy treatment.

What really happened at Liubukou must be known to the authorities, whose video monitors are being used so efficiently for the identification of 'counter-revolutionaries' and for selecting clips to discredit the student and worker activists of Beijing. We have to piece it together, discounting as far as possible the rumour factor.

A column of students, retreating from Tiananmen Square by a circular route, crossed the main avenue there at the exact moment that a column of tanks headed west. They scattered, but the last line of students – at least ten of them – were caught against the railings and crushed. Unlike many other killings, it was probably a real accident – if one accepts the grotesque logic that armoured vehicles had the right of way. But there is a particular horror about this form of death, and one day these students will undoubtedly be martyrs of a special kind. They will join the martyrs of the Cultural Revolution – such people as Zhang Zhixin (celebrated now by the Communist Party) whose throat was cut before execution to prevent her denouncing the Gang of Four with her last breath. The date will also be as fixed in the revolutionary calendar as 5 April (1976) when Beijing demonstrated against the Gang of Four, and 4 May (1919) when the Democracy Movement began.

The events of the past two months – and particularly the last week since the tanks stormed in – almost overwhelm analysis. It has shocked to the point of an alienating numbness almost every single 'foreign friend' or sympathetic observer. It has stripped away the illusions of millions of Chinese. 'Most of those who were killed,' explains one Chinese who manages to maintain a detached view, 'didn't even know as they died that they were making history.'

There was certainly an enormous naïveté on the night of 3–4 June. At 12.30 a.m. at Dongdan, east of the Square, I was being urged to inspect a bicycle damaged by an armoured personnel carrier as the ultimate example of the government's lack of conscience. At 1.30 a.m. in the Square, I was reproached for retreating from what most people thought could be nothing worse than tear gas, or perhaps blank shots.

The next morning, Beijing citizens still approached the Square, by now heavily garrisoned, to within thirty metres of the armed soldiers. Some rode on bikes, their girlfriends on the back. At least six times that day the soldiers fired when the crowd became too large or its appeal too irritating. And at least seven bodies fell in the first three-minute fusillade alone.

This amazing bravery was still largely based on the experience of the previous two weeks when troop movements had been deterred by non-violent means. On the morning of 3 June, less than thirteen hours before the first killings, I and about 6,000 Beijingers had watched, helpless with laughter, as several hundred unarmed soldiers shambled back to base after attempting to sneak in the night before.

'You must be tired; take it easy,' shouted the Beijing mums, straightening the collars of these almost boy soldiers, warning those whose shoelaces were undone, and clapping them like heroes. 'Come and bugger off from Beijing another time,' the working men shouted more rudely but still cheerfully.

Almost everyone failed to understand that this now set in motion a military plan of graduated escalation. On the afternoon of Saturday, 3 June, tear gas and truncheons were used as large numbers of troops suddenly emerged around the Great Hall of the People. By 7 p.m., riot police were attempting to penetrate from the west. Soon bogged down by the same popular resistance, they did not fire at first.

But by 10.30 p.m. orders had evidently been received to force a way through. The ground-floor windows of the apartment blocks near the Yanjing Hotel still show the marks of automatic fire which killed an average of two persons in each block. The local hospital would receive sixty-three bodies by the end of the next day.

The government videos show civilians burning troop trucks in this area early on the evening of 3 June, but there is reason to believe that the time sequence has been distorted, and that the burnings took place the next day after so many people had been slaughtered. But stones were thrown and troops were roughed up. Most importantly, the army was failing to get through. And after two weeks of hesitation, we must assume that Deng Xiaoping and his lieutenants were now determined to accomplish the objective of clearing Tiananmen Square at any cost.

With the first lethal shootings, the situation clarified brutally for those in the Square. The army would kill, at intervals, to clear the bystanders and sympathetic citizens, driving them east past the Beijing Hotel. It would then herd the students out to the south-east, peacefully if possible. While massive armour poured into the north of the square, the students debated around the Martyrs' Memorial. Finally a last-minute vote by shouting, around five o'clock, prevented more killings. The students marched out sadly but in good order, with their banners still flying.

Government propaganda has argued consistently that no one was killed in the Square during the crucial hour and a half when the students were evacuating. That may well be true. Most people died that night either because they were in the way or by accident. Some deaths occurred in areas well to the south and north-east where no foreign journalists were observing.

The figure of 10,000 deaths seems far too high. The official claim of 300 or so, including soldiers, is far too low. Bodies reported in central hospitals were in hundreds rather than thousands, but some victims were never brought in – including most of the crushed students at Liubukou who were, it is said, scraped off the street. Three and a half thousand deaths is a standard figure among Beijingers, but that includes subsequent shootings which continued until 7 June. The figure could even be as 'low' as 1,000 or so for the night of 3–4 June without detracting one jot from its horror.

At this point it is necessary to listen to the voice of a Beijing intellectual who believes the government was right to end the student occupation but left it too late. 'Beijing had become a city without a government,' he argues. 'No one can want China to fall into anarchy. A government has to govern, and if I don't have any confidence in it, where else can I put my trust? The government should have acted earlier, when it was still possible to avoid using live bullets. No one wants people to get shot. But the students could have avoided it if they had accepted a compromise earlier.'

This sort of argument may not be unattractive to middle-aged Communist Party members and others who were disturbed by the students' assault upon conventional political culture. It in effect requires the students – most of whom were only born in the mid-1960s – to have made a sophisticated tactical judgement allowing the government the traditional Chinese 'way out'.

A more profound analysis by some younger Chinese starts with the factors on the government side which prevented it from seeking accommodation with the students. This begins with the economic crisis and the political divisions within the upper Party ranks which are enmeshed with it. The lack of any real political reform, it is argued, means that the 'relations of production' – the whole bundle of relationships which govern ownership, management and reward for work – have lagged far behind the 'productive forces' – the actual physical capacity for production of the society. Inflation, corruption and irrational output of goods all stem from or are worsened by this mismatch.

It adds up to a deeper crisis in the Communist Party which has failed to reform itself. The crisis was already evident earlier this year when Party conservatives were moving against the reforms of Secretary-General Zhao Ziyang, and a crucial Party meeting had to be postponed. The accident of death and chronology then played its part. Chinese intellectuals revived their call for political reform to mark the tenth anniversary of Deng Xiaoping's reforms. And the death of Hu Yaobang triggered the students' protests.

The result of these catastrophic three months, argues one Chinese civil servant in his thirties, is that the people as a whole have now abandoned all hope in the Party, at least in anything like its present shape. 'The country changed,' he says, 'with the first shot fired.' The Beijing people, according to this still fundamentally optimistic view, are biding their time. Like the Chinese king who waited patiently to take his revenge, comments a hotel worker, 'We are sleeping on straw and tasting gall. The moment may come when Mr Deng dies, or when the economy collapses . . .' The problem with this perspective is that the first thing likely to come in either event is the tanks rolling back onto the streets of Beijing. The insurrectional route is now less likely than a modification of the regime – perhaps a drastic one – brought about by the accumulation of its own internal contradictions.

Repression creates new problems, because it is likely either to go too far or (in terms of the regime's survival) not far enough. Li Peng may also have to pay a high political price for securing the verbal support of the Party veterans. Most important, the economy can at best limp along. While no one will take the initiative to promote further reforms (and few will have the enthusiasm to work very hard), Mr Li's regime does not appear to have an alternative package to offer.

Recent events should have taught us that nothing is too remote a possibility. Some believe that the most likely way forward is a benevolent coup when the Li Peng regime starts to unravel – say in the next two to four years. It is also possible that China will simply regionalize: the hardliners in Beijing will formally dictate policy, supported by conservatives in the less advanced interior provinces. The coastal provinces, where a third of the population lives and the door has been flung wide open, will quietly get on with making money.

The brand-new factor is the army itself which, although formally an instrument of the state, might better be regarded as the instrument of the Communist Party. Its high-ranking officers appear to relish their exposure on television, expounding their vision of events and smiling toughly with an assurance which the political leaders lack. Its troops are fanning out now in the *hutongs* (lanes) of Beijing.

There will be no repeat of 3–4 June for a very long time. The Beijing citizens have, as always, a wry jingle to describe their situation: 'Eat a bit, drink a bit, have a meal, tomorrow you may not need one.' It helps people to deal with what may be a very long period of sleeping on straw and tasting gall.*

---

* There was to be no coup, benevolent or otherwise. The state apparatus tightened its grip, pursuing a list of wanted people and rounding up anyone who might still protest. The country – including much of the Communist Party and the army – was too stunned to challenge Li Peng. Jiang Zemin was brought in from Shanghai with relatively clean hands to take over running the Party. Then in 1992 Deng Xiaoping moved again, launching a new wave of economic reform which held out the promise that everyone – not only those in the coastal provinces – had a chance of making money. Quite a few ex-student survivors of the massacre decided that China would only change when it become prosperous, and joined in. But though the shock of the Beijing Massacre faded, it was still an unhealed wound at the heart of Chinese politics.

9

Tibet in the Shadows, 1989–94

Tibet had been devastated by the Cultural Revolution, when almost all of several thousand monasteries were destroyed and Buddhist clergy thrown into jail. Hu Yaobang visited in 1980 and wept for shame to see how poor the Tibetans still were. He lifted taxes, allowed monasteries to be rebuilt, and let the farmers grow barley again instead of the rice which they were forced to cultivate for the Chinese. Tibet was opened up to foreign tourists, ending the total isolation in which it had been plunged since the Chinese Communist occupation of 1950. A new generation of young Tibetans looked for inspiration to the Dalai Lama in exile. But talks between him and Beijing got nowhere, and local cadres in Tibet resisted Hu's reforms while increasing numbers of Chinese migrants set up business.

With incredible bravery young monks (and nuns) began to stage peaceful demonstrations in 1987–88, knowing they faced jail and torture. Demonstrators were shot in the streets, and the world began to take notice. In March 1989 martial law was declared for Lhasa by Premier Li Peng – two and a half months before he would do so in Beijing. Yet Tibet still seemed remote and exceptional – until the Beijing Massacre showed that repression was not confined to the 'national minorities'. Tourists continued to visit Tibet under tighter restrictions: they included journalists like myself who would be barred if they applied openly. Dissidents still found ways, at great risk, of communicating news to us about human rights abuses.

Tibetan society may have been a feudal – sometimes brutal – theocracy in the past, but most Tibetans today are completely alienated from the Chinese. Few of them believe that the Tibet Autonomous Region offers any real autonomy. Tibet is an amazingly beautiful country, close to the stars on 'the roof of the world', yet it is impossible to forget that this remains a country under occupation.

A city under martial law
27 September 1989, Lhasa

More than a thousand Chinese soldiers are guarding the Tibetan capital on the eve of China's National Day to prevent independence demonstrations. Monks are stopped from entering town and armed soldiers examine identity papers at checkpoints.

The streets are deserted. The sacred Jokhang Temple was closed on Wednesday – the second anniversary of the 1987 mass protest. Martial law, declared in March three months before it was imposed in Beijing, has deterred civilians from large-scale defiance. But activists are still risking severe punishment. Two groups of nuns were arrested this month after shouting independence slogans. Leaflets were handed out this week calling for self-determination and a plebiscite to 'free Tibet from China'. The centre of Lhasa was prohibited to foreigners today. The few tourists still visiting Tibet – less than 10 per cent of last year's figure – must travel at all times with a guide and an official pass.

Life seems almost normal at the start of Barkhor Street – the clockwise pilgrims' circuit around the Jokhang Temple. Hawkers thrust amulets, temple bells and leather money belts into the hands of tourists. Pilgrims in dusty clothes carrying babies, kettles and prayer wheels throng the circuit. Only the Chinese, especially plain-clothes police who are conspicuous in tinted sunglasses, deliberately walk anti-clockwise.

But within a hundred yards, the first narrow alley into the old Tibetan quarter is blocked by a tin sentry box and four soldiers with camouflage jackets and AK-47s. No one can leave or enter without showing an identity card. The soldiers may refuse to let people past if their hair has grown longer or other personal details differ. Old people with immensely wrinkled faces stand in line while a young soldier from Sichuan province decides whether they can go shopping.

It was from this network of lanes that hundreds of demonstrators emerged on 5 March and the next two days, when security forces shot at least a dozen Tibetans after a peaceful demonstration on the Barkhor. Independent activists say the death toll was far higher. Today there were brief shouts of 'Independence for Tibet' and 'Long live the Dalai Lama' by the few demonstrators willing to risk identification. Shops and street stalls closed in sympathy – perhaps also because there was no business to be done. Most supporters found it safer to stay home and read the scriptures in memory of those who died.

Tourists ending a hard bout of bargaining for a prayer wheel or scroll banner this week might find a thin square of paper folded into the change: 'Help us to free Tibet under the supreme leadership of his holiness the Dalai Lama. We do not want to stay under a foreign power – China. Tibet has never been a part of China except by conquest.' Longer leaflets have been tucked surreptitiously into the handbags of tourists. They allege inhuman behaviour by the authorities, including dragging injured suspects from hospital and deliberate acts of torture. The stories cannot be confirmed, but local Chinese do not deny that force has been used. A regular visitor to Lhasa, who is not opposed to the Chinese presence, says the security forces are out of control.

The authorities believe they were faced with a counter-revolutionary threat in March, when for at least a day Lhasa was virtually independent. Lhasa is now a garrison town. Army jeeps and trucks dominate the traffic. Off-duty soldiers photograph each other at the foot of the Potala or window shop in the empty stores. One estimate is that at least four regiments – more than 10,000 troops – are stationed in or around the city.

Some fraternizing goes on at the checkpoint behind the Holiday Inn, one of two hotels where all foreign tourists are confined. A bicycle-repair man and a maker of ashtrays from Coca-Cola tins keep the soldiers company. There is even a compliment book in which schoolchildren have written 'Uncle Soldier, are you well?' But the army's real message to the people was broadcast today from loudspeakers on a patrolling lorry. It warned people to stay away from the Barkhor. 'We must maintain iron discipline!'

China insists that it has saved Tibet from feudalism and

that the independence movement is instigated by a 'handful' with sinister foreign backing. But Chinese residents admit the strength of feeling against them. 'Before martial law I did not feel at all safe here,' says a tourist agent. 'Now I can do my work much better.'

Lhasa should be at its best in September. The nights are cool and the mountains rise clear in the pollution-free air. Yet no one, Chinese or Tibetan, can see a way to a future without troops and inter-racial tension. The independence movement stages small-scale demonstrations, but arrest is almost certain. Lamas who plan to demonstrate wear all their winter clothes, ready for prison.

Tibetan activists still hope for international pressure to be brought upon China. 'Lovers of peace and freedom,' says one leaflet, 'don't fail to give your support to Tibetans.' Another reads: 'Wake up champions of human rights. The UN's very foundation is being shattered beyond the Himalayas.' The room vacated by the Dalai Lama in 1959 on his flight to India still awaits him. But its location in the White, or secular, Palace rather than the Red, or religious, Palace symbolizes the main obstacle to his return. The desire for political as well as religious freedom is so widespread that China's intermittent efforts over more than thirty years to 'improve and educate' Tibet have been ineffective.

In retrospect, the 5–7 March demonstration in Lhasa has much in common with that in Tiananmen Square. A peaceful movement was answered with extreme force. Some violence was reported on the Tibetan side – a soldier died after being chased and stoned by the crowd. But this was vastly outweighed by the authorities' deliberate use of firepower to intimidate and kill. The dilemma of the Chinese authorities in Lhasa and Beijing is much the same. Martial law offends their version of normality – the maintenance of Party rule without big public protests. It cannot last for ever, yet its ending is likely to bring protesters back to the front of Jokhang Temple – and into Tiananmen Square.

The defiance of the nuns

October 1989, Lhasa

Out of the throng of Tibetan pilgrims on sacred Barkhor Street in Lhasa a few weeks ago emerged six young women in maroon gowns and bare heads. The pedlars of shawls and prayer wheels and bottles of Indian hair-oil scattered, knowing what would happen next. The six women – all nuns – cried out 'Independence for Tibet' and began to walk with short but determined steps around the clockwise circuit of the Barkhor Temple. They did not get far.

As the official indictment says, 'Officers on duty from the Lhasa Public Security Bureau seized them on the spot with the swiftness of a thunderbolt.' The nuns were charged with 'splittist activity' and condemned to three years' labour for being 'extremely arrogant'. For a group of young nuns to challenge the full authority of the Chinese state, visibly expressed by the tin-hatted martial-law troops standing guard only a hundred metres away, is an act of calculated defiance. In view of the treatment handed out to previous women demonstrators, it also displays remarkable courage, but it is not an isolated act.

The 'heroic nuns' – as they are described in the clandestine leaflets of the Tibetan resistance – have staged at least twelve protests in the past two years. Nuns, and lay-women, were prominent in the 1959 demonstration before the Dalai Lama's flight to India, and during the Cultural Revolution. The story of their latest protests is beginning to be pieced together from documents brought by travellers to Hong Kong and the West.

A list of the fourteen nuns who demonstrated in March this year gives their ages between eighteen and thirty-two, with an average of twenty-three. Four of them were arrested. 'In prison they were intensively tortured, including electric sticks to the breasts and being beaten by rifles, sticks, handcuffs and chains.' It goes on to state that the cell had no electricity and no floor covering, the prisoners were allowed few clothes and they received only two meals a day, one consisting of a single very small *momo* (steamed bun) and the other of a small cup of wormy vegetables. It also alleges that they were forced to put their heads into a bucket of urine and excrement.

Tibetan sources claim that two nuns who were seized after the March demonstrations were held in cells with male prisoners and raped. One, who had an electric prod inserted in her vagina, has disappeared since their release and it is feared that she has committed suicide. The written accounts suggest an array of special 'female' tortures, including the use of dogs, lighted cigarettes, electric prods and stripping prisoners naked. One young Lhasa lay-woman, a secondary school teacher, was sentenced to two years' jail for writing a manifesto. She was so badly tortured that the authorities had to send her to hospital. They first extracted a written guarantee of good conduct from her uncle and aunt, who are now required to pay for the medical treatment which, if successful, will allow the woman to return to prison.

Nuns have been prominent in all the large demonstrations which culminated in the 5–7 March demonstration this year and the imposition of martial law. But they have also staged their own protests. One was held in December 1987 and another five during 1988. Despite the repression, seven protests have been staged so far this year. It used to be possible to complete three circuits of the Barkhor before being detained. Since martial law was imposed, with army checkposts everywhere, and a heavy plain-clothes police presence, protests last only a few moments.

Nine nuns leapt onto the stage of a Tibetan opera at the Yoghurt festival in the Norbulinka Park on 2 September and were quickly seized. According to more than one witness, one of the nuns had her shoulder broken. Several came from Shung Sep nunnery, a day's walk from Lhasa, which had also supplied the heroic nuns of the March demonstration. Another was seen later with a breast wound. Others came from Ani Tsangkhang nunnery in Lhasa. Although this has a militant reputation, the abbess is a Chinese appointee and nuns have been known to climb out of windows to take part in the demonstrations.

The nuns are young because fresh recruitment – of monks

as well as nuns – was stopped during a decade of suppression and allowed only after reform in 1981 initiated by the then Communist Party Secretary-General, Hu Yaobang. Mr Hu, whose death in April this year sparked off the student democracy movement in Beijing, was forced to resign in 1987. The charges against him included that of being too soft on the Tibetans.

Most nuns come from the Tibetan countryside and may join the nunnery in their early teens or even when they are as young as nine or ten. They reflect a tough tradition among rural women of shouldering a heavy economic burden and speaking their mind. Their stand is not explicitly political, but the strands of secular and religious commitment to an independent Tibet, led by the Dalai Lama, are closely woven.

Women were active in March 1959 when thousands of Tibetans demonstrated in Lhasa believing that the Chinese were planning to kidnap the Dalai Lama. Members of the Women's Patriotic Association – originally set up by the wife of the Chinese army general as a pro-Beijing front – gathered on 12 March. One participant, Rinchen Dolma Taring, wrote in her book, *Daughter of Tibet*: 'The Lhasa women had made many anti-Chinese posters and when I joined them they were lined up around the Barkhor shouting slogans, 'From today Tibet is independent' and 'China must quit Tibet'. Our women were more fierce than our men. It was frightening to walk through the Barkhor, where Chinese soldiers with machine-guns were watching us from the roofs. All the shops were shut and no one was on the streets except the shouting women.'

In 1969, the destruction of monasteries and suppression of monks and nuns during the Cultural Revolution led to another desperate rising, largely unknown to the outside world. Its most famous leader, according to the only available account, was a Buddhist nun who led more than 1,000 people in an attack on government offices in the western suburbs of Lhasa. Defeated, the rebels fled to the mountains overlooking the Lhasa valley. Blockaded by Chinese troops, the leader was captured and executed at a public meeting.

Some say that more people died that year than during the rebellion ten years before.

The nuns' tales reveal that inhuman treatment was already standard practice before the declaration of martial law in March. An Amnesty International report, published in February, documented torture of Tibetan men as well as women. More first-hand accounts which have reached the Tibet Information Network in London have not been translated for lack of funds. After recent mass arrests and tortures in Beijing, it has become even more difficult to claim that the government is unaware of the excesses committed in Lhasa.

Official doctrine, first proclaimed by Chairman Mao Zedong forty years ago, insists that the state is entitled to use all the dictatorial weapons at its disposal to suppress its enemies. In Tibet this means suppressing a growing number of brave young people whose only crime is to write a leaflet or shout a slogan. The latest news from Lhasa is that six more nuns were arrested in mid-October. They had committed the 'counter-revolutionary crime' of celebrating the Dalai Lama's Nobel Peace Prize.

Tourism in an occupied country

August 1994, Gyantse

Tibet is the last place under Chinese rule where I expected to find a portrait of Mao Zedong being paraded through the streets. Had not 2,000 Buddhist monasteries been sacked during the Cultural Revolution, and in the Chairman's name? In mainland China these days, people would hoot with laughter to see the old man's picture aloft. Surely there was some mistake: should it not have been the Dalai Lama?

It was the first day of the big summer festival in Gyantse, third town of Tibet. Young women with braided hair and striped chupa dresses carried good-luck offerings. A cheerful band of flute and percussion players wearing felt hats opened the show. And there, up front, was Mao being carried by a young Tibetan not even alive when the Chairman died in 1976. The portrait was draped sacrilegiously in a white prayer scarf. The opening ceremony had already been inaugurated by two giant floats. One bore a painting of Gyantse's famous Dzhong, the craggy castle which shadows the town. The other bore a massive picture of – Chairman Mao.

Moments like these confirm the impossibility of being 'just a tourist' in Tibet. I was genuinely there, with my family, on holiday, at my own expense. A week in Lhasa followed by five days across the high plateau and over the Himalayas to Kathmandu. But it can never be quite the same as hiking in the Pyrenees or trekking in Nepal. It is impossible to forget for very long that this is tourism in an occupied country.

The Gyantse procession was followed by the yak races. This is a contradiction in terms: yaks don't like racing. Knots of yak fanciers in serge suits studied the form, while the competitors were dragged to the starting line. It was an achievement when more than two yaks completed the course. There was plenty of time to try to find out why Mao's portrait was on display. As we waited, a Tibetan quietly explained the reason. In Gyantse (and all over Tibet this summer) the Chinese authorities have been eager to promote local 'cultural traditions'. What better proof that the Tibetan people enjoy 'real autonomy' under the Communist Party's benevolent guidance?

Yet the authorities are still worried in case 'splittist tendencies' stage a demonstration. In Gyantse, the local leaders thought they should prove their loyalty beyond all possible doubt. Who could accuse them of secretly desiring the return of the Dalai Lama if they carried Mao's portrait on high?

China's presence is less obtrusive now than five years ago when I last visited Lhasa, then under martial law. The entire Tibetan core of the city was ringed by army checkpoints. Ordinary Tibetans had to show three separate passes to be allowed through. Foreign tourists travelled in guided convoy: any deviation from the route led to instant arrest. The army has now pulled back from the streets but it has not gone away. On the road into Lhasa from the airport, we passed three substantial military camps. One is brand-new with smart Chinese-style architecture and an unambiguous name-sign at the gatehouse. It reads *fang bao zhi dui* – The Prevention of Disorder Force. Another camp fills the entire valley next to Sera Monastery on the other side of town.

On Lhasa's main square in front of the Jokhang cathedral, the alleys through which demonstrators in 1988–9 rushed out waving Tibetan flags have been sealed off. A police station blocks one entrance; a public lavatory another.

Outside the Jokhang, Tibetan worshippers prostrate themselves after throwing handfuls of juniper into the always-burning furnace. Some have come for miles on their knees, flinging a mat before them to ease the pain. A stream of pilgrims follows the clockwise Barkhor circuit around the Jokhang. Only Chinese tourists and secret police walk the other way, from ignorance or spite. 'Watch out for the beggars and the monks,' warns a Tibetan friend. 'Most of them are spies.' A red flag stands in the middle of the square. Any Tibetan pausing next to it is moved on by the police: who knows whether they might not suddenly unfurl a flag?

The Jokhang is a Tibetan sanctuary: the monks force Chinese visitors to buy tickets and keep to official opening hours. The pilgrims with their prayer wheels, and sympathetic foreigners with their cameras, are allowed in free of charge and in the mornings. 'Be careful what you say,' warned a friendly monk. The Potala is being turned into a high-security zone with obtrusive TV monitors in the main halls and chapels. Beijing claims that the system is being installed as a gift to the people of Lhasa to prevent their sacred relics being stolen. 'Stolen!' a Tibetan exclaims. 'When the Chinese stole so many treasures of ours to pay back their debts to the Soviet Union!'

10

The Flowers that Bloom and Fade, 1979–91

Literature and art were always a political battlefield in Mao's China: the Cultural Revolution had begun with the denunciation of a play which Mao suspected of satirizing him. When I first visited China there were only heroes and villains on the screen and stage. Fiction was not allowed to portray 'middle characters', only those who were either thoroughly good or bad. Classical artists painted electric pylons on mountain tops and left their pictures unsigned. Some lively painting came from amateur groups in factories and villages, but the themes were resolutely black and white – or rather red and black. Propaganda posters were everywhere: many showed Mao as a quasi-religious saviour.

After Mao's death, young writers and artists soon seized the chance, braving Party disapproval to express pent-up feelings. A new wave of literature explored the dark side of the Cultural Revolution. Foreign art was published for the first time in more than ten years. In 1980 I was lucky to coincide with a brief show by an experimental art group – the Stars – in an ill-lit upper floor of the Beijing Art Gallery. Many older artists and writers were too numbed by their experiences to resume creative work. The younger generation was taken up by foreign patrons and many went abroad in the mid-1980s. At a popular level, Maoist parables were replaced by (often trashy) adventure and love stories: political journals lost readers to magazines devoted to new consumer themes.

Chinese culture suffered another setback after the Beijing Massacre, as more writers and artists left the country or ceased producing. Some persevered: in 1991 I interviewed Hsiao Ch'ien, a veteran from before the revolution, and Zhang Xianliang, a *younger writer who had survived nearly two decades in detention. From very different perspectives both were struggling to produce creative work in an airless environment —the 'iron cell' in Lu Xun's famous phrase. In an equally famous speech during his revolution, Mao had called for a hundred flowers to bloom, but long after his death most of those that managed to do so still faded very quickly. Others preferred to write 'for the desk' – just for themselves and their closest friends.*

Cultural stirrings after Mao
March 1979, Xinhua bookshop, Beijing

It would be too much to say that a Hundred Flowers are Blooming in the world of Chinese art and literature after the Gang of Four. But there are a number of promising buds, at least, which have begun to force their way through the hard cultural earth, particularly from the pens and brushes of the new ex-Red Guard generation.

'I was elated in a strange way. I looked up at the poplar trees, their buds and leaves vivid green in the sunshine, set against the blue sky. I knew that I had at last fallen in love'. It is not inspired writing, but *A Place for Love* by the young writer Liu Xinwu has opened up an area of life which was totally taboo during the Cultural Revolution.

The Chinese now acknowledge that the revolutionary high-mindedness of those years led to a very 'unhealthy' situation among young people. On the one hand, as the magazine *China Reconstructs* admits, 'All love was labelled sensual, vulgar, cheap and obscene. Young people could not talk about it, authors could not mention it.' At the same time, the looser social discipline of the Cultural Revolution increased the opportunities for affairs among young people, while society continued to expect them to choose a mate and get married at the recommended age.

The narrator in *A Place for Love* is a girl called Meng who has fallen in love with a cook, a young man who is not particularly handsome or brilliant. But he is kind and honest, and his 'thinking is good'. What will her friends and her family think? For in the absence of any open discussion of the morality of love, what continues to flourish in post-Mao China is the wholly unrevolutionary view that a girl should make a 'good match' in material terms.

They look for young men, Meng complains, 'as if choosing a woollen sweater to wear.' Her own best friend tries to warn her off the young man, arguing that 'you shouldn't find it too difficult to find yourself an actor or someone like that.'

The problem is resolved for Meng through the good advice of her aunt, who tells her that 'to deny the place of love in the life of a revolutionary is itself revisionist and decadent.' Real love should be based upon 'common ideals and interests', and Meng's love for her boyfriend is 'a fine thing'.

Questions of sexual morality have been discussed openly before in China during previous periods of cultural relaxation – particularly in the mid-1950s and early 1960s, and it is a relatively easy area to open up today. But the larger problems raised by the events of the last ten years offer a more complex challenge to contemporary Chinese writers. The current leadership, operating through the Propaganda Department of the Party Central Committee, certainly wants to see the 'crimes of the Gang of Four' exposed and satirized in literature and art. Yet the underlying faults in the style and structure of Chinese politics are mostly still present today. How far should they be exposed too?

An even younger writer, Lu Xinhua (still a student at Shanghai's Fudan University) has touched a raw official nerve with a story called *Scars*. It is tritely written but deals with the explosive subject of how many young people turned against their 'bourgeois' parents in the Cultural Revolution.

The narrator is a Shanghai girl who disowned her mother when she was labelled as a bad class element; then volunteered to go down to the countryside and cut off all ties with home. The story covers her journey home after the Cultural Revolution, having heard that her mother is ill. As the train speeds through the dark countryside, the young girl stares out of the window reliving her flight from home and her complicated emotions of the last few years. When she arrives in Shanghai it is too late; her mother died that morning. But here too a boyfriend is on hand to turn grief into strength and suggest hope for the future.

Scars was praised in the Beijing newspaper *Guangming Daily* on three separate counts where the author had 'broken through' the usual self-imposed restraints of recent Chinese literature. He had exposed 'the dark side' of certain aspects of the Cultural Revolution. He had also written a story in which the central figure was a 'middle character' (neither wholly good nor wholly bad) of the kind which vanished altogether during the Cultural Revolution. And he had succeeded in writing what the newspaper described as a 'socialist tragedy'.

But the new director of the Party's Propaganda Department, Hu Yaobang, has let his own less enthusiastic view be known. He said it was all very well exposing the scars of the past, but Chinese writers and artists should not let this task monopolize their attention. What is needed today, Hu told a literary tea party in Beijing at the beginning of this year, is for 'Chinese writers and artists to create their best works in praise of China's march towards the Four Modernizations.'

The scars which are exposed in novelettish style by Lu Xinhua are the same ones now being detailed, with real names and real circumstances, by student demonstrators for human rights and socialist democracy in Beijing and other main Chinese cities.

Lengthy accounts have been published on the walls by young people victimized for alleged misdeeds in the remote past of their families. Recent demonstrations in Shanghai have drawn attention to the plight of thousands of students who went 'down to the countryside' and now wish to escape. A cartoon which was on display showed some dejected members of a youth shock brigade in one of the border regions. They were clearing timber under a hot, hostile sun and they subsisted, according to the artist, on a diet of rice and peppers.

The dividing line between fact and fiction merges very easily in the sort of unofficial art and literature which now circulates among young people in China. The events of April

1976, when a demonstration in Tiananmen Square, mounted in memory of Premier Zhou Enlai, turned into a massive show of hostility against the authorities, has been the source of a great deal of recent unofficial writing.

Poems in all the main classical styles, penned on posters affixed to the side of the Martyrs' Memorial in the square, or simply chalked on the pavements, were copied down by student demonstrators and circulated widely in spite of being denounced as 'black documents' by the radical leadership (the so-called Gang of Four) who then controlled official propaganda.

Students at the Beijing No. 2 Foreign Languages College collected these poems with particular zeal. In November 1978 the authorities, after hesitating more than two years, finally allowed them to be openly published. Chairman Hua Guofeng himself, whose role in the events of April 1976 (when he took over at the expense of the Gang's chief enemy, Deng Xiaoping) remains equivocal, eventually wrote the lettering on the title page of one volume of the poems. One or two of the bolder wallposter writers suggested that he of all people had no reason to cash in on the literature of a movement which he had helped to suppress. Once again the poetry may not be exactly inspired. But it does reveal how strong the tradition of expressing political protest in literary forms remains among young Chinese today.

Meanwhile, after twelve years of suspension, the magazine *World Literature*, which is devoted to translations of foreign literature into Chinese, has appeared again, with poems by Biswas, a story by Dürrenmatt, and a satire by Tolstoy in its first issue. But in the present mood of 'learning from abroad', the main constraint upon translations of foreign works is only likely to be space and the shortage of skilled translators.

The real political problems still arise with what is written in Chinese, and by Chinese, about the realities of China today. How these problems are resolved must depend on the wider fate of the whole political struggle now taking place between a reformist Party leadership, willing to make certain concessions in the interests of the Four Modernizations, and an assertive movement of protest among the alienated youth.

August 1980, Beijing Art Gallery
During the Cultural Revolution, a well-known artist, Huang Yongyu, painted a picture of an owl with one eye shut – a light-hearted present for a friend. Madame Mao's cultural apparatchiks got to hear of it, and the painter was severely criticized for 'making fun of socialism'.

Recently, in an exhibition of unofficial art in Beijing, another owl picture appeared. This time the owl had both eyes firmly shut. It was the most obviously political item in the exhibition, but no one objected. The thaw after the Cultural Revolution in China – unlike the post-Stalin thaw in the Soviet Union – has produced official tolerance, on the whole, for the new Chinese experimental artists.

The first show of the 'Single Spark' group (otherwise known as the 'Stars') had met with trouble in 1979. Staged in the gardens outside the Beijing Art Gallery, it was broken up by a squad from the local police station. But the authorities relented and allowed it to move into the gallery. This year a second show was also given a ten-day slot, and the official *Art Monthly* has called for more freedom of artistic expression.

A poem attached to a self-portrait by one of the experimental artists declares:

> *I am a tree on the mountain top watching the passers-by;*
> *I am a footprint in the soil, filled with human sweat;*
> *I am wind, I am rain, I am human.*

To a generation of young Chinese brought up in the Cultural Revolution when most art was 'collectively' painted (or else the artist prudently did not sign his name) questions of identity and perception – who am I and what do I see? – are not the hackneyed ones they have become in the West. 'The world is getting ever smaller,' proclaimed the second manifesto of the Single Spark group. (Their name echoes an old saying, quoted by Mao Zedong during the Revolution, that 'a single spark can start a prairie fire'.) 'Today the only new continent lies within ourselves. To discover a new angle, to make a new choice, that is an act of exploration.'

On the top floor of the Beijing Art Gallery, several

hundred visitors at a time, mostly in their thirties or younger, crowded the two rooms of the recent exhbition. Many gathered round a set of questions and answers posted at the entrance by Wang Keping, one of the leaders of the group.

> **Q.** What is this sculpture about? I can't tell what it's meant to be.
>
> **A.** It is itself. It doesn't have to be like something else in order to be worthwhile.
>
> **Q.** I can't understand this picture. All I can see are some colours leaping about.
>
> **A.** You have understood it correctly.

In a cultural environment where foreign art magazines still have to be passed from hand to hand and it is a sensation for *Art Monthly* to have Van Gogh on its front cover, a lot of the new art is clearly derivative. Picasso, Munch, Léger and Klee can be recognized on the walls of the Beijing exhibition. The nude, the abstract, and the untitled picture are startling concepts in themselves, and need to be justified.

Several pictures are accompanied by subtle, allusive poems, written according to the Chinese custom by a friend of the artist, and expressing the disturbed thoughts of many young Chinese about their country. The owl has attracted this comment:

> *I loved you without reserve; I spoke to you without scruple.*
> *But now my eyes are downcast, my heart wounded. You have changed, boundless land.*

A dark landscape bears the title, 'Spring is still the Spring'. A self-portrait by Yan Li, one of the most assured and humorous of the exhibitors, shows 'The Artist at Peace' – with an escape ladder dangling behind him. In his 'Life, Friendship and Love', two shirts shake hands on the clothes-line.

Some of the most successful works are found among the woodcuts and other graphics which stem directly from the political art of the 1930s and 1940s. A powerful set of eight black and white sketches by Qu Leilei, on 'The Motherland', shows the Chinese people oppressed – in the final scene flattened to the ground – but still asserting their nationhood. Woodcuts by Ma Desheng show the patient weary faces of a peasant with his ox, an old ice-cream seller counting her money.

The story of art in China since the Communist victory in 1949 has differed in several important ways from that of Soviet art since 1917, and this affects the position of the experimental artist today. The tradition of painting in the 'national style' *(guohua)* survived and except during the great political campaigns actually flourished. Socialist realism was imported from the Soviet Union in the 1950s but never established itself as a coherent artistic doctrine. What emerged during the Cultural Revolution was a brand of revolutionary romanticism which contained elements of both socialist realism and the national style. Figures of model workers and peasants scaled the traditional mountain peaks. Electric pylons were placed in the most unlikely places.

The result is that the professional artist in China can now revert to the classic depiction of flower and bamboo, of legend and hero, by simply deleting the revolutionary symbols which they had added on. In China, unlike the Soviet Union, experimentation is mostly in the hands of non-professionals, who are also much less aware of post-war Western art. Many of those exhibiting in the Single Spark show work in publishing, design or other fringe areas of the art world. Thus it has been easier for the official art establishment – the Central Arts Academy and the Arts Association – to tolerate the unofficials.

To overcome this peculiarly Chinese problem of cultural isolation, the new movement needs more access to artistic stimuli from outside. It also needs more time. It was closely associated with the Democracy Movement which collapsed after activists were gaoled and wallposters were banned: so far the artists have survived.

The magazine boom
March 1987, Beijing

Half a mile west on the Avenue of Everlasting Peace from the Great Hall of the People where conservative Chinese leaders are now denouncing 'bourgeois liberalism', there is a display of amazing popular magazines on sale which hardly follow the socialist road.

It is not just the Honda lad on the front cover of *Motorbike* or the UFO depicted on *Flying Saucer*, or the generous picture of Sophia Loren presented by *World Photography*. Nor is it even the double-page spread from the innocuous sounding *Sports Illustrated*, in which a European girl called Julia Bergman demonstrates the joys of female bodybuilding in frontal, rear and pelvic poses – the secret of success, says Julia, is 'good posture, good physique, and a no-fat diet'.

What is really surprising to anyone familiar with Chinese political culture till fairly recently is the nearly complete secularization – an absence of almost any political values at all – of the new magazines. It is the natural result of deliberate attempts to stimulate a consumer society, aided by an open-door policy towards the outside world, in a climate of widespread political cynicism especially among young people who, in Mao's phrase, 'know nothing about the revolution'.

The post office where these magazines are on sale still stocks the Communist Party's theoretical journal *Red Flag*, now once again carrying lengthy polemics written by ageing leftists. But many Party members no longer bother to read them. A random sample of the top thirty magazines last month showed a fairly equal division into fashion, household goods, romantic fiction, detective stories, film and theatre (especially from abroad), popular medicine and 'personal advice'. The lead short story in *Flower Garden* is about a Chinese soldier on the Vietnam frontier who captures an enemy scout and discovers that she is a young girl. Compassionately, he sets her on her road home across the border. But she refuses to go: 'Please, let me stay with you,' she murmurs. 'My heart melted,' says the narrator. 'What should I say in return? Anything would be too much! I quickly gave her my arm. Resolutely we turned and headed for the dark woods . . .'

This sort of magazine is read by lift girls and shop assistants or factory hands to occupy their long dull hours of work. For the young married and new urban middle class, there is another range of magazines offering advice on how to brighten life at home.

Last December's issue of *Sino-Foreign Consumer* carried a photo supplement on a new shopping arcade in Istanbul, a selection of 'international hairstyles', a profile of an American–Chinese TV presenter (her motto is 'Beauty, Brains and Breeding') and a wide range of consumer hints. There are articles on what the Queen eats, what Prince Charles wears, and whether black is a fashionable colour.

Police and detective magazines also sell well, especially on street corners where evening crowds linger. They contain some factual information on legal problems, as well as 'real life' tales of crime and disaster from home and abroad. There is also a new genre of shocking tales about the evil behaviour of the Gang of Four, recently including a study of the dubious relationship between Madame Mao and Kang Sheng, head of secret police during the Cultural Revolution. But in a society where half the population is below thirty, and a tentative sexual revolution is under way, the most popular sections in most magazines are often the pages of 'medical' advice. These range from sensible tips on everyday hygiene to more dubious propositions about sexual technique.

A recent issue of *Young Generation* – favourite reading matter on long-distance trains – carried a tale called 'It happened on the wedding night' which cannot help the cause of true sexual liberation in China. This told of a young man who was rushed to hospital after making love three times with his new bride. The first couple of times were on his initiative; the third was on hers. Moral: Female passion is hard to arouse but even harder to satisfy. The myth of the voracious snake-woman who can never be satisfied lurks unpleasantly close to the surface of Chinese male fantasy.

In theory those now denouncing 'bourgeois liberalism' can cite as evidence the surrender of much of Chinese popular culture to market forces and the appeal of largely Western-based trivia. Soldiers in the People's Liberation Army – which is now being promoted again as a political model – were recently warned not to buy unsuitable books and magazines. They should be 'educated to take the right attitude towards love and marriage without reading literature that describes sexual relations'.

Yet the real targets of the leftist 'conservatives' are the neo-Marxist scholars who were calling last year, with support from reformers led by Mr Hu Yaobang, for political as well as economic reform, including democratization of the Party itself. Some magazine front covers will now be toned down, but the contents may not change so much. The Party ideologues are not nearly as worried by pop publishing for the broad masses as by the attempt to create a new politics.

Literary voices from an iron cell
April 1991, Beijing

My search for Chinese *wen* or 'culture' begins in the northern town of Anyang, where the word was invented 3,000 years ago. Diviners at the royal court of the Shang dynasty scratched early Chinese characters on the back of tortoise shells, applied heat, and interpreted the cracks which then appeared. The Chinese classics are *wen*, the arts are *wen*, civilization is *wen*. Mao's Cultural Revolution was the *Wen Ge*.

How much *wen* is to be found in the New China Bookshop on Liberation Street in Anyang, serving a population of a quarter of a million? The answer which will surprise no one familiar with China today is very little. Bestsellers: romantic novels from Taiwan; books on the mystical arts; the complete translated works of Dale Carnegie. None of the critical Chinese writers of the 1980s whom we can read in the West. Politics: military memoirs; 'Why socialism must replace capitalism'; history of the Communist Party. Nothing about the Cultural Revolution or the Beijing Massacre. Foreign translations: *The New Professional Woman*, *Megatrends 2000*, *The Godfather*, various Arthur Haileys. No Orwell, Greene, or any serious modern writer. Art: traditional 'mountain and water' landscapes; posters of Mao and army hero Lei Feng; 'famous persons in cartoons', from Giotto to Marilyn Monroe. Nothing modern or experimental, not much Chinese.

Mao once said of literature and art that what people needed was not 'more flowers on the brocade' but 'fuel in snowy weather'. Here in Anyang there are neither flowers nor fuel. An article in the Beijing *Guangming Daily* complains that people no longer read books. Confucius praised those who studied without wearying, it says, but now people are only interested in 'watching TV, playing mahjong, and looking in shop windows'. The *Guangming Daily*, once known as the *Guardian* of China, must share the blame for a society which tries to keep the masses docile with consumerism but denies them intellectual nourishment. Friends in Beijing curse the newspaper's name. It led the campaign against 'bourgeois liberalism' among intellectuals, and loudly denounced the 'conspiracy' of the 1989 Democracy Movement.

Most of those intellectuals have now either left China, or are writing 'for the desk'. 'No one minds what you do at home,' explains one prominent writer. 'No one bans you from being published – it's just that the publishers find they have run out of paper.' The relationship of mutual contempt between writers and regime is expressed in one of those simple Chinese phrases: 'You say your thing, and I'll say mine.'

Most intellectuals have much grimmer memories against which to measure today's sloppy repression. From 1957 to the late 1970s thousands of writers, labelled as 'Rightists' after Mao's Hundred Flowers movement, often then relabelled with worse crimes, were sent to the countryside or labour camp where there was no desk and no pen. The politics of that period can still only be talked of obliquely. A poet recalls, 'We were all fooled by the Great Leader. He summoned us to the Zhongnanhai (China's Kremlin) and told us that Wang Meng's criticisms were good. Who could say that the Beijing Party was blameless?' Wang Meng would be 'sent down' for twenty years for writing two critical short stories; so was the poet who tells the tale – then begs me not to quote his name.

I have come to Beijing to interview two writers in particular, both victims of the 1957 'anti-Rightist' movement, whose books have been recently translated into English. Hsiao Ch'ien, novelist and journalist, now eighty-one, was a wartime correspondent in Britain who covered the founding of the UN. His autobiography, *Traveller without a Map* (Hutchinson) is dedicated to the memory of the Quaker Margery Fry and the campaigner Dorothy Woodman, life-long companion of Kingsley Martin. One of his greatest sorrows during the Cultural Revolution was the destruction all of his letters from E. M. Forster. Hsiao still looks on the bright side with the dignity and elliptic humour of his generation of intellectuals.

Except for one terrible night in the Cultural Revolution, he recalls, 'I have borne the hardship and disgrace quite dispassionately and have never lost my smile. I took myself to be a reporter and treated life as the ground I was to cover.

'During those six years when my family and I had to live in a tiny gatehouse, I had to go and queue up for a place in the public lavatory on our street, sometimes even during the rain. We had five pits over which we could squat. I might have a tricycle pedlar or a carpenter on either side, or a brick-layer or a factory worker. Ignoring the foul smell and the rain that dripped from the roof, we would chat quite boisterously. These people widened my horizons.'

While Hsiao Ch'ien smiles, Zhang Xianliang – thirty years younger but much better known in China – rages. Unlike Hsiao he was sent to labour camp (where he almost died) and state farm with all the most important things of life still unlived. The reason why he is so famous in China is his reputation as a 'sexy writer'. If he really wished to write a sexy novel, he says cryptically, it would have no women in it. His best-known work, *Half of Man is Woman* (Penguin, 1988), tells the story of a man released from a labour camp who finds he is impotent. His new novel, *Getting Used to Dying* (Collins), interweaves the prison experiences of an

embittered Chinese writer with his post-prison experiences
in bed. Death – past, present and future – hangs over all.

Zhang scorns the suggestion that those two decades may
have enriched him. He was not planning books in his head in
the labour camp: he was 'thinking about food and how to stay
alive'. When he fled, it was 'because of hunger, not politics'.
His horizons were never widened by contact with the peasants.
'Why should I feel for them?' he asks. 'They had something I
didn't have – a house and family. If a peasant came home in a
bad mood, he could beat his wife. If he was feeling happy, he
could make love to her.' It is another, harder sort of honesty.
Hsiao tells some twinkling anecdotes of romance in wartime
Britain, admitting that 'sometimes I got over-involved with
emotional episodes'. Poor Zhang was too innocent to
understand a labour camp leader who boasted about making
love in a ditch while supervising the workers.

Both writers are cautiously unpolitical. Hsiao is protected
by his age and a well-honed art of indirection. 'I think I have
learnt my lesson,' he says. 'I know that one can be the guest
of honour one day and a prisoner the next. I now have the
habit of never saying anything rashly. This can be very
irritating to my wife, for sometimes she finds me equivocal
even on some small domestic issues.' (When I visit she is
wholly absorbed in the study next door, six chapters into a
translation of Joyce's *Ulysses*).

Zhang locks himself away obscurely in Yinchuan, capital
of the Ningxia Autonomous Region where he was first
banished. He insists he is not a political writer – foreigners
who want to know about Chinese politics should read the
newspapers. But Zhang believes that we all have inside
ourselves an accumulated deposit of memory – our own and
that of hundreds of generations before. It is just that his
labour camp experiences have stirred up this deposit more
powerfully than anything else. Now he is slowly confecting a
novel based on the notes of a prison diary. Perhaps he is
taking his time till the publishers can find paper again.*

---

*The first volume of Zhang's prison diary, translated into English
as *Grass Soup*, was published in 1992.

To discover who else is writing, I consult a member of the *Wen Xie* – short for the Chinese Literary Association of Writers. Not many are actually writing, just a few hundred out of 4,050 members. 'One third are retired, another third are old or senile, the remainder either want to write but cannot be published or don't want to write because the situation is not clear. How can anyone start a novel without knowing what the climate will be like when it is finished?' There are a few exceptions: historical biography is doing well, with 'unofficial' histories of modern leaders – communist and nationalist – almost as popular as Dale Carnegie.

There is a new Last Emperor craze. The young historian Jia Yinghua has taken up where the Last Emperor's own biography left off, with his release from prison in 1959 – before he married a bank clerk's daughter. Less gripping perhaps than life in the Forbidden City, but it has sold a hundred thousand copies and Mr Jia is planning more volumes. There is also good money to be made writing 'enterprise literature' – books which puff one of China's new market-orientated business firms and are distributed gratis.

An old friend confirms this new trend. 'There is a cruder, uglier group now,' he says. 'After all, people have to live, and there is money to be earned from the new entrepreneurs. These people go with the tide, making money, getting new cars. They are more vigorous and less civilized.' He adds that 'XX' – a distinguished writer much translated in the West – now belongs to the past with that whole generation of serious, still moderately socialist, writers with public consciences who re-emerged in the 1980s. We run through the list: who has left, who has stayed, who has given up, who has an ambitious spouse and is trying to keep in with the Party.

Wang Meng (whom Mao had mendaciously praised in the Hundred Flowers to smoke out the opposition), became Minister of Culture in the 1980s but stepped down after the Beijing Massacre insisting he just felt tired. Now he writes essays about the *Dream of the Red Chamber*. The Writers' Association is thick with intrigue. Its President, the aged writer Ba Jin (author of the 1930s *Family* trilogy), has been asked by the Party to step down at the next Congress in September. They plan to replace him with the generally loathed Maoist poet He Jingzhi, acting Minister of Culture. A thousand intellectuals signed letters protesting that he should not become full Minister.

The anecdotes continue, while wisps of willow fluff float outside in the dusty afternoon air. It's time to check in the *China Daily* to see what's on in Beijing. The listing for Saturday 4 May – it happens to be the anniversary of China's first Cultural Revolution in 1919 – is depressingly skimpy. There is the usual *Monkey Creates Havoc in Heaven* for tourists at the Beijing Opera Theatre, and a fair amount of acrobatics performed by Chinese railway workers. Plenty of Western music, not much Chinese: Mozart, a lecture on Gounod's *Faust* and a non-stop concert of American film and British TV serial themes. No plays this year. Last year I remember a cautiously satirical play, *The Fields*, which hinted at rural contempt for the Communist Party and did not last long. Someone says that Ying Ruocheng (ex-deputy Minister of Culture, the jailer in *The Last Emperor*) is staging Shaw's *Major Barbara*, which will be scrutinized for hidden meanings.

Paintings? traditional landscapes, bird and flower, mountains and waters. Opera? *The Magic Flute* . . . and, surely not, one of Madame Mao's famous Beijing Revolutionary Operas. The regime has encouraged a modest revival of the old heroic themes, though the emphasis has shifted from the individual to the heroic Party. The heroine in *Azalea Mountain* is the Party's representative in a rural area fighting the Kuomintang. Her real name is rarely mentioned. 'Party Representative, please help me to find the Right Way,' cry out the honest peasants. There are some good tunes and, for those who wait to the end, some fine fighting acrobatics. One actor somersaults eight times into the lap of a Chinese violinist, smashing her chair, which goes down particularly well. Most of the audience is paper – free tickets for morally improving plays or films are frequently distributed at work units. I buy my ticket from a Beijing Construction Company worker who could not face it.

But there is a nice joke going around Beijing about this practice of papering politically worthy productions. The film *Jiao Yulu* tells the story of a Party secretary in a poverty stricken rural area who laid down his life. It is quite a moving reminder of how well some Party cadres used to behave, and audiences shed real tears. Hundreds of Beijing citizens have thoughtfully bought tickets and sent them to the Communist Party Headquarters and to City Hall, with polite notes expressing the hope that senior Party leaders will learn from Jiao Yulu's good example.

So what has happened to *wen*? The only book on literary theory in that dusty Anyang bookshop was *Deng Xiaoping Jiang Wen Yi – Deng Xiaoping On Literature and Art*. I search it for clues. It starts with a speech to writers in 1979 telling them that they 'enjoy the respect, trust and love of the Party'. But by 1985 Deng is warning them that 'bourgeois liberalization means taking the capitalist road'. That was the first ideological shock which led many writers to burn their manuscripts, and prepared the way politically for the suppression of the Democracy Movement in 1989 and the conservative backlash. The collection ends, appropriately, with a document which does not contain a word about 'literature and art' but which shook Chinese writers to the core.

It is Mr Deng's speech 'to the cadres of the Beijing Martial Law Units,' dated 9 June 1989. 'Comrades,' he begins, 'you have had a hard time!' He congratulates the army on its restraint in not using tanks. Only soldiers' blood was shed, he says, in Tiananmen Square.

The massacre was on 4 June. A writer tells me quietly how he turned on the television that evening and saw the newsreaders dressed in dark colours for mourning (they had refused to wear their normal clothes). 'I was eating my supper,' he says, 'and I knew immediately something awful had happened.' Then, with the precision Chinese always use in describing bodily functions, he describes how he vomited uncontrollably. 'It was not because I had a cold or anything like that. I brought up all the food that I was eating. Then I continued to vomit with nothing left inside.'

The self-disgust of the Chinese intellectual smells pervasively in these twilight months in Beijing. The history of repression has repeated itself – this time in a less deadly and often more farcical form. But for those growing old in spirit or body it is one time too many.

11

Launch of an 'Economic Miracle', 1992-5

They called it Deng Xiaoping's Southern Expedition – the term once used to describe the travels of a Chinese emperor through his domain. Yet it had a very modern purpose: to lift China out of its post-1989 gloom, and kick-start the economic revolution into a higher gear. Deng did not hide his aim: economic development, he said, guaranteed political stability. He also sought to make sure that China did not fall behind the other 'Asian tigers', and that it participated fully in the new global economy.

Deng was physically shaky and had to be steered in the right direction by one of his daughters, but he summoned up – for the last time – a reserve of mental strength. He did so in the Special Economic Zones of Shenzhen and Zhuhai, away from conservative Beijing. Deng jettisoned the old labels. It doesn't matter, he said, whether a way of doing things is labelled socialist or capitalist. The whole of China should follow the Zones in developing the market mechanism and seeking foreign investment. Within months a new 'development fever' had swept the land. Deng himself – Tiananmen Square forgotten – would be hailed in several Western newspapers as Man of the Year.

Shenzhen had the highest incomes in Guangdong province, and Guangdong the highest in the country. Thousands of officials from all over China came on 'investigation tours' to see how it was done. They studied the modern factories, the highways and department stores – and the four-star hotels and the night-clubs. Millions of peasants from the interior migrated to the coast seeking work. They sent money home to support families left in poverty, but thousands were forced into prostitution and hundreds died in factory fires.

Over the next three years I travelled widely to see the effects of Deng's new revolution. I began in 1992 on Hainan island, the wild southern frontier where Guangdong's Red Guards had once been exiled to open up new rubber plantations (with disastrous effects on the subtropical environment). Hainan was now a favoured area for would-be entrepreneurs seeking to make their fortune, by legal or other means. In 1993 I returned to Zhengzhou, capital of Henan province in the northern heartland of Chinese civilization. When I first visited in 1971, the famous museum was closed because of the Cultural Revolution. Now the galleries were closed because of the economic revolution: one whole wing was rented out as a furniture salesroom. Two hours by bus from Zhengzhou life was still very different. I visited a village where the peasants had protested against illegal taxation, and met one brave peasant who had been jailed – and his brave son who campaigned for his release.

In 1995 I decided to test the success of the new policies in the most obvious place of all: Deng Xiaoping's home town deep in Sichuan province. Guangan was a painfully long bus journey from the provincial capital of Chengdu: I found it booming with not one but two new industrial zones. The association with Mr Deng had given it a special advantage: the rural counties on either side were much less favoured. As elsewhere in China, development was patchy and uneven. Progress depended partly on natural resources and communications, but also upon having good guanxi, or connections with the right people. A speech by President Jiang Zemin was a reminder that corruption, in spite of a decade and a half of official campaigns against it, was more widespread than ever. Deng Xiaoping had successfully flung the economic revolution into higher gear but there was a price to be paid.

Mr Deng's new expedition

August 1992, Shenzhen

To follow in the footsteps of Deng Xiaoping has become the best way of studying China's Special Economic Zones. It only needs a copy of Deng's 'spring tour' itinerary, and a walletful of Hong Kong dollars. To recognize his calligraphic style also helps. The giant red characters on the marble front of Shenzhen railway station, the newest and cleanest in China, were penned by him. It is as if John Major were to write the sign for the new Channel Tunnel terminus.

Here, just yards from the Hong Kong border, 87-year-old Deng Xiaoping alighted from a train last January, supported by his watchful daughter and a few doctors, and made a little speech: If China does not 'open up' and improve the living standards of the people, he said, it will head up a blind alley. Though speaking in the South, he meant his words to be heard by the conservatives in Beijing.

A new Shangri-La hotel is rising next to the station. Across the square, prowling minibuses compete for fares to Shenzhen City, to other parts of the Economic Zone, and beyond the zone's internal frontier with the rest of Guangdong province. Deng recalled how eight years ago, on his last visit, Shenzhen was still a town with ponds, mudpaths and old cottages. Now he surveyed the 'wide boulevards and high-rises' from a revolving restaurant at the International Trade Centre.

My taxi-driver had his own perspective. 'Land is gold here. Any local person who owned land then now has his own house and car.' The local paper invites investment in the Blessed Commercial Centre, a new development which looks like a Chinese John Lewis. 'Immediate returns; safer than shares!' it appeals to the property speculators who have flocked from all over China.

I wanted to find the Xianhu Botanical Garden where Deng planted a tree – an alpine banyan – which his grandson then watered from a red pail. (No detail of the visit was too small for the *Shenzhen Special Zone Daily* to report.) Shenzhen has Hong Kong's shopping malls and karaoke clubs (admission six pounds), but not its traffic discipline. Outside the Trade Centre, battered taxis interrogate prospective clients on their currency holdings. Motorcyclists with strapless helmets offer a dubious pillion alternative. I was lucky to escape alive from my first ride in a taxi when its bald tyre exploded after fifty yards.

The Botanical Garden is in a wooded valley just short of the Hong Kong border at Shataukok. Deng's alpine banyan is surrounded by a messy heap of stones and turf. Until it has been turned into a proper shrine it remains anonymous. Children with bright plastic satchels on their backs play tag around it and another tree planted by the Chinese president. Yes, they both looked very healthy, said the souvenir stall manager, and then we walked along the lake to see the boats shaped like swans.

Shenzhen is all about making goods and money with the benefit of Special Zone tax reductions and looser financial controls. The roads are dense with lorries and minibuses – few bicycles and no handtrucks in this part of China. The petrol stations are Mobil and Esso. There are factories, science parks, curved-wall apartment blocks and clusters of villas behind marble-faced walls. There are also construction sheds with matting on the roof for the temporary workers, often in the zone illegally, who provide cheap labour.

Deng Xiaoping stopped at the Folk Culture Village and Tiny China, both owned by the Splendid China Development Co Ltd. He rode in a golf buggy and was photographed by foreign tourists – a subtle way of leaking the news of his Southern Expedition to the world at large and wrong-footing the conservatives in Beijing. It is China's most famous theme park. Here are the Potala Palace and the Great Wall in miniature, replicas of non-Chinese 'minority' villages to be compulsively photographed, and at night a stunning show of stilt-walkers, acrobats with kids on their shoulders, and a wedding procession with gongs and other ethnic attractions. The show ends in approved Western theme park spectacular style with multi-coloured lasers playing rhythmically on the pulsating waters of a computer-controlled fountain. It would do very well at Alton Towers, but the entry ticket for a British theme park would avoid Splendid China's warning: 'Obey instructions given by the inspector. Whoever violates rules and regulations will be subject to proper disposal.'

Later, Deng bumped across the great scar of earth where the new Shenzhen–Canton–Macao motorway is being built, on his way to Shekou port at the end of the zone. A 14,000-ton liner berthed there carries his calligraphy. He named it 'Sea World', but it was once called Ancerville and was launched long ago by General de Gaulle. Sold to China, it

paid friendship visits to Tanzania and Japan for many years
before being turned into a rather scruffy hotel with gift shops
selling jewellery and pots of Pond's Cream.

Deng had some parting advice for the Shenzhen
leadership as they drove to the port: 'First, do not be afraid
to make mistakes; second, correct them as soon as they are
discovered.' He then crossed to Zhuhai, the next Special
Zone, where from another revolving restaurant he surveyed
the view of Portuguese Macao. It would be nice to have a
copy of the speech he gave there about 'Marx, the Three
Kingdoms, Slave and Feudal Society'. He then spent a
comparatively quiet week in Zhuhai. He was reported to
have visited several 'typical enterprises' in Bus No. 2. But
Hong Kong's China Watchers believe he also held a series of
crucial meetings with military commanders from all over
southern China. Just like Chairman Mao before the Cultural
Revolution, he needed to get the army on his side before
launching his new economic revolution.

My visit to Zhuhai ran into problems of which Deng
Xiaoping is unaware, but I had only myself to blame. In the
spirit of 'opening wide', the Special Economic Zones allow
foreigners to buy a visa on the spot. One can arrive in
Shenzhen and buy a visa for eighty-five Hong Kong dollars
with no fuss. One can arrive in Zhuhai from Hong Kong and
do the same. But the visitor who buys a visa for Shenzhen,
then crosses to Zhuhai and seeks to buy another one, is in
trouble. I had my own crucial meeting with the border police
as I attempted to leave for Macao. In the end I wrote a one-
line letter saying that I had an appointment with a high
Portuguese official in one hour's time. I then paid a fine,
properly receipted, of 400 Hong Kong dollars.

It was all done in a spirit of friendly enterprise. As Deng
said, 'You should open wider to the outside world, repeat,
wider!'

China's wild southern frontier
May 1992, Hainan province

The 'chickens' are drinking lemon tea at the Haikou Hotel

before their evening business begins. The grand piano on its green baize platform is still covered with bright crimson cloth. More spectators than customers are sitting on pink-cushioned chairs, viewing the chickens – girls from Guizhou, Guangxi and Shanghai. This is Hainan island, China's new frontier. The girls' features are as almond-shaped as those of Chinese opera singers, though the clothes range from shimmery blouses to jeans. The whole café, raised on a dais in the hotel lobby, is a piece of theatre the Haikou police do not bother to interfere with. In Shenzhen, next to Hong Kong, the authorities at least go through the motions, but Hainan is a 'more special' Special Economic Zone.

Hainan island was known for a very different sort of performance in the Cultural Revolution twenty years ago. Young Red Guards all over China sang the tunes from the famous ballet *The Red Detachment of Women*. Personally supervised by Jiang Qing (Madame Mao) – who used to winter by the beach at Sanya in the south of the island – it was a work of revolutionary feminism. Women fighters leapt through the air flourishing pistols against a background of Hainan's tropical vegetation, in a tale of triumphant struggle against the wicked Kuomintang. 'Forward march, forward march,' they sang. Hainan is now engaged upon a very different kind of forward march. It is either China's frontier zone of opportunity which will become (Deng Xiaoping hopes) the first of 'ten new Hong Kongs' or – his conservative opponents complain – a sink of exploitation and spiritual pollution.

Plans for China's first free port, at Yangpu on the island's western coast, have burst back to life after Mr Deng kick-started the new reform movement earlier this year by his visit to the Special Economic Zones near Hong Kong. 'We hoped he would come here,' one ambitious economist in Hainan explained. 'We even prepared a room for him at the Luhuitou hotel in Sanya, where Jiang Qing used to stay.' Mr Deng's protégé, ex-mayor of Shanghai Zhu Rongji, did come and he is now personally in charge of Hainan's 'second revolution'. The Hong Kong company Kumagai Gumi (in which the parent Japanese company has a 35 per cent share) has finally clinched a deal to lease thirty square kilometres of territory at Yangpu for seventy years.

The managing director, C. P. Yu, is touring Asia's little dragons – starting in Seoul and Taipei – to entice investors. He lists the advantages: no Chinese bureaucracy; companies will lease directly from Kumagai; there will be direct approval from Beijing – he does not have to wheedle with the Hainan authorities. There is a virtually tariff-free regime plus a five-year tax holiday on profits. An excellent natural deep-water harbour has already had some port facilities developed. Vietnam is just ninety miles across the South China Sea and is already sending trade delegations to Hainan. Relocating the sparse local fishing population will be cheap. Land is cheap and, above all, so is labour.

No one knows just how many mainlanders have slipped across the straits from Guangdong province illegally. Hainan's population has certainly risen by several hundred thousand in a year to just under 6 million, and contractors in Haikou's property boom know where to find cheap labour for dirty work. Young men with no tools but their hands sit under bridges or on street corners, waiting to be hired. Digging sand from the river may only earn a few Chinese dollars a cartload, but it can bring in 300 *yuan* (thirty pounds) a month – what a 'chicken' gets from a single customer.

Like all frontier regions, Hainan carries the prevailing trend further. During the Maoist years it was a closed zone where the army and navy watched China's southern door. In the Cultural Revolution, ferry-loads of Red Guards sailed from Canton to hack down primeval forest in Hainan, plant rubber trees, and 'learn from the peasants'. In the changed climate of the 1980s, the whole island was designated a Special Economic Zone, several hundred times larger than the small zones fringing Hong Kong. Then for two years after the Beijing Massacre, conservative censure prevailed. Now thanks to Mr Deng, the city of Haikou is awash not just with typhoon season flash storms but with hot speculative money. The property market is booming and the stock exchange opened in April. At least 400 property companies have been grabbing land earmarked for luxury housing, golf courses, hotels or for development zones around Haikou.

Much of the money is from the mainland, although planeloads of eager Taiwanese are beginning to arrive. The get-ahead officials are mainlanders too. Some confess they too hope to dabble in property; others just do it. Hainan officially allows government cadres to move directly from public office into private business. It already has a reputation for colourful dealings and it lost two governors in the space of four years.

Ex-governor Lei Yu, sacked in 1985, is still a folk hero. He allowed the island to import 79,000 foreign cars and trucks in one year for irregular resale to the mainland, generating enormous profits. The young entrepreneurs recall those exhilarating months when anything went in Hainan. 'He had the whole army, navy and airforce out delivering cars,' says a chauffeur with thousands of *yuan* in the bank. 'Lei Yu didn't waste time talking. If you had a good idea, he just let you make money.' Lei Yu has just turned up in the nearby Guangxi province on the mainland, where he is in sole charge of its 'opening up' plans, and no doubt will have many more good ideas.

Lei Yu's successor, Liang Xiang, sacked after the Beijing Massacre in 1989, was another economic innovator but with a very different reputation. The people he allowed to make money included his wife and son. But the Liang Xiang case also has a political aspect. He thought he had bought Beijing's backing for the Hainan boom by inviting the off-spring of high-ranking officials to sit on the boards of Hainan-based state trading companies. But he backed the wrong side. One of those he brought in was Zhao Erjun, son of the Communist Party Secretary-General at the time, Zhao Ziyang, who was disciplined for opposing the army's suppression of the Beijing students.

Property speculation drives the new stock market – four out of Hainan's first five quoted shares were for property companies – but it has had a stormy start. After a week in operation, Mr Zhu flew down from Beijing to warn his Hainan protégés that they were going too fast. For this little island to open a new exchange, with only Shanghai and

Shenzhen already fully operating, would upset too many people.

When I visited, a compromise had been reached: the exchange was only trading in Shenzhen shares. But Hainan entrepreneurs are confident that full permission cannot be withheld for long. 'You have to give a baby a ration-book even if the parents have exceeded the one-child policy,' says one. 'This baby has been born and they can't kill it off.' No one has yet been stabbed to death outside the Hainan stock exchange – unlike in Shenzhen where rival triad gangs fight to control places in the queue. No one has yet followed the unfortunate speculator in Shanghai who, unused to the law of the market, committed suicide when he lost a hundred pounds.

There is still enormous excitement on the pavement outside, where prospective customers jostle to squeeze through an iron grille, or copy down the latest figures from Shenzhen pasted up on the wall. My own informal visit added to the excitement. Did the foreigner know something they did not? But these are small potatoes. Anyone with connections had already bought the new Hainan stock through inside trading before the exchange even opened.

Hainan island is not quite such a familiar location globally as, say, Taiwan or Cyprus or the Seychelles. It is, in the not entirely fortunate phrase of the Tourist Bureau, China's End of the Earth. In imperial days, out-of-favour officials were banished to it. Yet it is the size of Taiwan, warm, wet and tropical and deserves to be better known. Water buffaloes, straw-hatted peasants and deeply pregnant sows amble across Lei Yu's new straight roads. Roadside stalls sell coconuts, mangoes, wild birds and snake. The eastern route from Haikou to Sanya plunges through deep-green paddies and plantations of half a million coconut palms. The western route crosses wilder flatlands where little but cactus grows. The most interesting road – through the centre – climbs into mountains where some virgin forest has survived the Red Guards. There are thatched Miao villages with yellow walls of adobe, and old Li women in black shovel hats. Touristically, it is still a blank on the Western map, but

Hainan is aiming high. The resort at Sanya has 100 miles of beaches, ten bays, coconut palms and plans for an airport able to take Boeing-747s.

The plan is to make Sanya an International Tourist Beach. City officials sit till late at night awarding contracts or handing out hotel concessions. Land prices have multiplied six times in the last two years. Mainland money is searching for investment opportunities. One hotel is owned by the Tourism Bureau of Nanjing in Central China, another by the Cigarette Corporation of Yunnan province. 'Tourism will be the motor for economic development.' Sanya's planners are too gripped by the concept to listen to any gentle suggestion that, in the Chinese phrase, 'the conditions may be lacking'. Sanya's tourists are up from nearly 350,000 in 1988 to 435,000 last year, but the big increase has come in domestic tourism and in the arrival of more 'compatriots' from Hong Kong and Macao.

The numbers of 'real foreigners' have actually fallen in the same three year period from an already modest 13,000 to only 7,500. An international beach? In the main Sanya stretch the only hotel from which guests can walk to the sea with ease has stained carpets and surly clerks who try to evade tax by not writing out receipts. There is very little seaside atmosphere and excavation is taking place behind the best sands. With great enthusiasm, foreign travel firms are being invited to set up bureaux in Sanya and foreign supermarkets will also be welcomed. But no one seems to understand that the Western travel market operates on tight margins and quality controls which Sanya will find it hard to meet.

Sun Yat-sen, father of the first Chinese revolution, first dreamt of developing Hainan island. Much later, so did the far-sighted prime minister Zhou Enlai. Now the dream has become the test of Deng Xiaoping's doctrine that the new Special Economic Zones can 'get rich first' by opening trading windows to the outside world, which will then trigger economic development throughout China. If some dirty capitalist flies get through the mesh, the price is worth paying. The zones bordering Hong Kong and facing Taiwan are indeed outward-opening windows, but Hainan is less certainly so. Its main success so far has been to offer speculative opportunities through which surplus profits from mainland companies can be soaked up. 'Industry is slightly above zero,' Hong Kong reporters were recently told.

Mr Yu of Kumagai Gumi is a gleaming exception – at least for Hainan's future. He was guest of honour at the First International Coconut Festival in April, a new addition to China's rapidly expanding list of manufactured events. A prominent commercial rival of Mr Yu in Hong Kong, deeply involved in Guangdong, dismisses Hainan as a project for the twenty-first century which will take twenty years at best to begin. Certainly, Mr Yu's own optimism must depend upon remaining the 'freest of free zones'.

Will some of the wealth sloshing around in Haikou wash through to the rural parts of Hainan? Less than twenty-five miles off the main central highway, villagers growing tea and rubber still struggle on an average personal income of twelve pounds a month. State farm leaders search for new outlets for agricultural produce in an uncertain market where last year's boom in green pepper prices has been wiped out this year by cheap imports from Indonesia. They have the same enthusiasm as the planners in Haikou and Sanya, but they are still living at the end of the world.

Market fever and rural unrest
March 1993, Henan province

The splendid museum in Zhengzhou, capital of one of China's largest inland provinces, is noted for its ancient bronzes and a giant statue of Chairman Mao. The statue is still there but the bronzes have disappeared. One wing of the museum has become a furniture salesroom instead. Armchairs and vanity tables occupy the space once reserved for the kings of Shang (circa 1200 BC). 'Isn't it strange?' I cried out to the men heaving sofas past Chairman Mao. 'A furniture shop in a museum!' No one seemed surprised. At last one of the salesmen paused briefly. 'Ancient things are out of date,' he said. 'Everyone's doing business now. That's all.'

The whole of China is gripped by what the papers call the Market Fever. Deng Xiaoping's famous Southern Expedition a year ago gave the signal that the economic revolution which had begun in the Special Economic Zones along the coast should now apply nationwide. Communist Party restraints on the free market were to be swept aside, and every province, even every county, could have its own special zone. Middle China, the vast intermediate region between the coast and the inner frontier regions, is the test of Deng's reforms. This heartland includes fertile plains and barren mountains, drab industrial towns and still-tranquil hillside hamlets, modern industry and ancient remains. Its central provinces contain a third of the Chinese population, with Zhengzhou, capital of Henan (population 78 million) as its northern gateway.

This week the National People's Congress in Beijing formally endorsed the 'socialist market economy'. How is it working in Middle China? The chaotic vigour of the new economic drive is visible everywhere, from Zhengzhou's High Technology Zone to the 1,000 private shops in Shaoshan, Mao Zedong's home village in the south, now cashing in on the hundredth anniversary of his birth. Hong Kong-style shops and restaurants stay open late with showers of fairy lights outside. There are businessmen everywhere. Dark-suited dealers in real estate and transportation carve out their own empires in what is still nominally state enterprise. Leather-jacketed entrepreneurs with mobile telephones make more dubious deals, exploiting the margin between state-controlled and free market prices.

The sleeping mounds of job-hungry peasants at every big railway junction tell another part of the story. So do the scavengers running up the track to retrieve plastic lunch boxes thrown out of passing trains. No one denies that the gap between rich and poor is widening. Zhengzhou's High and New Technology Industrial Development Zone, now spreading over five square miles of farmland, is one of twenty-seven hi-tech zones approved nationally by the State Council in Beijing. It sits on the new east–west rail link from the East China Sea to Kazakhstan which will carry freight right through to Europe. China's new north-south motorway will skirt the zone. An international airport is under construction.

There is development zone fever in China. Two thousand new zones have sprung up in the provinces, occupying 3.7 million acres of scarce land. Thousands more have been set up by local counties, often no more than an office, a banner across the road, and the occasion for another banquet. The zones offer valuable tax breaks for foreign investors – two tax-free years in Zhengzhou followed by a 50 per cent rebate until the sixth year. There are tales of 'phoney joint ventures' where the rebate is shared with a shell company abroad. Although the zones still 'belong to the state', they are run by autonomous development companies under local Communist Party patronage. The larger ones will provide schools, hospitals and high-standard housing for their employees. Some economists complain that scarce investment funds and farmland are being squandered. But the zones offer a tempting route out of politics into business for China's newly emerging managerial class.

An hour out of Zhengzhou the peasants are taking another way out. The flight of millions from the land (one million from southern Hunan province alone) has been widely reported but not so well understood. It is much more than a seasonal migration of surplus labour from deprived areas. Many peasants are driven off fertile land permanently by high taxation and low prices for farm produce. And although they disrupt transport and are blamed for increased crime in the cities, their cheap labour is fuelling the urban economic boom.

In an ordinary village a half-mile off the national highway, I listen to a string of ordinary complaints. The peasants smoke, and drink hot water: tea leaves are reserved for their guest. 'The taxes are too high: we can't bear the burden. But if you don't pay up, they'll seize your furniture or smash your roof in.' I am shown a tax demand for last year. One third of the family's wheat crop goes to pay the agriculture, education and irrigation taxes. Another third is deducted for village-level 'administration and services'. Most of the rest goes to the local *xiang* (township), supposedly to subsidize schools, army dependants, local militia and roads. The peasants complain that *xiang* officials buy new cars and consume fine banquets with public money. With wheat selling at only seventy *yuan* (eight pounds) per 220lbs, this family is left with a net income from the land of thirty *yuan* for the year. For the people it is cheaper to grow a few vegetables and seek work in the nearest town.

The peasant Hu Hai is famous in these parts. He was jailed for three years after leading a tax protest. The local police paraded him first through the villages, hands bound behind his back. His fearless son, Hu Desheng, who escaped rural poverty to graduate from law school, continues to petition Beijing. Hu Hai (whose case was adopted by Amnesty International) has now returned home on parole, still insisting that he acted in defence of 'truth and justice'. Other peasants appeal instead to the gods: the village has two new Buddhist temples.

Beijing has issued new instructions but provincial leaders have a vested interest in defending rural exploitation. Peasant migration, some argue, is a necessary form of 'social mobility' through which new urban skills can eventually be transferred back to the countryside. The truth is that most work available is dirty and unskilled, but cheap peasant labour has become a structural part of the urban economy. The Zhengzhou zone is being built by cheaper peasant gangs from another province who have undercut local Henan labour.

China's scholars and intellectuals, victims in the past of Communist persecution but protected from economic extinction, are also obliged to worship new gods. The writer Zhang Xianliang, famous at home and abroad for his prison novels, now chairs an advertising company in remote north-western Ningxia. A senior cultural official in Mao's home province runs a children's magazine, against the day when his state subsidy will be withdrawn. An assistant is organizing the export of peasant labour to prosperous Guangdong.

In Zhengzhou. the elegant Liu Xinxin, who used to sing in revolutionary operas, now runs her own private bookshop, the best, perhaps, in all of North China. The windows are clean, with bright advertisements, the shelves are well-dusted and there is a lively (but safe) selection of books. Ms Liu's husband is the famous calligrapher Pang Zhonghua, a member of the non-Party National Consultative Conference. She had no difficulty in obtaining the permits to start the business.

Some delegates at the National People's Congress in Beijing have complained that regional economic policy was barely mentioned in the report by the prime minister, Li Peng. The lack of a clear regional plan is not really so surprising in the new age of market economics. The socialist market economy, Chinese economists explain, is intended to 'place the market mechanism in a key position to distribute all social resources' and to reduce government 'interference' to 'macro-control of the economy'. Government investment is promised in energy, communications and river control, but the state's efforts are likely to be limited in coming years by its budgetary deficit and a declining share of national revenue.

Schemes for regional development are familiar from the past. None has lasted more than a few years. There is talk today of forming seven 'economic regions', or linking provinces in Middle China with a partner on the coast. But Beijing's ability to impose any supra-provincial economic structure, never very strong, is becoming weaker. Plans will depend on provincial leaders who must listen to their own emerging business communities. And they in turn will be guided by their balance sheets.

Lei Feng, the soldier hero of the 1960s who 'served the people', is still tediously offered up on television as a national model. In Middle China, the Communist Party is more likely to hand out medals to those who have 'made money'. In Yueyang on the Yangzi river, the local newspaper carried profiles of two dozen model entrepreneurs. Their average income was 40,000 *yuan* (5,000 pounds), about eighty times the national average for peasants. 'Chairman Mao used to say that Marxism was our magic weapon,' comments one Chinese economist. 'Now it is the market.' The fever is raging in urban Middle China. Only the peasants, on their pathetic bundles outside the railway station, shiver at night.

Doing good business in Sichuan
March 1995, Guangan

Ms Wang's entrepreneurial efforts in Guangan, hometown of Deng Xiaoping, would win the approval of the old man himself. Her Elegant Restaurant, just a few tables in the open ground floor of an old wooden building, is packed with customers eating chicken with red hot chillies. There is a queue for her Elegant Hair Salon across the road when it opens each morning. The tag is hard to resist: here in the provincial heartland of Deng's new revolution is the Good Businesswoman of Sichuan.

Wang dresses in eye-catching clothes for a small county town in the middle of China: high heels and a fur-lined outfit one night, a denim suit the next. But the elderly man in an old raincoat, helping out with the bills, is the real key to the operation. He is her father, and also the Communist Party Secretary (or boss) of a large factory, a crucial position from which to get the permits for opening a shop. Party officials are debarred from going into business but there is nothing to stop their family members from fronting the operation.

In Guangan's 'get rich first' atmosphere, Ms Wang has some serious competition. Outside the Elegant Salon last week, a leaflet was being distributed for International Women's Day. But the text was not so internationalist: 'To celebrate this important day, the Flying Geese Restaurant invites you to join a banquet on favourable terms. It costs 237 *yuan* for six starters, seven main dishes, soup and fruit (drinks not included). See you tonight!'

Guangan is a traditional market town of the kind which has driven the Chinese rural economy since the development of urban commerce a thousand years ago. On the pavements are mounds of vegetables, the intense colours attributed to the fertile Sichuan earth, hanks of suspended meat dripping into the dust, piles of beans and pyramids of sugar cane. The shops sell tools, twine, spare parts; all that the peasants need. But Guangan has also embarked on a new Leap Forward which transcends the traditional economy. There are stores stocked with electronic goods, eighty new private taxis hooting through the streets and two new Economic Development Zones.

The economic reforms of the past fifteen years mainly benefited coastal China and the big cities. But Deng's strategy since 1992 has been to inspire a fresh wave of entrepreneurial activity across the country by extending the tax and other concessions the coast had. What better place than his hometown to study this phenomenon of economic boom and its uncertain effects on society.

Guangan still has a sense of civic responsibility which has been weakened in other towns where the economic revolution has gone further. Army officers sweep the road in support of a new health campaign – even if some look unused to handling a broom. The Women's League of the Guangan Electrical Company hands out essential information on 'What the Peasant Should Know about Electricity'. Don't explode fireworks near cables or dig ditches next to pylons. Don't confuse washing lines with electric lines. Don't divert power for private use to deter thieves, stun fish or kill rats.

The start in Beijing last week of the National People's Congress – China's mainly advisory parliament – did not cause much of a stir on the streets of Guangan. I found only one friendly policeman who had heard the opening speech by Premier Li Peng. But Sichuan's delegation to Beijing boasted of Guangan's connection with Deng and claimed that the lives of the peasants in his home village of Xie Xing, five kilometres away, had been transformed.

That was not the view of one angry farmer in the Guangan market place who displayed his heavily worn hands to me as credentials. 'Deng Xiaoping's birthplace is all for show. You don't know what we peasants really live like: not enough food, poor housing, while the officials get rich. I know what I'm talking about. I fought for Deng in Vietnam. The problem is: he's a good man but we are cheated by the people beneath him.' A couple of young men in cheap suits, come from the big city to check out business opportunities in Guangan, told me to ignore him. 'He's an old fool.'

Conflicts of evidence between official statistics and popular perceptions are frequent; so is the mutual contempt between many city-dwellers and peasants. In 1993, serious peasant riots broke out over excessive taxation in Renshou, an impoverished county only sixty kilometres from the provincial capital of Chengdu. Yet people in Chengdu today barely know what happened and insist that peasants everywhere are doing well. A 400-mile journey across the Red Basin of Sichuan – from Chengdu via Guangan to Chongqing (the wartime capital known to Westerners as Chungking) – suggests that this is far from being the case. At an average speed of thirty kilometres an hour, long-distance bus travel offers a close-up view of the parts of China other methods rarely reach. Sometimes these journeys pass through areas technically 'closed' to foreigners. That is no problem if one has a convincing destination. The real disincentive is the bone-bruising ride and knowledge that most road fatalities in China are caused by overloaded buses.

Cutting across country proves the obvious but overlooked point. Even if the gross statistics are correct (and China's own Statistical Bureau has warned they are often boosted by local officials eager to claim success), the effects of the economic boom away from the coast and big cities are localized and patchy. I travelled across eight counties with a population of as many millions. Away from Chengdu and Chongqing, the only sign of economic take-off was in Deng's home county – a remarkable coincidence, or is it more than that?

Elsewhere life seemed much the same as ten years ago after the first post-Mao Zedong reforms had restored peasant markets and led to some new building of peasant homes. The broad-bladed hoe is still the most common tool. Farmers work barefoot in the paddy with red mud stains up to their knees. There are no roadside advertisements, only one or two cars, and the main form of transport is still the bicycle or a bamboo shoulder-basket. The county towns are dusty and bare: one or two karaoke bars with tattered curtains give a whiff of modern life. Hairdressing is much less elegant than in Guangan. I saw one customer having her hair hosed down on a pavement stool. Here the pressure of population growth has swelled the flow of peasant migrants to the south with special force. Slogans put up by the local governments stress the point. 'Warning to all citizens: the Chinese population has reached 1.2 billion.'

Other slogans hint at a rural lifestyle which has been lowered, not raised, in recent years and appeal in dated language for a return to socialist values. In one short stretch of road I noted down the following: 'Everyone get organized and smash down the criminals.' 'Politics in command is the key to the socialist road.' 'Those who refuse to pay taxes will be punished according to law.' 'Unite to abolish all illegal religious activity' (probably a reference to the Protestant 'house churches' which flourish in parts of Sichuan and other deprived provinces).

What on earth was going on here? These glimpses through bus windows more often black than grey with dust can only lift a tiny corner of a rural reality even harder to gauge further away from what counts for the main road. Guangan's building boom is all the more startling by contrast. Hilltops have been tipped into valleys to form two new 'Economic Development Zones' to the north and south of the city. Clusters of shacks with matting for roofs have sprung up to provide shelter and food for the peasant contract workers. The red dust blows in everywhere.

Pursuing my historical research into Deng's early life, I was greeted with simple kindness. One encounter led gently to another. Some old folk chivvied a group of teenagers to practise their English on me. Two of the boldest invited me to their school. I gave an impromptu lesson to a class of 100 – I had to count to believe my eyes (the average across the school is seventy). I was hijacked by an English teacher, struggling amazingly well with a language she had learnt only from fellow Chinese and tapes. The headmaster told me, proudly, that here they were able to pay the teachers' salaries on time. Elsewhere educational funds are diverted for prestige development projects and teachers – like peasants – may get paid with IOUs.

Will the next generation of Guangan teenagers aspire instead to work for a joint venture or run a nightclub? My friends took me to see the new South Guangan Economic

Zone. One of the roads, I was told with pride, is forty metres wide. First to be finished are a set of eighteen five-storey apartment blocks, nicely faced with tiles. Some are maisonettes of the kind built for foreigners on the outskirts of Chengdu and Chongqing. Lavish substitute housing, perhaps for the inhabitants of old Guangan's wooden houses, with their attractive balustrades but no sanitation? No, these are new apartments for the cadres of the Guangan Prefecture. Once again, the Party connection. It begins to make better sense.

Guangan recently had a crucial promotion from the status of county (*xian*) to the much larger prefecture (*diqu*). This favoured and highly unusual treatment also explains a great deal. To do this it has sliced off a great chunk of the neighbouring prefecture to which it used to belong. With that territory, plus the immeasurable factor of Deng's connection, comes investment funds both from the three counties now absorbed into Guangan and from Beijing.

A special edition of the *Guangan News* offers tax incentives for foreign investors and a list of projects ranging from a paper factory to new classrooms at the local technical college. But Guangan has bigger plans than an assortment of light and medium industry. It aspires to build 'the biggest power station in south-western China' – a coal-fired plant generating nearly 2.5 million kilowatts at a price of 350 million dollars – if it can get Beijing's go-ahead. The story is long and involved. Guangan's main backer in Beijing, a close friend of Deng, has died. New pledges are being sought. They will have to hurry up: the Deng connection may not outlive the man. Deng does not seem to have personally championed the cause.

Mao went back home twice in his later life, seeking inspiration at crisis moments of the Great Leap Forward (1959) and the Cultural Revolution (1966). Deng left home in 1920 to study in France, and never returned to Guangan. The road to the Deng family farmhouse climbs high above the Qu river – one of many tributaries of the Yangzi – into a hilly but intensively cultivated terrain. The land is sculpted in man-made fields shaped to make the best use of water run-off. Rape seed and wheat are intermixed, with fruit trees on the margins and patches of vegetables sown between the other crops like embroidery.

Several dozen peasants were rehoused when the farmhouse was turned into a museum less than ten years ago. It is a substantial tiled building with three wings – a landlord's home. One of Deng's brothers was an opium smoker whom Deng failed to save from being 'persecuted to death' during the Cultural Revolution. There are canopied wooden beds. A room of photographs disconcertingly includes Margaret Thatcher – twice. Monty is also there, being told by Mao that Deng (this was before the Cultural Revolution) is second in line for the succession. Outside, parties of schoolchildren and small groups of Chinese on vacation pose for the obligatory picture under the signboard saying: 'Deng Xiaoping's old home'. There are exactly two souvenir stalls selling postcards, notelets and medallions in praise of 'our great architect of reform'. Mao's birthplace in Hunan province has several hundred shops, hustling restaurant owners and its own railway access.

A 500-character poem, displayed on either side of the door to Deng's bedroom, celebrates in classical Chinese the modern concept of 'importing European capital and American technology'. Not far away, Deng's mother and grandmother are buried in an auspicious site overlooking the valley. Children play while their mothers hoe the vegetables. Mist floats up. There is a shimmer of fruit blossom. The loudest noise comes from above: a sandstone bluff, known as the Buddha's Hand, is losing its fingers to hammers and crowbars. The appetite for stone of an expanding Guangan must be satisfied.

What does Guangan tell us about the big 'after Deng' question? Poised for economic take-off, at first sight it seems to confirm the argument that there should be no big problem. The good businessmen and women of Sichuan and elsewhere will carry on regardless of whatever arcane struggles take place in Beijing. Yet there must be a limit to the number of Guangans that China can support, sucking investment from elsewhere. There is a limit, too, to the amount of land which can be swallowed up for construction. If the Party is to survive, it must somehow also limit the appetite of officials aspiring to maisonettes and the profits of indirect commerce.

The biggest question remains in those villages off the road which itself is already off the beaten track. Migrant workers send back funds to keep their families alive, and provide cheap labour for the urban boom. No one really knows whether this will prove to be a satisfactory new social contract between town and countryside or the cause of more lethal friction when the boom subsides. Guangan is still a place where one is woken by the cockcrow and there are fields through the back window. But not for long. In its headlong rush to modernize, it is like everywhere else in China which seizes the hour in a cloud of frenetic dust – even if it means smashing Buddha's fingers.

The curse of corruption
March 1995, Chengdu

China's top Communist Party leader has sounded the alarm against the growth of corruption and abuse of power, in a speech which even tells Party officials not to frequent red light districts. The lengthy warning by the Secretary-General, Jiang Zemin, was published nationally yesterday on the front pages of every newspaper. Delivered in January, its release is timed in advance of the National People's Congress, when popular concerns about corruption will be widely expressed.

In a passage which may be unique in Party history, Mr Jiang rebukes officials who have been 'intoxicated by wine, women and power, and give themselves up to all forms of pleasure'. He then warns these 'comrades' not to be seduced by 'white wine and red lanterns' – a transparent reference to the nightclub and brothels appearing in many parts of provincial China.

The main thrust of Mr Jiang's speech is to urge the Party to return to the by now semi-mythical standards of hard work and self-sacrifice, and to reject the 'unclean' aspects of capitalism, imported along with China's economic reforms. He denounces the ideological influence of capitalist corruption in terms usually used by old-guard critics of the reforms. He suggests, also unusually, that the influence of China's former 'exploiting classes' has survived to take advantage of new opportunities for corruption.

This is a loaded formula which may worry some Chinese entrepreneurs in high places who come from families which wielded power before 1949. But Mr Jiang insists that the general aim of the economic opening up under the veteran leader Deng Xiaoping is entirely correct. He claims that it amounts to a new revolution which should strengthen rather than weaken socialism. This may be a difficult concept for many Chinese today – including Party members – who welcome the reforms but are much less sure what socialism means.

In his speech, delivered to the Party's disciplinary commission, Mr Jiang demands that local officials should not cover up crimes committed by their colleagues, nor frustrate legal action when it is taken against them. This is regarded by many people as the nub of the problem. The ability of officials to protect officials has caused widespread cynicism. Mr Jiang also warns against government cadres who 'swallow up state property' – a common device by which officials profit from enterprises still technically in public ownership.

Mr Jiang's warning on sexual morals reflects alarm at the appearance of an organized sex industry in areas where economic reforms have created a class of new rich with money to burn. Country towns in the hinterland of booming cities such as Chengdu, capital of Sichuan province, have begun to invest heavily in night-clubs, which then attract a surrounding district of sleazy karaoke bars where prostitutes work. While the metropolis will ban such blatant activities within its own boundaries, they appear to be tolerated at a safe distance.

Mr Jiang's speech is far more than a routine denunciation of Party malpractices. Though it follows a long line of similar complaints, its much more urgent note reflects the worsening situation despite successive anti-corruption campaigns.

Corruption, crime and inflation are now the main popular concerns in China, according to a poll by the Chinese Academy of Social Sciences.

In political terms, Mr Jiang's speech will to some extent tilt the balance against the more radical reformers who tend to regard corruption as an unavoidable price to pay while China is in the midst of disorderly but necessary change.

Many Chinese intellectuals are sceptical about the chances of yet another appeal for a return to traditional moral standards. They say that Mr Jiang will need to tighten discipline so that top officials can no longer protect their subordinates in return for favours: that has never been achieved in the past fifteen years of official efforts to stamp out corruption.

12

Revisiting an ugly past, 1993

In 1968, at the peak of Red Guard violence during the Cultural Revolution, rumours circulated in Beijing of wholesale murder being committed in the region of Guangxi. Some of the trussed bodies which ended up in the harbours of Hong Kong and Macao must have floated all the way down the West river from the south-eastern corner of the province. It soon became known outside China that the killings in Guangxi had finally persuaded Mao Zedong to call a halt to the mass struggle and send in the army to restore order throughout the country. In Beijing an even darker story was already circulating – that people had not only been killed but eaten in Guangxi.

In the mid-1980s the poet and novelist Zheng Yi, who had heard the story while a Red Guard himself, decided to investigate on the spot. Equipped with his credentials as a writer and journalist, he found some local officials and witnesses, and even a few people who had killed and eaten human flesh, who were quite prepared to talk. This was the period when the Party, led by Hu Yaobang, was making a serious effort to deal with the past and to carry out internal reform. Zheng Yi was given printed copies of evidence compiled by special government and Party 'work teams' which had recently investigated the killings and had documented the evidence of mass slaughter accompanied in a number of rural counties by cannibalism. These reports were dry and detailed, listing names, dates, and methods of killing and consumption.

After the Beijing Massacre Zheng Yi spent three years on the run, pursued as a 'counter-revolutionary', and his wife was imprisoned for a time. He decided to smuggle the material he had gathered on Guangxi out of the country and later the couple were able to reach Hong Kong. His articles gained little attention when they were first published in one or two Hong Kong magazines. The *subject was distasteful and even many Chinese dissidents felt embarrassed that it reflected badly on their country.*

I obtained copies of the original material gathered by Zheng Yi: it was detailed in a bureaucratic style and appeared to be authentic. But in the end there was only one way to be sure. I looked at the map of Guangxi: Wuxuan County, where the worst episode of cannibalism was said to have occurred, was surprisingly close to the immensely popular tourist route (which now attracts a million foreigners every year) of the Li river with its karst limestone formations and fishermen who use cormorants. Five hours by train from Guilin, where the tourists stay in international hotels, took me to Guiping. From there it was another five slow hours up the Qian river – past scenery every bit was beautiful as the famous sights along the Li – to Wuxuan.

In Guiping I spoke to riverside dwellers who remembered those awful years, and the bodies washed up by their front doors which had floated downstream. Wuxuan was much poorer than Guiping and had a dismal air. It was still officially closed to foreigners, but I arrived on a public holiday and wandered freely. It was not long before I found someone prepared to talk there too. Just twenty-five years after I wrote about the bodies in Hong Kong harbour, I had arrived at one of their sources. There was no doubt about the truth of the story: the harder part was to try to understand why it happened.

A journey to Wuxuan
October 1993, Guangxi Autonomous Region

From China to the former Soviet Union, the history of the former Communist bloc is being rewritten. Its achievements, mythical or real, are being discredited in the cold light of the post-Cold War era: Beijing still claims to be 'socialist' but has done its own demolition job on the revolution; in the West, wildly exaggerated tales about Mao Zedong's private life have surfaced ahead of the hundredth anniversary of his birth. More accurately, the starvation of the Great Leap Forward and the suffering of the Cultural Revolution is now fully acknowledged. But one secret skeleton has remained hidden until now.

Earlier this year a dissident Chinese writer published the claim that people had not only been killed but eaten in South-west China during the Cultural Revolution. Could this really be true or was it just another piece of backstreet gossip? Abroad, former 'friends of China' were particularly upset. So many of their illusions about the Mao era had already been shattered: this was one revelation too far.

The only way to be absolutely sure was to visit the town of Wuxuan in the South-western province (technically an 'autonomous region') of Guangxi where the worst cases had allegedly occurred. Beneath the covered market in Wuxuan's main square, sacks of rice and bundles of tobacco were being traded in an early-morning grey mist. The subject of cannibalism is not an easy one to raise, even twenty-five years on, in a country where history is entangled with politics. But within half an hour, I had secured an unambiguous answer.

'Yes, the killings were really bad in Wuxuan,' said Mr Li, a friendly middle-aged local government clerk. 'Just over there' – he pointed towards the old town – 'I saw them rushing down. Then there was a big explosion, right next to the market, and bodies everywhere!'

But were people really eaten as well? 'Of course they were; it's absolutely true, not false at all! And in Wuxuan,' Mr Li added with a touch of pride, 'we ate more people than anywhere else in China!' Li is not his real name, although he wrote that down readily with his address in my notebook.

His cheerful confirmation was both depressing and enlightening. Suddenly everything around me began to make historical sense. Old Wuxuan has hardly changed in the last quarter of a century and many of its walls still carry the faded slogans of the Cultural Revolution. The market square lies on its eastern side, the broad Qian river to its west. The town's main street runs between the two, descending to the water's edge in a flight of flagstone stairs. Most of the killings in May–July 1968 followed the logic of this simple geography. The market was where the victims were put on show; the river was the scene of the worst butchery. On the streets in between, these 'class enemies' were paraded, hands and feet lashed with electric wire, forced to kneel and confess their crimes.

The fast-flowing Qian river rises near the Vietnam border, loops through Guangxi province and eventually – 500 kilometres downstream from Wuxuan – debouches not far from Hong Kong. These days it carries small smoky freighters, river steamers with narrow bunks for human sardines, and tiny barges towing enormous rafts of timber. At the height of the Cultural Revolution, it carried bodies.

The Hong Kong police fished dozens of corpses out of the harbour in the summer of 1968. There had been reports of fearsome fighting between Red Guard factions in Guangxi, and even Mao Zedong was said to have expressed alarm. But Wuxuan was too distant for its worst horrors to become known.

Some large, flat rocks near the water's edge were Wuxuan's killing stones. They made a convenient butcher's table for human dissection, and the unwanted bits could be disposed of easily in the river. Two typical cases are quoted in the official (but secret) chronicle of events which the dissident Zheng Yi obtained.

In the first, Zhou Shian was dragged to the town crossroads by a barber called Niu Huoshou and forced to kneel down. Beaten half to death, he was pulled down the long flight of stone steps to the riverside. Wang Chunrong then used a five-inch knife to cut Zhou open and extract his heart and liver. Others joined in and soon stripped him to the bone. Then they used a wooden boat to dump his remains in the river.

In the second, a raiding party from across the river seized three brothers from the Li family, and dragged them to the vegetable market where they were knifed to death. Their bodies were then carried down to the river, where the gang removed their livers and cut off their penises. The bodies were thrown into the river. That night they raped one of the widows, killed her pig and held a feast to celebrate the 'great victory of the people's proletarian dictatorship'.

The secret report, compiled with bureaucratic thoroughness, also lists the 'different forms of eating human flesh'. These included: 'Killing and then having a feast, cutting up together but eating separately, baking human liver to make medicine, etc.' And it catalogues the 'eleven different ways in which people were killed'. These were: 'Beating to death, drowning, shooting, stabbing, chopping to death, dragging to death, cutting up alive, squashing to death, forcing someone to hang himself, killing the parent and raping the daughter, raiding to kill.'

These documents were the result of secret Communist Party investigations finally carried out fifteen years after the events. Most of those involved were punished, but with relatively light sentences: loss of party membership and/or jail terms of between one and fourteen years. When Zheng Yi visited Wuxuan (and four other Guangxi counties where cannibalism had occurred) in 1986 he was warned not to go out at night. Some of the killers still had powerful local connections.

After the Beijing Massacre, Zheng and his wife, Bei Ming, went into hiding. Last year they escaped via Hong Kong to the US where he now works on Princeton University's China Project. Zheng is determined to the point of obsession to make the tale known and has just published *Red Monument*, a 700-page book, in Taiwan. The *New York Times* carried a report on Zheng in March this year (excerpted in the *Guardian*) and the dissident journalist Liu Binyan wrote a powerful article in the *New York Review of Books*. But reaction has generally been muted, especially among the overseas Chinese. Cannibalism is a distasteful subject and it reflects badly on the motherland. Why rake up the past?

Wuxuan County, with its population of 300,000, is tucked into the western folds of the grey and misty Great Yao Mountains in central Guangxi. It grows rice, vegetable oil, tobacco and sugar cane, but crop yields and incomes are much lower than the provincial average. Rural industry employs less than 2 per cent of the working population.

Wuxuan has always been 'backward' in Chinese terms, and is only just beginning to be touched by Deng Xiaoping's consumer revolution. I arrived by boat from the lively port of Guiping after a five-hour journey which only passed one or two small villages. The scenery, almost as beautiful as that of the famous Li river near Guilin, is little-known to foreign or even Chinese tourists.

There were no street lights in Wuxuan's main square: a single food stall served oily noodles in the dark. I heard before I saw the large sow rooting through piles of rubbish on the broken pavement. Rats ran down the outer wall of a cinema showing an old kung fu film. I bought a stale moon cake and some chocolate in the dingy department store before it closed its shutters, but soon abandoned them to the pigs. In Guiping there had been shops with neon lights selling video recorders; cheerful street stalls with bright displays of fresh fruit; and an evening parade of teenagers in Hong Kong-style clothes. Here it seemed like the China of ten years or more ago.

Yet there are a few splashes of light in Wuxuan's darkness. At the new end of town, along the modern highway past Party headquarters, cultural palace and government guest-house, the first scouts of Mr Deng's revolution have arrived. These are the hairdressers and karaoke bar operators (often using the same premises). A young entrepreneur from the city of Liuzhou, newly established in Wuxuan, asked me to approve his window display of fashion posters and cut-out Chinese characters. But he complained of the high rent (500 *yuan* or fifty pounds a month) and the poor business. Too many people still have their hair cut in the market with a mirror hung against the wall.

The karaoke bars in Wuxuan are simple affairs, without giant screens or strobe lighting. A few tables are crammed into a small shop serving beer and peanuts: the screen is an ordinary TV set, but it has the latest videos. I stood on the mud-smeared pavement, watching a well-shaped young lady in one-piece bathing suit (no bikinis yet) floating on a surfboard somewhere in the South China Sea. 'My heart leaps in the honey-sweet moon,' she mouthed, 'I want to whisper that I love you . . .'

On the ground, the Great Leap Forward from cannibalism to karaoke is the distance between old and new Wuxuan, from the harbour steps to the new highway. Culturally, it is the distance from a society sealed from outside influence to one where every teenager knows who scored the goals in the European Cup. Those of the same age in 1968 were 'revolutionary youth', rank-and-file fighters in the Red Guard struggles. Dozens of them died in the fierce battle which led to Wuxuan's summer months of slaughter. The children of those who are still alive will be the next generation of karaoke fans.

Not only Wuxuan but the whole of Guangxi province had been torn by political struggle for over a year (1967–8) between rival Red Guard factions each claiming to defend Chairman Mao to the death. These were manipulated by political cliques in the provincial capital and, through them, from Beijing. After a lull early in 1968, the more radical groups – known as the Small Faction because of their numerical weakness – were stirred up by signals from the 'ultra-left' (Madame Mao and her 'gang' in Beijing) to a last-ditch struggle. The Large Faction, controlled by Guangxi governor and army boss Wei Guoqing, then moved in literally for the kill. All Communist Party officials, right down to the village level, were ordered to 'wage a Force 12 typhoon against the class enemy' and to carry out a 'merciless class struggle'. The official (and minimum) estimate is that 90,000 throughout Guangxi died in what are now termed 'unnatural deaths'.

On 4 May 1968, the Small Faction in Wuxuan had seized the harbour office and requisitioned its funds. In confused skirmishes a Large Faction leader was shot dead. The Large Faction called for reinforcements from two neighbouring counties and on the night of 12 May captured the Small Faction's base. The survivors, mostly teenagers, fled to a rocky outcrop in the harbour where they were rounded up early the next morning. At least thirty were killed on the spot.

At a memorial meeting for the dead of the Large Faction, two prisoners (both students) were hung on trees as a 'sacrifice' and butchered. They were the first to be eaten. Their hearts and liver were removed, cooked with pork and eaten communally. The head and feet of the Small Faction's leader, Zhou Weian, were displayed in the market place and his wife was forced to come and 'identify' them. (Zhou Shian, whose slaughter is described above, was singled out because he was Weian's older brother.)

I shall only quote sparingly from the official account of the horrors which followed. Many school teachers were killed and at least two were eaten by their students. The headmaster of Tongling Middle School was the object of many struggle sessions. Although a guerrilla in the revolution, he had come from a landlord family. One night the students got tired of guarding him and killed him instead. The first person to eat his flesh was the girlfriend of his eldest son who had broken off the relationship.

A victim might be paraded and abused for some time before one or two individuals 'dared' to kill him – watched with horrified fascination by the 'masses', and by local officials who feared for their own lives. At first the victims were dragged to a secluded place before dismemberment, but within a month they were being openly butchered on the main street. The official record frequently notes in a chilling phrase that other people then 'swarmed around to remove the flesh'. The most active killers were young men in their teens and twenties, including former members of the defeated Small Faction who sought to prove their new loyalty.

The taboo on eating human flesh was eroded by degrees. Zheng Yi suggests the following sequence: (1) furtive eating by night, by individuals or families; (2) human and animal flesh are mixed together: those eating can delude themselves that they are 'only eating pork'; (3) as the blood craze spreads, eating becomes a vogue. Different parts of the body are prized for their therapeutic value and cooked in a variety of ways. At the peak of the movement, human flesh is served at banquets with wine and loudly shouted guessing games.

The special horrors of Wuxuan finally became known in Beijing as the result of a remarkable act of courage which must have saved many lives. Wang Zujian was a former official – 'upright' in the best Chinese tradition – who had been sent to a state farm in Wuxuan for criticizing Party policies in the late 1950s. Released from the farm, he was now working quietly in the town's cultural office, hoping to keep out of trouble. Every day, as he walked to work, he was confronted by the slaughter on the streets. His wife, pregnant at the time, had arranged an abortion at the local hospital. She was so terrified that after two attempts to reach it she gave up. Wang resolved to denounce the cannibalism to the authorities, knowing that if his letter were intercepted he would probably get eaten too. He wrote to a relative, asking him to forward his letter to an old friend from the revolution, who in turn sent it to the capital. The ruse succeeded with dramatic results.

One morning early in July the rumour spread that a 'big chief' was arriving to inspect Wuxuan. Soon a long convoy had arrived at the river port. Soldiers quickly fanned out to cover their commander as he entered the town. He was Ou Zhifu, commanding officer of the Guangxi Military District. Striding through the carnage, he confronted Wen Longsi, the head of Wuxuan's 'revolutionary committee', and went straight to the point.

'How many people have you eaten here? Complaints have been made to Beijing! Why didn't you stop it? Why didn't you report it?' Pointing directly at Wen, he thumped the table. 'Wen Longsi, from tomorrow, if one more person is eaten I'll make you pay. I'll blow your head off!'

The killing stopped immediately. Wen wished to save his head – so too did the Guangxi commander whose career would be blighted if Beijing blamed him for the 'Force 12 typhoon'. The heroic Wang was identified after a friend revealed his name under torture. Wang was sent back to labour camp but not harmed. The town leaders feared subsequent investigation if they killed him too. His wife had the baby – their fourth child.

The eating of human flesh in Wuxuan and elsewhere in Guangxi had nothing do with the 'famine cannibalism' recorded in China when millions have starved through war or natural disaster. It was 'revenge cannibalism ' in which the victor demonstrates extreme contempt for the defeated foe by consuming parts of his body after (or sometimes before) death. Chinese dynastic history has recorded many such cases over several thousands of years. The philosopher

Mengzi observed that 'when men depart from righteousness and benevolence, they become like animals, even devouring their fellows'.

Not all cultures resort to cannibalism to take revenge on the vanquished. Western society prefers to humiliate the dead by mutilating and then displaying their remains. A typical modern example is the posed photograph of victorious soldier with severed head (US Marines in Vietnam, Indonesian rangers in East Timor, etc). Though any attempt to 'explain' a society must be treated with great caution, the psycho-cultural view of China as an extremely 'oral' culture seems to be relevant. Chinese attitudes towards food also suggest a therapeutic aspect. Bread soaked in the blood of an executed criminal was popularly believed to have powerful medicinal properties. A short story by the famous writer Lu Xun, *Medicine*, is based on this theme.

Cannibalism is a commonly used metaphor in China for the most destructive aspects of social behaviour. Lu Xun's most famous short story, *A Madman's Diary*, describing the patient's delusion that he is threatened by people wanting to eat him, is a powerful allegory for the misrule of warlord China after the failure of the 1911 revolution. Similarly, a recent short story by a young contemporary writer, Wen Yuhong, describes an atmosphere of mounting blood lust which a witness to the events in Wuxuan would have readily recognized. In Wen's *Mad City*, a pair of ferocious butchers set a new fashion in slaughtering dogs for food. Everyone starts doing it too. Then one day they butcher a young man, and . . .

Can we be completely sure that the Wuxuan tale is not also fiction? Ever since the Conquistadores first traduced the Aztecs, Professor P. Arens has argued in *The Man-eating Myth*, Western societies have used the slur of cannibalism to de-humanize those whom they conquer, especially in the so-called Dark Continent. But apart from the Wuxuan documents and eyewitness accounts, there is substantial evidence of cannibalism in China in the past.

The distinguished anthropologist Wolfram Eberhard has identified five types of cannibalism, including acts committed in revenge and for medical reasons. The majority of examples are found in South China among those ethnic groups known as 'national minorities'.

Wuxuan's own population is 60 per cent 'Zhuang' and the nearest county to the east is a 'Yao' minority area. This offers a comforting alibi to friends in Beijing who can argue that what happened in 1968 was not really 'Chinese' at all. In fact, most Zhuang have lost their original language and have been sinified by the dominant 'Han' Chinese culture. But there is certainly an element of geographical history involved.

In another fold of the Great Yao Mountains, south-east from Wuxuan, the great Taiping Rebellion which rolled up half of China in 1851–64 began in the foothills of Mount Thistle. One of its leaders, the 'western King' Xiao Chaogui, came from a Wuxuan peasant family and the Taipings' first military foray was launched into Wuxuan. Is this a clue to what happened a century later? Certainly the Taipings had a reputation for eating the hearts of their prisoners to make them bolder in combat (though so did the Manchu soldiers of the imperial armies with whom they fought). The official Party report also notes that, during the 1940s, Japanese soldiers who raped Wuxuan women were sometimes killed and eaten.

These local factors help to explain Wuxuan's unhappy claim as the place where 'we ate more people than anywhere else in China'. But why did it happen anywhere in a China which should have been transformed by socialism and the revolution?

For Zheng Yi, passionately anti-communist in the Solzhenitsyn mould, the answer is simple. The Communist Party and Mao were more savage, more inhuman, than Chiang Kai-shek or even Hitler and there is no need for further explanation. His sole concern is to reveal what has been covered up by timid or complicit party officials for the past twenty-five years. These and other dark secrets certainly do need to be exposed. It is impossible to imagine real political progress in China – whether towards pluralist democracy or a more democratic communist regime – unless Beijing can 'settle accounts' with the past honestly and fully.

The final reckoning will have to include the persecution of hundreds of thousands of intellectuals in the 1950s (barely admitted because of Deng Xiaoping's role in this 'anti-Rightist' campaign); the millions of famine deaths in the Great Leap Forward (only properly recorded in local histories which are not easily available); and the real responsibility for the Tiananmen Square Massacre which no one yet dares to admit. Cannibalism in Wuxuan is another such 'negative lesson' to be learnt.

There is a broader justification, transcending China's own frontiers, for exploring these events. Crimes against humanity take many different forms, from Dachau to Dresden, from Angola to Cambodia, from the great Indonesian massacre of 1966 (when at least 100,000 died without the world noticing) to Wuxuan – and currently from Bosnia to Burundi. Why, we have to ask, does the impossible-to-believe somehow persist in happening? How can humans behave so frequently with such extreme inhumanity? The 'special case' of Wuxuan is part of a much wider pattern which we need to understand.

In Wuxuan, as in most of China during the Cultural Revolution, a desperately poor community was expected to act out a political drama which it barely understood. Conflicting signals from Beijing destroyed the authority of those party officials who still believed in 'serving the people'. If the people of Wuxuan had been as politically mature as Beijing propaganda pretended, and if they had enjoyed a reasonable standard of living and education, it might have been different. But control was seized by the ignorant, the insecure, the power-hungry and the pathologically violent. A primitive kind of class struggle did indeed take place in which those with more education and slightly better jobs (particularly teachers) were vulnerable targets. The rest was tyranny by a few, terror for the majority, and a growing mob hysteria.

Might it happen again in Wuxuan or elsewhere in Guangxi? It hardly seems possible as China moves into a new quasi-capitalist age. Yet the gap between the masses and the elite is still dangerously wide in the Chinese hinterland, and economic change is still far too slow. Only three hours by bus from the city of Liuzhou, where the streets glow with neon lights and the jewellery shops are always full, Wuxuan remains 'backward'. Its young high-schoolers have only one ambition – to pass the national college exams and leave. Those who stay must settle into a society still isolated by physical and political barriers from hope and enlightenment. In this respect, Wuxuan is typical of a large swathe of China away from the booming coastal zones and rich provincial capitals.

Earlier this year I visited Mengshan County on the other side of the Great Yao Mountains. The Taiping rebels set up their first headquarters here in 1850 after they left Wuxuan. Mengshan, Zheng Yi tells us in *Red Memorial*, was notorious as a place where even the youngest children of 'class enemies' were killed in 1968. Several were dragged to their death and dumped in an old air-raid shelter. One mother pleaded to be allowed to 'keep just one' of her three children. Not one was spared.

Mengshan is now on a popular route for foreign backpackers, though their buses do not usually stop there. Surely there can be no child murderers now? I lunched in the town's only good restaurant, next to a noisy table where bottles of Maotai liquor were being drained. The dozen men and one woman were hard-faced and swaggering, instantly recognisable as local bosses. I asked the waitress, already half-sure of the answer. Yes, this was 'the leadership of Mengshan Public Security Bureau'.

Most of them would have been children themselves at the time when their peers were dragged to their deaths. Now they belong to a new exploiting elite which imports foreign cars, over-taxes the peasants and takes corruption for granted. Watching them belch and boast in the restaurant, lords of their domain, I could imagine them still getting away with murder. Or something even worse?

13

After Deng: New Directions, 1997–8

Twenty-one years after Mao Zedong's death, 1997 was another turning-point for China. Deng Xiaoping had vowed he would stay alive to witness the handover of Hong Kong: he did not quite make it. His death on 20 February preceded the return of Hong Kong 'to the motherland' on 1 July. Both events had been anticipated by many people with apprehension. Would China be plunged into new political confusion? Would the lights of democracy be darkened in Hong Kong? The new regimes in both cases made a much less dramatic start: the leadership under Jiang Zemin in Beijing was well aware of the need for a smooth transition in Hong Kong and on the mainland.

After the Beijing Massacre a million Hong Kongers held candlelight vigils and the territory's own democracy movement became a real political party. In October 1992 governor Chris Patten had enraged Beijing with his proposals for a new more democratic electoral system. China suspected a British plot to retain influence in Hong Kong and asked why Britain should suddenly champion democracy there after denying it for more than a century? The Council elected in 1995 under the new system was disowned by Beijing, which set up a Provisional Legislature to take over. Britain and China continued to bicker over the handover arrangements till the last moment. Eight thousand foreign journalists converged on Hong Kong for the handover: foreign tourists stayed away for fear of trouble.

Travelling in Guangdong province before the handover, I tried to fit Hong Kong into the context of the country which it was about to rejoin. Though the province was the richest in China, there was

*still poverty in the villages of hilly eastern Guangdong. Migration
to the Special Economic Zones or – for the luckiest ones – to Hong
Kong itself was the only way out. I explored the growing network
of roads and railways from Guangzhou to Beijing, which will link
Hong Kong more closely to the mainland. I visited Humen on the
Pearl river where, in 1841, a Chinese commissioner burnt more
than 20,000 chests of opium imported by British traders – the cause
of the First Opium War and the opening of China to the West.
Now Guangdong has its own narcotics problem. I also visited new
cities booming with light industry which had been transferred from
Hong Kong to take advantage of cheaper labour costs.*

*The Hong Kongers approached the handover in a practical
spirit: it was the opportunity to have a good feast, and it provided a
wealth of souvenirs. A few shed tears at the British withdrawal,
rather more waved flags to welcome the incoming token forces of the
People's Liberation Army. Most people took it calmly: Hong Kong
carried on with daily life and accepted the logic of geography. The
handover was peaceful and the outside world quickly lost interest.
In May 1998 a new Legislative Council was elected under more
restrictive rules, but the democrats still became the main opposition
party. The first stage had gone well: the long-term evolution of
relations between Hong Kong and Beijing would depend on how
China evolved – and on economic developments affecting both of
them in Asia.*

*In Beijing the post-Deng leadership settled into shape at a Party
Congress in the autumn and a National People's Congress in
spring 1998. Zhu Rongji, known as China's 'economic Tzar' with
a reputation for practical dealing, replaced Li Peng as Premier.
Returning to the Yangzi valley, I found the Three Gorges Dam –
Li Peng's pet project – well under way. From Chongqing above the
Gorges to Wuhan below them, urban China was being rebuilt in a
haze of pollution. There were encouraging signs of more tolerance
for political argument – within limits. Blackboards outside private
bookshops announced the arrival of the latest best-sellers from
Beijing, which dealt outspokenly with corruption, poverty and the
other 'negative consequences' of economic reform.*

*Tiananmen Square could still not be mentioned, although the
new radical thinkers called for a fresh start to political reform. Two
prominent dissidents – Wei Jingsheng and Wang Dan – were*

released as a gesture to Western countries which were looking for reasons to justify improving relations (and boosting trade) with China. The new British Labour government said that the experience of Hong Kong should be 'a bridge and not a barrier' to Beijing.

Jiang Zemin visited the US in November 1997, paving the way for President Clinton to visit China in June 1998. Dissidents continued to be harassed even as Mr Clinton was arriving, yet he was allowed to take part in an unprecedented live TV debate with Mr Jiang covering subjects such as human rights, democracy and Tibet. There was a new atmosphere of debate over critical social issues including crime, unemployment, poverty and corruption.

The summer floods of 1998, the worst for over four decades, forced the government to admit how much the environment had suffered from years of neglect. Political change was still beyond the margin of permissable discussion, but many Chinese privately believed that it must lie ahead. China had long since left behind the age of Mao: now the age of Deng was beginning to fade too. A new age was emerging, even if no one could yet give it a name.

Exit the patriarch
21 February 1997

The two faces of China, one peering stolidly backwards and the other looking ahead with mixed feelings, were visible in yesterday's reports from Beijing. From the official apparatus came solemn music and stern appeals to the Chinese people to Uphold Party Unity with Comrade Jiang Zemin at the Core. Out in the streets, on the packed trains and new highways, people bustled up and down the country with hardly a pause.

Should he have died before? Certainly Deng's reputation would have been hugely improved if he had met Marx before the Beijing protesters were met by tanks. But his passing is also the fading of a political style which to most Chinese seems anachronistic – even laughable. This is not to underestimate the huge importance of the Communist Party as a nation-running machine. It has also delivered a lot of goods to a lot of Chinese in the past two Dengist decades. No one, not even the dissidents abroad, has any real idea what to put in its place. The notion which has been taken up by some Western analysts recently of a China about to fall apart as Beijing loses its grip is too facile.

The provinces may try to dodge the central directives, but the key appointments are still made from the centre. The map of China is an interdependent mosaic of new roads and railways: the Party is a vast human web which networks energetically, at meetings and, especially, at 'working banquets'.

Yet being irreplaceable does not mean being popular – nor will it necessarily solve China's problems. Millions of Chinese believe the Party under Deng has brought them a better life. But they still denounce its deadly mix of bureaucracy and corruption. Millions more cut profitable deals with local apparatchiks, but still despise those with whom they deal. And many tens of millions of rural Chinese curse the local Party officials who tax them till it is hardly worth farming the land. Most of these millions end up as sweated labour to fuel the urban construction boom, eyeing the bosses sullenly, and regarded with fear by the new urban middle class as a source of fresh disorder.

Most of the advertised achievements of the rural economic revolution come from areas close to the big towns or in the more developed coastal provinces. Elsewhere Mao Zedong's famous efforts to 'bridge the gap between town and countryside' have gone into reverse. When peasant riots broke out in the countryside of Sichuan (Deng Xiaoping's home province) three years ago, most people in the provincial capital – just forty miles away – neither knew nor cared.

The great divide is beginning to be acknowledged. It is over a year since the Party's Central Committee revived the call to fight poverty, and warned that too-fast economic growth could tear the country apart. It became respectable to say that economic development should be put 'within the larger context of resources, environment, society and population'. Whether these concerns will produce results – any more than the annual official campaigns against corruption – is another matter. The targets have a habit of fading or changing shape.

The Western chorus of enthusiasts for China's 'economic miracle' share the responsibility. Take what should be a straightforward question: how many Chinese live below the poverty line? The answer in September 1993 from the World Bank, which has been reporting on China for over fifteen years, was fewer than 100 million. The answer in September 1996 was . . . 350 million – a more than threefold increase. Whoops, said the World Bank, 'we are now using recently improved data.'

The destruction of the environment may be an even more massive item on the new agenda. Anyone who travels in China and sees the thick scum of effluent on the rivers (when they are not dried up) knows that only too well. Beijing is spending more funds on cleaning up – but the problem continues to gush out from the same dynamic which drives the economic reforms. There is more awareness generally of these problems. TV programmes and radio chat-shows discuss peasant migration, pollution, corruption and crime quite openly, only steering clear of politics.

The Party elite has had months, probably years, to get its act together for the post-Deng age. There will be no excuse if it descends to factional infighting for the spoils. The challenge of guiding this vast nation into an uncharted transition should be much more rewarding – if only they are up to it.

Images at a funeral
23 February, Hong Kong

There are many different Deng Xiaopings to be recalled in Hong Kong on the eve of his funeral. It all depends which of the versions on sale is chosen. There is Deng the hero, who after the age of Maoism set China on a new course of 'stability and prosperity' for the next century. There is also the Deng who ordered the tanks to Tiananmen Square and whose death will lead to 'new disorder'.

There are fascinating glimpses of Deng struggling to regain Mao's favour in the Cultural Revolution, twenty-five years ago. And even earlier glimpses of the young Deng visiting pre-war Hong Kong.

Every bookstall carries up to a dozen instant publications, ranging from *The Great Architect of China* to *Deng's Secret Life*. Up-market Deng kitsch is also going fast. A thousand holographic watches with his face were sold from a shop on the Peak.

Deng's *Selected Works* are less in demand, but there is plenty of easier material. The headline of one sympathetic magazine says simply: 'Death of a good man'. Another recalls Mao Zedong's aphorism that death can be lighter than a feather or heavier than Mount Tai, depending on the worth of the deceased. Deng belongs to the mountain category.

More critical supplements have pictures of the troops in Tiananmen Square, or quote Deng's congratulations to the armed forces after they 'quelled the rebellion'.

A couple of small publications, apparently edited by former Red Guards, have capitalized on material from the Cultural Revolution, when the Communist Party's archives were ransacked. They feature Deng's abject letter to Mao in 1972, praising him for his brilliance in exposing the 'counter-revolutionary plots' of enemies such as Liu Shaoqi (the ex-head of state and Deng's close colleague).

Another magazine reveals some 'little-known facts' about Deng, including a visit to Hong Kong disguised as a businessman in 1931, while on the run from Chiang Kai-shek's police. The story says he stood next to the tallest building in Central District and joked: 'If people see me against this big chap, they'll really think I'm short!'

Deng's large family network also comes in for close scrutiny, with names, charts and pictures of the 'princelings' for whom connection to China's most famous leader has been no hindrance. A chart lists the Hong Kong companies in which Deng's family has invested money.

Hong Kong's appropriation of his name will continue in other ways. There is a good chance of the colony's new airport being named the Deng Xiaoping airport. The chairman of the colony's main pro-Beijing Party has urged Deng's widow to spare a few of his ashes to be scattered on the historic day of the handover.

Everyone acknowledges the huge significance of Deng's intervention in the Hong Kong negotiations with Britain, which led to the formula of 'one nation, two systems'. But there is less detail than might be expected on his involvement in Hong Kong policy, which continued for nearly a decade after the 1984 agreement was signed. This included Deng's insistence that the Chinese army should be stationed in Hong Kong.

Yet without Deng, the pivotal formula guaranteeing Hong Kong's autonomy – even if it now looks less secure than it did in 1984 – would not have been reached. Deng's reputation slumped in Hong Kong after the Beijing Massacre, though it was partly redeemed by his later success in revitalizing the Chinese economy – to the colony's financial advantage.

More than 20,000 people paid their respects before Deng's portrait at the New China News Agency in the first three days. But most of Hong Kong is more interested in looking to the future than the past. As an editorial in the independent *Ming Pao* says, China's new leaders will have to 'go beyond' Deng to tackle many new problems.

Hong Kong will also have to find out whether the wide range of opinions on mainland affairs which is now available on the news-stands will continue to be tolerated after 30 June.

25 February, Shenzhen
The city which Deng Xiaoping has made the richest in China said a modest goodbye to him yesterday: it was not enough to stop the traffic. Sellers of yellow chrysanthemums did good business around the huge billboard from which Deng's portrait surveys Shenzhen's modern skyline. Office workers from the new banks and businesses laid flowers and a few wreaths before his image.

There were no tears or visible grief. It was something to be done for history, and to be recorded for the family album – though plain-clothes police harassed many of those who stopped to pose. Some mourners took calls on their mobile phones as they filed past the creator of post-Mao economic reforms. Deng would have approved of their entrepreneurial commitment.

Their respect for Deng appeared genuine, but was expressed briefly, in conventional terms: he had been a world leader, he was the great architect of China's new enterprise – phrases from headlines in the *Shenzhen Economic Zone Daily*.

The hour of 10 a.m., when all over China people stopped to mark the beginning of the funeral service in Beijing and sound whistles and horns, attracted less attention in Shenzhen. A few cars and buses did sound their horns on time at the busy junction next to the billboard memorial. But they were hooted at when they tried to remain stationary after the lights changed. Some stores relayed the Beijing memorial service on television, but the Shenzhen government had ordered that there should be no official ceremony.

There was rather more solemnity across the border in Hong Kong, where nothing is being taken for granted as the handover approaches. Ferry-boats sounded their sirens, solemn music was played in the underground, schools stood to attention, and the work stopped briefly at the container terminals.

Though there was not a single poster of Deng on the streets of Shenzhen, his 'Southern Expedition' five years ago is well remembered. He used the visit to revive economic reforms which had stalled after the Beijing Massacre. He surveyed a Shenzhen already much changed since a previous visit when, he recalled, it was a small town with ponds, mud-paths and cottages.

From the forty-ninth floor of the International Trade Centre, he praised the 'wide boulevards and high buildings' below. Photographs show him, already frail, peering at the sights with almost child-like enthusiasm. The Shenzhen Museum behind the Deng billboard is staging an exhibition to celebrate Deng's 'modern miracle', which has raised Shenzhen incomes to eight times the national average.

Hong Kong to Beijing
June 1997, Shenzhen

Of all the projects to mark the return of Hong Kong to China, none is greater than the one that starts here. A new railway has been completed from Beijing to the Shenzhen Special Economic Zone – 1,500 miles of track which open up a swath of eastern and southern China and join the line into Hong Kong.

'Greet the return of Hong Kong by promoting railway safety', a huge banner proclaims at the just-completed station of Jinggangshan, high in the mountains of Jiangxi, where Mao Zedong founded the Red Army in 1927. The *Jing-jiu* (Beijing–Kowloon) line is the latest addition to a transport and communications grid that now knits Hong Kong to the mainland interior. A network of motorways in the Pearl river delta was expanded this month with the opening of a bridge across the river at Humen, cutting travelling time from Hong Kong to the western side of the delta by up to six hours. It will also provide the link for a new southern highway the length of Guangdong province.

Travellers on the *Jing-jiu*, and its branch line in Guangdong, will encounter unusual treatment by Chinese standards. Stewardesses introduce themselves by name and can be summoned by a bell. As the train leaves each station, they stand to attention and salute. Lavatory paper is available, and is actually replenished during the journey. And instead of a surly sweeper cleaning the floor, there are litter bins, described in the promotional literature as a modern innovation.

At present the through train from Beijing terminates short of Hong Kong at the Shenzhen border, but before long it will complete the journey into Kowloon. The *Jing-jiu* opens up the eastern provinces of Anhui and Jiangxi. There was fierce competition to become a 'railway town', and several have already attracted foreign investment, including Jinggangshan. Its real name is Taihe: Jinggangshan, it turns out, is still sixty miles from the station. Passengers arriving at night bed down in the local police station, which makes a useful income from the service. The line into Guangdong alternates between tunnels and viaducts of equally impressive length, passing through a jumbled mountain plateau where seventy years ago communist guerrillas struggled for survival.

The growth of infrastructure between Hong Kong and the mainland has transformed travelling, and it more subtly reinforces the sense that Hong Kong is an integral part of China. More than two dozen bus services, starting in central Hong Kong, cross the border for towns all over Guangdong, reaching most destinations in three or four hours by the new super-highways. A new western crossing is planned. Entry from the mainland to Shenzhen – and to Hong Kong – will continue to be regulated, but experts predict that post-handover traffic will rapidly increase.

The *Jing-jiu* railway has been an almost unnoticed engineering feat. Most of the work was completed within four years. More than 200,000 labourers worked on the project, which cost three billion pounds. It has reached a population of 200 million – one-sixth of all mainland Chinese – previously far from a railway. It has been financed from a variety of sources, such as bonds and bank loans, previously unknown in China. The branch line to the Special Economic Zone of Shantou, in eastern Guangdong, is run by an independent corporation.

In spite of these innovations, some features of the new transport grid reveal an uncertain transition. The new motorways are under-used because toll fees have been set too high. And local services on the new railway still use battered rolling stock, smoking restrictions are ignored, the average speed is less than twenty-five miles an hour – and the lavatories quickly run out of water, let alone the unheard-of luxury of paper.

How democracy came too late
June 1997, Hong Kong

Mao Zedong saved Hong Kong for the British in 1949. Struggling to rebuild the country, his new government shelved plans for regaining Hong Kong – which historians believe a strong Chiang Kai-shek regime would have pursued vigorously. But Mao's successors made absolutely sure that Hong Kong should return to the motherland: British hopes that some form of new arrangement – perhaps even a new lease on the New Territories – could maintain its control beyond 1949 were a foolish delusion.

Margaret Thatcher's attempt to argue this case got the 1982 negotiations off to a bad start, nourishing Chinese suspicions of British perfidy which have never been entirely dispelled. But after two years of tough negotiations, the 1984 Joint Sino-British Declaration seemed to many Hong Kongers to offer a reasonable prospect for the handback in 1997. But it was a hostage to history, both past and future.

The Beijing Massacre in June 1989 shattered Hong Kong confidence: how could the Chinese Communist Party be given any longer the benefit of the doubt? Popular support from Hong Kong for the student protesters in Tiananmen Square encouraged paranoia among the Party elders in Beijing that the territory would become a base for 'subversion'. But the most significant result of the massacre was to force the British government to respond to public opinion – against its own inclination – by toughening the commitment to make Hong Kong more democratic by the time of the handback. And here the past history of British colonial neglect of democratic reform caught up with Hong Kong.

In 1946 the first post-war governor proposed giving Hong Kongers 'a more responsible share' in local government. The next governor proposed elections for more than half the 'unofficial' members of the Legislative Council (Legco). The scheme was even approved by the British cabinet in 1952 – but then shelved. The Korean war and the refugee crisis in Hong Kong diverted attention, and there were fears that elections would lead to conflict between local communists and nationalists, which could then antagonize Beijing.

But at heart the British administration and the Anglo-Chinese business establishment were happy to have an alibi for opposing democratic reform. They fostered the image of a Hong Kong economic miracle, guided by enlightened paternalism, which offered every immigrant the chance of making good. China made clear its opposition to any changes which might lead to self-rule. They insisted that Hong Kong was not a colony which might one day gain independence but a piece of their own territory temporarily under foreign control. But the real issue was not granting dominion status to Hong Kong – an obvious non-starter – but making a start in giving the Hong Kong people a voice in their own affairs. Foreign Office papers for 1966, only released this year, show FO officials conducting a desperate search to find mainland statements indicating that Beijing would object to greater democracy.

Political parties continued to be banned in the 1970s. New 'pressure groups' for social and political reform were reluctantly licensed and kept under surveillance by Hong Kong Special Branch. Senior government officials spoke of them contemptuously, and mocked their efforts to raise serious issues. The minority of civil servants who favoured democratic reform, according to John Walden, who was director of home affairs from 1975 to 1980, 'were regarded as disloyal or even dangerous'. The government also argued that the local population was easily 'stirred up' by agitators, citing the 1967 riots, though these had occurred in the abnormal context of the Cultural Revolution.

The mood changed dramatically after negotiations with Beijing began in 1982: British politicians talked publicly about the need for 'representative government' – though the Hong Kong elite on the Executive and Legislative Councils was still lukewarm. The argument from London was un-ashamed: democracy had been irrelevant under enlightened British rule but was now essential to preserve Hong Kong's 'way of life'.

China agreed at the last moment that the future legislature should be 'constituted by elections'. Within two months of the Joint Declaration, a White Paper suggested indirect elections by 1985 for two-fifths of Legco. Crucially, it also proposed 'a very small number of directly elected members in 1988 building up to a significant number . . . by 1997'. But

Britain backed down under Chinese pressure. After carrying out a consultation exercise widely regarded in Hong Kong as bogus, the first element of direct elections was postponed till 1991. The then governor, David Wilson, has defended the postponement arguing (a) that Hong Kong opinion was divided, and (b) that 'we had a real issue in terms of China's concerns'. But his financial secretary, Piers Jacobs, believes that if Hong Kong 'had gone straight to direct elections after the Joint Declaration' the issue would not have become so contentious later.

Instead, the move towards direct elections began in a far worse atmosphere after Tiananmen Square. Agreement was eventually reached on allowing one-third of the Legco (twenty members) to be directly elected in 1995. The remaining two-thirds were to be elected indirectly – thirty by 'functional constituencies' and ten picked by an 'election committee' – but crucially there was no decision on how these procedures should work. Enter Chris Patten in 1992, to announce a cunning new plan: to tinker with the 'indirect' procedures so as to involve millions of electors instead of the few thousands envisaged by Beijing. And though he emphasized it was only a proposal, he had not consulted the Chinese first.

Some British officials barely bother to conceal their view that Mr Patten bungled it. 'China had notice [of the Patten plan] but no negotiations,' says one very senior figure. The result was that from the moment he made it public, Mr Patten was 'substantially in baulk and not on the bridge'. Talks in 1993 ended in failure, and China announced that it would repudiate the 1995 elections, making it impossible for the Legislative Council elected then to continue after 1997. The famous 'through train' would have to stop at the frontier on 30 June, and all the passengers dismount.

Britain's reluctance to introduce democracy earlier turns out to have been a fatal error – an opinion now held at the highest level as well as by democracy campaigners. 'Of course, if one had known that those things [the 1984 handback agreement and Tiananmen Square] were going to happen, a decision would probably have been taken much earlier to move more quickly down the road towards greater democracy.' That is the view of Anson Chan, who as Chris Patten's chief secretary has managed to hold her job and, like millions of Hong Kongers, will be adjusting to a new age. Those who have to make the transition will remember Britain's colonial rule more critically than those who pack their bags on the night of 30 June.

Just another Red Bean Day
1 July 1997, Hong Kong

Hong Kong was a city of different worlds yesterday: some areas buzzed with excitement; in others the great event hardly seemed to matter. In affluent central Hong Kong, Tony Blair and Chris Patten were mobbed by a cheerful crowd in Pacific Place. This is the all-glass multi-storey development where young Hong Kongers love to shop: it is almost New Labour.

There were admiring Cantonese cries of *wa! wa!* as Mr Blair worked his way down the line on the marble floor. It looked like Downing Street after the election all over again. Some of the spectators probably had been in Downing Street: many of them were tourists or Hong Kong expatriates, home for a big Party.

The Prime Minister signed one autograph and was besieged by hopefuls offering baseball hats, banknotes and shopping leaflets. These may become treasured items – or valuable commodities in the current mania for handover collectabilia. The Pattens enjoyed genuine affection. Lavender Patten was applauded when she hugged a baby, her husband when someone hugged him.

The Blair Party moved slowly past McDonald's and Marathon Sports, while ingenious members of the crowd photographed their reflections in the shiny underside of an escalator. They then took the escalator past the Body Shop's ingratiating display of Chinese flags (they did not pause for pictures), and on upwards and out of sight.

Two subway stops away, on Possession Street in the Western District, there are no boutiques or canned music.

The name commemorates the spot where Captain Charles Elliot planted the British flag in 1841. The shopkeepers selling dried mushrooms and other traditional goods take their history calmly. 'I shall watch it on TV – I've got a 29-inch screen,' said the manager of a shop selling nothing but one brand of rice wine. 'China? I liked the Great Wall. But as to what happens, I'll wait and see.' The manager of the Number One Tea Shop, which offers a choice of ginseng tea and sour plum drink, comes from China herself. 'I don't know,' she said slowly. 'Of course China has improved, but . . . I don't know.'

Not everyone had the street's historic significance entirely clear. 'Yes, it's famous,' said the local baker. 'There used to be a lot of foreign prostitutes around here.' But he wasn't going to take the day off: there were red bean buns to be made. Next door the customers and owners of a hardware shop agreed on one thing: 'We don't have any opinion. We'll just let it come.'

Thousands did come out in the evening to watch the fireworks after the British farewell ceremony. The Star Ferry, which otherwise only stops for a typhoon, came to a halt. There were more choruses of *wa* and huge applause for a show so brilliant that the rain did not matter. A student of engineering and his girlfriend studying accountancy said that no previous fireworks display had contained so many varieties. As for Hong Kong going back to China, they, too, had no opinion: they just want to graduate.

Many people in Hong Kong ended up doing what they always do on a public holiday – having a big evening meal in a restaurant. But in the north Kowloon housing estate of Wong Tai Sin, the dinner organized by a patriotic association had some special features. The chairman made a speech saying that, with the return of Hong Kong to China, the wishes of the legendary Yellow Emperor (circa 3,000 BC) had been fulfilled. And in the large dim sum restaurant they had hired, exactly ninety-seven tables were laid to make the obvious point.

New hopes of reform
May 1998, Wuhan

A new debate on the Chinese reforms which is now sweeping the country has raised issues barely mentioned in public since the upheaval of 1989. The events which led to the Beijing Massacre on 3–4 June nine years ago still cannot be referred to directly. But new books and articles are attacking the Maoist die-hards in the Communist Party who backed the suppression of the students.

More liberal-minded Party leaders have encouraged a new generation of intellectuals to take a hard look at the darker side of China's economic and social revolution. Criticisms include the claim that 70 per cent of Chinese state assets have now been 'siphoned off into private pockets'. The new critics also warn that the 'leftist' forces in the Party are preparing for another battle. This time, they say, it will be fought over the 'reform of political structures' which the die-hards fear could lead to more democracy.

The biggest hit on the booklists is *Crossing Swords*, written by two journalists on the official *People's Daily* newspaper. It has already sold 300,000 copies and can be found on railway bookstalls here in Wuhan and in small-town bookshops all over the country.

One of the authors, Ma Licheng, recently had a well-publicized meeting with former Vice-Premier Wan Li, who congratulated him for exposing the 'bad ideas' of the leftists. Nine years ago the students in Tiananmen Square had high hopes of Mr Wan's support when he returned from travelling abroad, but he was prevented by the hard-liners from coming to Beijing.

Crossing Swords warns that recent documents issued by the 'left' have the same dogmatic ring as Maoist diatribes in the Cultural Revolution thirty years ago. The book avoids saying what happened in 1989, only referring elliptically to 'various reasons' which led to a harsher political climate in the early 1990s. But it denounces the hard-liners for taking advantage of the crackdown to call for a renewal of 'class struggle' and to oppose Deng Xiaoping's efforts to revive the faltering economic reforms.

Another bestseller – *The Trap of Modernization* by young economist He Qinglian – provides a detailed account of the climate of corruption and widening gap between rich and poor. Ms He provides a list of twelve different types of illegal operations in the 'black economy'. They range from drugs and prostitution to currency fraud, insider trading, illegal sale of planning permits, producing counterfeit goods, and wholesale traffic in false invoices.

She lists the sex and pornography business as 'one of the main areas of black income'. She also cites statistics showing that up to four out of every five cars imported from Japan have escaped paying customs duty.

The popularity of these books reflects a new spirit of debate in a previously numb intellectual climate, but it does not yet amount, as some optimists have suggested, to a new 'springtime' of liberal thought in China. The authors avoid delicate topics such as the treatment of dissidents or the kind of democratic change now needed. This is not just because of political inhibitions: they also strongly believe that the only secure route towards liberalization is through continued economic reform. They back the current supreme Party leader Jiang Zemin and hope to stiffen his resolve by presenting a strong case for pushing ahead.

But in describing the struggle between the dogmatic 'left' and the enlightened supporters of reform, they throw important light on the darkest episodes of recent history, and suggest that the struggle is still continuing. *Crossing Swords* has been attacked at seminars organized by academic journals in the hands of orthodox Party intellectuals. They complain that its arguments are undermining ' the Party's basic line'.

The book was rejected by a dozen publishers who feared it might 'cause difficulties' for them, before being accepted by a new popular series called *China's Problems* – the title appears in the current fashion both in English and Chinese.

14

A Nation of People, 1995–8

Without the people, Mao Zedong used to say, we are nothing. (The tragedy is that he forgot his own advice.) And without the people, any attempt to understand China also means nothing. Even during the Cultural Revolution, the individual Chinese whom we met were never 'faceless' as Western writers often described them – although it might be hard to read their features. Developments since then have made it easier for Chinese people to express their feelings and their personalities. Anyone pronouncing on contemporary China should bear in mind the simple fact: there are 1.2 billion Chinese and they are all individuals.

So often in my travels I have briefly chanced upon persons whose life stories I wish I had been able to learn from beginning to end. The list of them would include: the itinerant bee-keepers of Fujian, seen on the road in Shaanxi; a circus troupe in a small Zhejiang town who invited me to travel with them; the would-be entrepreneurs whom I met in railway restaurant cars as they were heading south or north to seek their fortune; all sorts of people from outside Beijing who congregated in Tiananmen Square in May–June 1989; restless junior officials drinking in cheap hotels and chafing at their empty lives; and, up and down the country, students, teachers, painters and poets, some merely marking time but many clinging to high ideals.

There are others more fortunate, with money and connections, who aspire to a modern Asian lifestyle, eating and shopping in the new fast food restaurants and department stores of the big cities. If I have identified less with them in these pages, it is because their aspirations are more familiar, but they now form the most dynamic sector of Chinese society. Their lives and those of the parents have changed immensely in the last ten or twenty years. And when the grandparents die, they leave behind life histories containing unimaginable tales of upheaval and of often tragic drama.

Chinese officials too are people, with their own complicated past and ambivalent views on the future. Though the bureaucratic tradition maintains its strong and deadening grip, some officials do show a sense of responsibility, an eagerness to help their nation modernize and reform itself. The other tradition of the upright official, asserting what is right even if it should offend the imperial authorities, also survives among a minority.

In the course of nearly thirty years of travel, how many of this vast nation of individuals have I got to know? If I am honest, it is only a tiny handful compared to the multitude. Yet however few they may be, they provide a small window into the huge complexity of human existence which is China. Whatever we may understand about China can only be achieved through their words, their feelings and their lives.

The beggar girl
March 1995, Guangan, Sichuan province

Reading the walls in China opens windows to human experience which cannot easily be gauged by other means. In these post-Mao entrepreneurial times there may be no revolutionary slogans or manifestos, but there is still life, and death, in plenty.

Li Meiying, aged thirteen, has turned herself into a living wallposter. She stands against a plain brick wall in the main street of Guangan, Deng Xiaoping's home town in Sichuan province. With silent bowed head she displays, hung around her neck, a plea for help.

It is market day in Guangan: peasants with bamboo baskets, students on their way to school, and passers-by gather to read. Hers is an everyday story of the kind of tragedy which can so easily overwhelm a Chinese family now that state employers or communes no longer provide all their needs.

Meiying – her name means 'beautiful and courageous' – comes from a family of five. Her father, a rural tractor-driver, had dumped a load of sand one day and was returning home with some passengers on the back. He skidded in the rain and plunged 300 yards down a hillside: three passengers were wounded and one died. Insurance is almost unknown. He was jailed and ordered to pay compensation to the wounded and provide for the schooling of the dead man's son.

Meiying's mother sold their livestock and furniture, but it was not enough. Distraught, she has become mentally ill. She also suffers from heart trouble. The family cannot afford medicine for her. 'I beg all the aunties and uncles who read this to show their generosity,' Meiying's placard concludes. 'I shall never forget your kindness!'

Such a tale might arouse scepticism in cynical Beijing, but not in small-town Guangan. 'It's a very sad story: you must give her some money,' the spectators urge.

Written Chinese has a visual and cultural power not easily comprehended by those used to the Western alphabet. Writ large, it conveys a graphic sense of urgency commanding attention. Writ small, it packs a surprising amount of human detail into the most laconic account. During the Cultural Revolution, most notices were ritual denunciations of officially targeted 'capitalist-roaders'. But small groups of Red Guards turned the 'big-character poster' to their own purpose, arguing for a genuine revolution instead of the one stage-managed by the sycophantic elite around Mao Zedong.

In 1979 and 1980, when Deng Xiaoping was challenging Mao's successors, a wider range of radical arguments appeared on Beijing's Democracy Wall. Ten years later, these blossomed in the leaflets and posters of Tiananmen Square.

Any notice soon attracts a crowd puzzling over subtle allusions. But, with politics banished from the walls, the most topical subject is now crime. The most compulsive reading remains the 'execution poster', easily spotted because it carries a large tick in red ink to signify that the job has been well done.

When I visited Guangan it had just completed the traditional Chinese New Year purge of those on death row. The Guangan intermediate court's proclamation listed twelve names. Their appeals to a higher court had been rejected and all were 'dealt with by shooting'. The details make tawdry, pathetic reading: six murderers, two persistent robbers, two rapists and two guilty of serious wounding. Who knows what inadequacies, frustrations and perhaps miscarriages of justice these may conceal.

In each case the court pronounced that 'the crime was severe and the circumstances atrocious'. The accused were sentenced to death and – as if it mattered – to 'deprivation for life of all political rights'.

Amnesty International's partial list of Chinese executions for 1993 totals 1,419. The real figure may be twice as high. The sentences are intended to deter, but the number of violent crimes is rising. Photographs of young men paraded in the streets on their way to execution have been smuggled out. Some show defiant gestures. In pre-Communist China, the boldest criminals sang snatches of opera to the waiting crowd. What do they call out today? Long live the socialist market economy?

Next to Guangan's execution poster is a more hopeful list, of high-school graduates who have been successful in college entrance exams. For the spectators, many of whom are young and unemployed, they are the ones who will escape.

The 'revolutionary'
October 1996

Wang Li, who has died aged seventy-seven, had his finest day on 22 July 1967, at the height of the Cultural Revolution. With his foot in plaster, he was greeted by almost the entire Chinese leadership at Beijing airport, after winning a fierce battle between rival Red Guard factions in the central city of Wuhan. He had scored a revolutionary victory, the banners proclaimed, against the dogs' head counter-revolutionaries.

Six weeks later, when his 'ultra-left' faction was itself condemned as counter-revolutionary, Wang was denounced as a traitor against Chairman Mao. Confused? So were thousands of Red Guards who took their lead from him: famously, one group had seized control of the Foreign Ministry and stormed (setting on fire) the British chargé d'affaire's office in Beijing.

Wang did not exactly have 'revolution' written on his face. Nancy Milton, a foreign 'polisher' of official documents at the Chinese news agency, described him as a handsome man, 'stout in his khaki padded overcoat, his suave bankerly appearance seeming strangely out of place amid the admiring swarms of excited Red Guards'.

No youthful worshipper himself of the Red Sun, Wang was one of a group of middle-aged ideologues who took Mao's side against the Communist Party bureaucracy for mixed reasons. Like many left-wing intellectuals, the ideologues were attracted by Mao's idea of building communism at full speed – even if the country was not ready for it. Joining Mao's camp also protected them from being labelled 'bourgeois scholars'.

Born to a property-owning family in the central province of Jiangsu, Wang joined the Party in 1939 and worked his way up the national hierarchy of propaganda departments. By the early 1960s, he was helping to produce anti-Moscow polemics as part of the bitter Sino-Soviet dispute. Wang was closely connected to the mayor of Beijing, Peng Zhen. But when Peng became the first target of the Cultural Revolution in the spring of 1966, Wang made a quick switch to the Maoist camp.

The ultra-left excesses of this camp led to the first split a year later. Mao's wife Jiang Qing and her group gained political space by ousting Wang's clique. Wang was accused of seeking to undermine Premier Zhou Enlai. (Jiang Qing had exactly the same intention but went about it more circumspectly later on.)

Wang's downfall came about through two errors. Mao personally criticized his speech encouraging the Red Guards to seize the Foreign Ministry; the Chairman knew that revolution must be kept within the family. Wang also erred by sponsoring a controversial play, *Madman of a New Age*. Its real-life hero was a young man, Chen Lining, who had denounced Mao's main rival, the Head of State Liu Shaoqi, several years earlier when Mao and Liu were still officially on good terms. Chen had then been certified as mentally ill. Wang now claimed that the unfortunate patient was a political dissident suffering from 'fascist persecution'.

Whether the claims could be substantiated or not was never discovered; but it was foolish of Wang to get involved in the theatre which was, as everyone knew, the domain of ex-film actress, Mao's wife Jiang Qing. In 1967 Wang was imprisoned. He spent the next fifteen years in jail without being charged with a crime. Outside, Mao died, others rose and fell – including, eventually, the Gang of Four.

Wang emerged in 1982 to rejoin his wife, filing more than 100 petitions for rehabilitation by the Party. Wang denied that he had ever encouraged violence and claimed to have been the scapegoat for the chaos which almost destroyed China in mid-1967. He also claimed to have helped Deng Xiaoping write a letter of 'self-criticism' which saved him from the fate of Liu Shaoqi, who was beaten and died in prison. More recently Wang has claimed that Deng was prepared to rehabilitate him, but that other leaders objected.

He spent his last years in Shanghai where he was said to live comfortably in a spacious house – with a red carpet. Wang said that he would take the secrets of his brief period of fame to his grave. They were not really so mysterious. Revolutions have a habit of getting hijacked by the ambitious and the amoral. Wang may have looked 'suave', but he was out of his depth.

The drivers
November 1996, Yanzhou, Shandong province

Sitting on a stone bench in front of Yanzhou station I look across the square. It is vast, like most such places in China. A plinth in the centre carries a rusted statue of a worker, labelled 'Building the nation'. He is shown guiding the hook and tackle of a hoist, which descends from nowhere. Yanzhou, in the eastern province of Shandong, is an industrial centre – although the rural birthplace of Confucius is just down the road.

In front of the plinth there is a parked bus: it turns out to be a public lavatory. In a little booth, its custodian hands out small wedges of paper to customers in exchange for tiny sums. He also provides a public telephone service.

An idle group of waiting passengers peer at my note-taking. 'Your writing is hard to read,' says one, as if I were writing in Chinese. They comment, laughing, on my left-handedness, and drift away.

A beggar in cotton shoes, black felt hat and padded coat, approaches me. Suddenly he pulls back his coat to reveal that his right arm is no more than a fingered flipper attached to the shoulder. Startled, I give him a note so large that he is surprised in turn.

It is time to move off before I become an object of general interest. I walk over to a magazine stall, with rows of periodicals displayed behind glass. The practice is to ask for one, study it carefully, then either buy it or toss it back with a casual *buyao* – 'don't want'. I am making a general collection, so cause a stir by buying a dozen different titles without reading them first.

They include a military magazine with a picture of a British UN soldier on the front, a fashion journal, one advising young people on how to set up home, a short story collection, several police and romance titles, and what proves to be a remarkable exposé of the hardships of peasant life, part of a series called 'an eye on the real China'. (Afterwards I regret not buying them all.)

Some taxi-drivers come up with friendly curiosity. Where am I from, where did I learn Chinese? The conversation moves quickly to another familiar topic: how 'backward' China is compared to Britain. And yet China, they lament, is a nation with 5,000 years of history!

I am asked how long ago England was 'established as a nation' – *jianguo*? In this special sense, China was only 'established' in 1949 when the communist revolution succeeded. England has been established for several hundred years, I loosely reply. This helps to explain why we are more 'advanced'.

The conversation takes a different turn. How many wives are you allowed in England? Some disbelief that it is only one. This leads on to Aids and drugs, and a less favourable comparison between the West and China. But the balance tips again.

Is the government corrupt in England? Here, in China, it's really terrible. There are laws but they are worth nothing. The ordinary people have no trust in them. And we finish on another familiar topic: China's population is far too large, its social discipline is too bad. Singapore is mentioned admiringly.

I move on, past the bus station. The most popular routes are lined up on the square, waiting for passengers from the trains. They include buses to Qufu where Confucius was born, one of China's best-known tourist destinations.

There is a trick to catching buses here. No one wishes to board one – especially the private minibuses – till it is nearly full, because it may wait for ever. A few exhausted train passengers are lured in, while people linger outside. Then the driver gets in: there is a quick rush. He cunningly moves a few feet, and switches off again.

I take out my camera to photograph the line of buses: some are grimy beyond belief. One of them has broken down and is being pushed away by hand. Husbands, sisters and children are urged to look at the Old Foreigner Taking a Picture (Old as in Honourable, I must explain).

I continue the circuit, past the plinth with the statue and the lavatory bus. I now see several large vats behind it, some empty and some full, serving an obvious purpose.

At the foot of the square is a huge department store of the type which every town in China now requires. It has lots of tinted blue glass and a dome on top. The store calls itself Nine Oceans Goods Store. There is a much smaller globe above the traffic cop at the road junction. This contains the lights and – an ingenious device widely used in China – a countdown showing the number of seconds till they will next change.

On the last side of the circuit, I pass the 'Calfnia Restaurant' and the 'YZBG Hotel', both in Roman lettering. California is easily recognized, but YZBG? Like many modern shop signs, this one has taken the initial letter of each word in its title (as spelled in the Chinese phonetic alphabet) to form a meaningless acronym. YZBG stands for *Yan Zhou Bin Guan* or Yanzhou Guesthouse.

Finally, the female touts outside a couple of small restaurants urge me to eat, but accept with good humour my reply that I have *chihaole* – 'eaten well'.

It is time to enter the dim waiting hall and see whether this is a railway station with good or bad social discipline. It is good, to a fault. The smartly uniformed staff makes us line up in twos and march onto the platform. Travelling in China can be exhausting but it is always full of surprises.

The upright official
25 June 1998, Xi'an

Chinese security officials have ensured that human rights will remain a source of contention during the visit of President Bill Clinton by taking heavy-handed action against critics of the Beijing regime even as the president was on his way to Xi'an.

A former government official in Xi'an, Lin Mu, well-known for his advocacy of political reform, was barred from receiving visitors today. The *Guardian*'s attempt to pay a quiet visit to his home was frustrated by half a dozen plain-clothes police.

It was a journey that quickly exposed the limits of Beijing's tolerance of dissidents. An unmarked black car stuck close to my taxi through the morning rush hour of Xi'an and plain-clothes police were waiting at the gate as I tried to enter. Forced to leave the car, I walked quickly into the compound but was soon surrounded by a group of people tugging at my clothes and demanding to know my identity.

They were sharp-faced and agitated, wearing the anonymous uniform of loose trousers and white shirt. 'You would not just walk into the house of the British prime minister, would you?' asked one accusingly.

Back at the main gate, I was shoved to one side when the distinguished ex-official I was trying to visit emerged, furious at the news of my detention. He denounced one policeman he knew by name to the gathering crowd in this side street in the city's south.

'It is my right under the constitution to entertain guests,' he shouted. 'Calm down, old Lin,' another policeman said patronizingly. Mr Lin became even more furious.

I was told I had to register as a visitor before I could see a resident within the compound. On trying to register, I was told that according to unspecified 'regulations', no visit could be made. The argument that Mr Lin was entitled to speak freely to a foreign journalist because China had now opened up did not impress a Mr Han – the only policeman willing to show his identity card.

'Yes, China is an open country,' he said. 'But openness has its limits.'

It was a stalemate. I walked away slowly to have a late breakfast – a bowl of hot spicy noodles on a pavement stall – and consider what I had seen. For many Chinese it was an everyday incident, but it provides a sobering counterpoint to assertions that China's human rights policy will improve if the regime is left to its own devices.

Two dissidents in the Xi'an area were reported to have been sequestered by the police the previous day. They were taken to separate hotels, presumably to ensure they could not be contacted by foreign journalists.

Mr Lin is a former Communist Party official who has petitioned the government urging reform. He was dismissed from the Party for supporting the student movement in 1989 but is still a free citizen. Last month Mr Lin and eleven other critics of the regime sent an open letter to the National People's Congress calling for the release of Zhao Ziyang, the Party Secretary-General who was ousted after opposing military action in Tiananmen Square. One of the men detained in Xi'an yesterday has also signed a letter urging Mr Clinton to meet Mr Zhao while in Beijing.

It is beginning to look as though any reference to Mr Zhao, whose job was appropriated by Jiang Zemin – now China's president – touches a highly neuralgic nerve in Beijing.

In a letter to the Communist Party leadership apparently written earlier this month, leaked to Reuters agency yesterday in Beijing, Mr Zhao called on it to admit that the massacre was 'a historical mistake'. Otherwise, he argued, the incident would continue to undermine China's reputation. He welcomed the Clinton visit as a 'turn for the better', but he said that relations with the West continued to be marred by the human rights issue.

The more open atmosphere of debate which has emerged this year focuses, often outspokenly, on the harmful social effects of economic reform, including corruption, widening income gaps and unemployment. But the concept of political reform is still left on the margin.

The letter takes issue with this gradualist approach. A repudiation of the Beijing Massacre, it says, 'would bring one hundred benefits and no harm'. It is time to give a fair appraisal and 'not carry a historical burden into the next century'.

As a Party member, Mr Zhao is entitled to petition the leadership: there is a long tradition going back to imperial times of exiled officials who refused to remain silent. Even some of Mao's colleagues spoke out and are now hailed for their courage.

Mr Lin belongs to the same tradition as Mr Zhao of 'upright officials' who refuse to be silenced. Before the Cultural Revolution he worked for Hu Yaobang who, as Party Secretary-General in the 1980s, encouraged talk of political reform. Mr Hu was ousted by hard-liners and his death sparked the 1989 democracy movement.

Last year Mr Lin issued a manifesto appealing to the leadership to tackle corruption, release political prisoners and begin a transition towards multi-party democracy. By doing so, he argued, the Party would actually win back the trust of the people, and it would 'retain the status of the ruling party in future democratic elections'. The present rulers appear to have no intention of taking any such chance.

'It is only democracy and the rule of law that China can turn to,' Mr Lin wrote, 'not the cult of violence or the suppression of dissent.' He said repression only aggravated social tensions, citing growing unemployment.

Most Chinese would regard the small scuffle at Mr Lin's

gate yesterday as the norm. 'This is just the way they behave,' said one witness with contempt. 'They go their way and we go ours.'

Those responsible may be minor officials who are not used to national diplomacy. 'Beijing is Beijing,' one of the policemen said, 'but this is Xi'an.' But they are part of a countrywide policy to stifle dissent during the American President's visit. It is a paradox that Mr Lin is able to send messages and articles to the outside world – although his telephone was being tapped yesterday – but still may not be interviewed in his home town.

The missionaries
June 1997, Jinggangshan, Jiangxi province
Seventy years after Mao Zedong launched the Red Army on the path of peasant revolution from these mountains in southern China, some young Chinese are adopting new ideals.

These come in a strange assortment, as I have just discovered while travelling in a wide sweep through Guangdong to Jiangxi province. Many young people are too busy looking for work to set their sights higher, but others claim a sense of missionary zeal to do something 'good for the nation'. The nationalist students of the 1920s would have recognized the sentiment, though it can take dubious forms today.

In a filthy hard-class carriage on the new railway which passes through southern Jiangxi, I was greeted by a band of modern evangelists. Their cause was not immediately apparent, but the commitment was clear in their shining eyes and almost over-warm handshakes. The mission, they told me, was too complex to be explained here among the peanut shells and banana skins, against the noise through broken train windows. Fortunately we were heading for the same town. When we arrived late at night, their leader was met by a dozen followers, clasping his hands and vying to carry his luggage.

I extracted the truth in a long session the next day, probing the philosophy they expounded to reach, at last, a solid material basis. This took the form of a glossy pamphlet for the Futian Oxygenating Health Machine, with a cover picture of two dozen happy Westerners, including dog and baby, beaming behind a moulded plastic box with two indentations at the top. It was an electric foot massager of the kind sold in Hong Kong health shops.

The young evangelists insisted they were not just selling a product: they were engaged in 'cultural communication'. They were forming a network of like-minded people 'of high moral worth' to disseminate advanced market information which would improve the people's health and contribute to the nation's wealth. They quoted the writings of an American guru whose name I could not quite translate back from the Chinese.

It is true that they were not selling the Health Machine as such: they were selling information about it to a network of those who would then sell it. It was, in other words, a classic pyramid scheme. Members of the network paid a 'premium' – a figure of 700 *yuan* (fifty pounds) was mentioned – before setting up their own subsidiary network. It was possible, I was told, for an individual to earn 200,000 *yuan* in a month: just think how profits of this size could then be invested in successful industry for the good of the nation!

The actual gadget (if anyone buys it) is marketed for 3,900 *yuan* (300 pounds). The user puts his or her feet in the indentations, plugs it in, and it will then, says the brochure, 'communicate oxygen to the autonomic nervous system'. It is to be found, I was told, in every three-star hotel in Japan. Did they have another product in mind to 'culturally communicate' to the Chinese nation? Yes, indeed. The next item to be disseminated to those of high moral worth was an electric lavatory seat.

Spooky though they were, the Futian Net display in an extreme form the connection – and confusion – between personal and public goals which characterizes this former revolutionary society. The ambivalence is often shown in answers to the standard conversational question: 'What is your *lixiang*?' The dictionary translation of the word is 'ideal', but it can also denote 'ambition', and answers range uncertainly between the two.

An out-of-work graduate in English replies she is heading for Guangzhou to look for work, preferably in a firm with foreign connections: that is pure ambition. Another with a degree in physics hopes to go abroad to make money, and also 'learn new ideas' which will help his country. A language student says she has no 'ambition' but just wants to be a good teacher – an unfashionable ideal these days.

Around the economic zone of Shantou, in eastern Guangdong province, I came across some actual missionaries. Just 140 years after the first Presbyterians built a church in Shantou, an amazing revival is under way. Most of the 600 who turned up for the weekly bible class at Shantou West Church were in their twenties or thirties. Many rode scooters and wore brightly coloured helmets. But they were not just attending for social purposes. A visiting Hong Kong Chinese minister was envious of the congregation's commitment. 'They're not content with an hour's bible class but insist on more,' he said. 'In Hong Kong our young people have too many distractions.'

Out in the Shantou countryside, new churches have been built as high as blocks of flats. One fine example stands alone by a wooded hill, dwarfing the pagoda on the summit, and blocking the view from several dozen Chinese tombs on the hillside. Such conflicts of interest between Christian missions and local tradition led, 100 years ago, to the Boxer rebellion. Today there is still resentment, but money speaks louder. In another county town, a new church of more modern design gleams with blue reflective glass. Together with a smaller church, it baptises 100 people every year; they have a combined congregation of 2,000. The pastors of both churches are young and open-faced, too young to remember the dark years when the faithful could worship only in secret.

The missionary impulse in China today is not confined to charlatans or to the Christian Church: it infuses much of what we might regard as normal commercial activity. Perhaps the traditional contempt with which entrepreneurs were regarded still requires a higher purpose to be invoked.

The impulse is so well internalized that those who invoke it may be unaware of the mental sleight of hand. This is particularly true of the overseas Chinese investors who put their money in the motherland.

The Shantou West Church has been an incidental beneficiary: the Hong Kong tycoon Li Ka-shing gave it three million Hong Kong dollars (240,000 pounds) to rebuild on the old site. He has put up 100 times as much to build a university on the hillside overlooking Shantou, complete with swimming pools, conference centre, and a 600-bed teaching hospital. Other investments in Shantou include new ports, a power plant and a bridge.

Mr Li, praised as a patriot by China's President Jiang Zemin, is the best-known of a number of overseas Chinese tycoons who sustain much of the coastal economic boom. They are regarded as gurus as well as investors. Guangdong television portrays the superior wisdom of men such as the Indonesian Li Guihua, who is shown lecturing communist cadres on the virtues of competition and efficiency.

Li Ka-shing is the hero of books and magazines, preaching his own religion: that success depends upon knowing when to give ground. 'Why did the Yangzi become a long river?' he asks. 'Because it can accept smaller rivers and can become big. If you're too powerful and reject the smaller waters, you cannot become a long river.' Such sentiments delight native Chinese entrepreneurs. They are written up in a monthly magazine called *Rich People*.

It is obvious – and has been for some time – that these new evangelisms have filled a gap left by the declining appeal of the Chinese Communist Party. Yet some of the Party's 50 million members still believe in making a contribution to society – though 'serving the people' has given way to 'making the people rich' – and they take a tough view on law and order.

The question of what will emerge out of this ideological jumble in present-day China is difficult but vital for the future. Quite a large minority seeks some sort of intellectual prop, whether fashioned from superstition, religion, business mantras or socialism turned into muscular patriotism.

Perhaps none will prevail: will this mean that China evolves into a more pluralist society of ideas, or descends into universal cynicism – or will some new -ism arise to sweep the country again?

Chronology

1949	(Oct.) Liberation – victory of Chinese Communist Party led by Mao Zedong over Chiang Kai-shek's Nationalist Party (Guomindang).
1950	Sino-Soviet Alliance; Korean War (China intervenes to help North Korea after it has invaded US-backed South Korea).
1950–7	Land reform leads to rural cooperatives; national health and education systems set up; heavy industrial base established.
1958–61	Great Leap Forward seeks short-cut to communism and fails; People's Communes set up; millions of deaths from starvation; Defence Minister Peng Dehuai replaced by Lin Biao; Sino-Soviet split comes into open.
1962–5	China isolated by both superpowers; Mao on defensive against critics of Great Leap, his radical supporters prepare counter-attack.
1966–8	Cultural Revolution (first stage), Red Guards encouraged to attack and overthrow Mao's rivals; Liu Shaoqi and Deng Xiaoping ousted; Party bureaucrats and intellectuals humiliated; Red Guards split into warring factions.
1968–71	Red Guards sent into exile; Mao's successor Lin Biao dies after alleged failed coup; secret contacts with the US; schools reopen.
1972	(Feb.) President Nixon visits China.
1973–6	Deng Xiaoping rehabilitated by Mao; 'Gang of Four' led by Mao's wife (Jiang Qing) struggles for power; second stage of Cultural Revolution.

1976   (Jan.) Death of Premier Zhou Enlai.

          (5 Apr.) Tiananmen demonstration mourning Zhou, condemning Gang; Deng dismissed.

          (9 Sept.) Death of Mao, succeeded by Hua Guofeng; Gang of Four arrested a month later.

1978–9   Policy of Four Modernizations; Deng Xiaoping ousts Hua from control; Democracy Wall and unofficial magazines briefly encouraged, then closed down; border war with Vietnam; Wei Jingsheng and other dissidents jailed.

1980–3   People's Communes replaced by rural 'responsibility system'; higher wages and urban consumer boom; large numbers of foreign leaders and tourists begin to visit China.

1983   (Oct.) First hard-line backlash – campaign against 'spiritual pollution'.

1984   Hu Yaobang becomes Party General-Secretary, encourages rethink of Marxism, urges liberal policies in Tibet.

1984   (Apr.) President Reagan visits China.

          (Sept.) Sino-British Joint Declaration on Hong Kong agreed.

1986   Reformists argue for political liberalization; students resume demonstrations.

          (Oct.) Queen Elizabeth visits China.

1987   (Jan.) Second hard-line backlash – campaign against 'bourgeois liberalization'; Hu Yaobang replaced by Zhao Ziyang; reformists sacked from Party.

1987–8   Hainan declared a province; Special Economic Zones and coastal regions flourish; migrant peasants seek work in cities.

1989   (Mar.) Martial law declared in Lhasa after pro-Dalai Lama demonstrations.

          (Apr.) Death of Hu Yaobang leads to student demonstration and occupation of Tiananmen Square.

          (May) Zhao Ziyang ousted by Li Peng; martial law declared in Beijing.

(3–4 June) Army occupies Tiananmen Square – Beijing Massacre; Li Peng becomes Premier; Jiang Zemin appointed Party Secretary-General.

1990–1 Nationwide repression of those who protested; economic slowdown.

1992 (Jan.–Feb.) Deng Xiaoping's 'Southern Expedition' launches new economic drive; new 'development fever'.

1993–4 Hundredth anniversary of Mao's birth creates 'Mao fever'; increase in foreign investment; high economic growth leads to 20 per cent inflation.

1995 Vice-Premier Zhu Rongji tackles overheated economy; growing concern over crime and unemployment; Wei Jingsheng sent back to jail.

1996 Chinese war games in Taiwan Straits; new efforts to tackle rural unrest, pollution, corruption.

1997 (20 Feb.) Death of Deng Xiaoping.
(1 July) Hong Kong returns to China.
(Oct.) Jiang Zemin visits US in role of State President.
(Nov.) Wei Jingsheng released on medical parole.
(Dec.) Collapse of Asian 'economic miracle' – China claims it will be unaffected.

1998 (Mar.) National People's Congress – Premier Li Peng replaced by Zhu Rongji.
(June) Bill Clinton visits China.
(July–Aug.) Flood disasters in Central and North-east China – 3,500 die.
(Oct.) Tony Blair visits China.

1999 (3 June) Tenth anniversary of Beijing Massacre.
(1 Oct.) Fiftieth anniversary of Chinese Communist victory – 'Liberation'.

Note on Chinese Political Structure

The Chinese constitution provides that China should be ruled by the Communist Party. Some small parties are tolerated as part of a 'united front', but opposition to the Party has never been allowed. The Party is run by a Secretary-General (the exact title has sometimes changed) and a small Politburo. A Party Congress should meet every four years (it has not always done so) to elect a Central Committee which then chooses the Politburo and its even smaller Standing Committee. Party secretaries and committees should be found at every level of society, including the armed forces and right down to the village and the factory, although gaps are beginning to appear in the structure. They are supposed to act as a link with the people and to ensure that Party policies are carried out.

A separate State structure exists side by side with the Party, and ultimately under its control. A National People's Congress is elected by local People's Congresses. It appoints a State President, and a Premier and Vice-Premiers who form a State Council. This functions as the effective government of China. Until now all such appointments have followed the Party's recommendation. The President represents China in exchanges with foreign heads of state.

Most senior officials hold parallel Party and State offices. The current Party Secretary-General, Jiang Zemin, is President of the People's Republic of China and also chairs the Central Military Commission which controls the armed forces.

Attempts have been made with varying success to lessen Party control over the ordinary running of the government. Many government leaders in the provinces, while belonging to the Party, now act much more on their own initiative, particularly in taking economic decisions. An increasing number of village officials are now elected by secret ballot without prior Party selection. But the Chinese leadership says that one-party rule must continue for many more decades. Chinese dissidents who attempt to register opposition political parties have so far been harassed or arrested.

The armed forces (People's Liberation Army) is supposed to be subordinate to political control: the Party controls the gun. At times of crisis – e.g. in the Cultural Revolution (1966–76) and after the Beijing Massacre (1989) – the PLA acquired greater influence. It has never usurped political power, although in 1971 Minister of Defence Lin Biao died while fleeing China after allegedly seeking to stage a coup. In recent years the PLA has acquired widespread economic interests in industry, commerce and tourism.

In spite of the apparently monolithic structure described above, Chinese politics since 1949 has been ridden with factionalism and struggles for power, in which the contestants each claim to be defending the correct 'line'. The Party almost disintegrated during the Cultural Revolution when Mao used the Red Guards to purge his political opponents, and his supporters then split into rival factions. These pro-Mao forces were often called 'radicals' or 'ultra-Leftists' by foreign commentators. Confusingly, those leaders who still support radical policies today are more likely to be called 'conservatives', in contrast to moderate leaders who are usually labelled 'reformers' or 'modernizers'.

Sources

All items appeared in the *Guardian*, on the date given, unless another source is indicated.

1: 'The floods of violence', *Far Eastern Economic Review (FEER)*, Hong Kong, 4 July 1968; 'Student power in China', *FEER*, 27 June 1968; 'Stifling the students', *FEER*, 29 August 1969; 'Sweet and sour', *FEER*, 6 February 1969; 'The pied piper of Kweichow'. *FEER*, 5 June 1969.

2: Excerpted from the series 'Report from China', 30 April, 3, 4, 5, 6 May 1971; 'Whose boom down on the commune?', 21 January 1972; 'Biking in Beijing', 29 May 1976; 'The revolution without resolution', 31 May 1976; 'Chinese hero becomes a clown', 8 December 1976.

3: 'China in ferment: character assassination', 23 November 1978; 'Why the children of China are on their marks' (excerpt), 24 November 1978; 'Chinese national minority begins to bridge the cultural divide' & 'Separate development among the national minorities of China' (excerpt), 2 & 4 December 1978; 'The great leap sideways', part 1, 14 April 1980; 'The great leap sideways', parts 2–3, 15 & 16 April 1980 (excerpts).

4: 'Hard life of China's peasants on the plain', 19 April 1980; 'Peking encourages peasants' enterprise', 24 February 1981; 'China now: the long march from famine', 12 March 1982; 'From blossoms to bricks?', *China Now* (London: Society for Anglo-Chinese Understanding, No. 109, Summer 1984, pp. 3–5); 'How Dazhai caught a wind of change', 4 September 1987.

5: 'Not-so-inscrutable Chinese give clear message to Reagan', 28 April, & 'Reagan visit still marred by discord' (excerpt), 1 May 1984; 'Governor sells a deal and pays tribute to colony', 27 September 1984; 'Who'll lead the new Hong Kong?', 5 October 1984; 'Queen gets first glimpse of Deng's reformed China', 'Royalty goes to the wall', 'Noodle stew', 13, 15, 18 October 1986.

6: 'Rough ride to reconstruction', 8 July 1980; 'The new seats of power', 16 November 1984; 'How Wenzhou rediscovered its place in the Sun scheme', 4 October 1985; 'Progress caught in a pit-fall', 29 August 1987.

7: 'Why the Chinese revolution nearly went West' & 'The dark side of China's festival of light' (excerpts), 17, 18 November & 16 December 1983; 'Deng's economic reforms face last hurdle', 16 October 1984; 'China's breath of intellectual courage expires', 5 February 1987; 'They do like to be beside the seaside', 10 August 1987; 'Beijing's dissenting voices find common platform', 1 March 1989.

8: 'Beijing rings to calls for democracy', 5 May 1989; 'Army held off by the unlikely street fighters of Beijing', 'Poem gives Deng a push', 23, 24 May 1989; 'Cyclists crushed by tank tracks', 'Anger and despondency on the street corner', 5 June 1989; 'A new history code for the capital', 'Triumphal convoy lacks cause for celebration', 'Soldiers sweep up debris of mayhem', 6, 8, 9 June 1989; 'Tasting gall', 15 June 1989.

9: 'China tightens rule of iron discipline on Tibetans', 30 September 1989; 'Tibetan nuns defy might of China', 8 November 1989; 'Chinese whispers – Tibet', 12 November 1994.

10: 'China's shock brigade of the arts', 12 March 1979, & 'Bright sparks in the new dawn of Chinese art', 24 December

1980; 'In the East, *Sports Illustrated* is read', 9 March 1987; 'Voices in a hostile silence', 30 May 1991.

11: 'Mudpaths paved in gold', 1 August 1992; 'Chinese capitalism's frontier island', 23 May 1992; 'The Middle Kingdom drops Mao for market fever', 3 April 1993; 'Leaps and binds', 14 March 1995; 'Chinese leader denounces seductive joys of power', 3 March 1995.

12: 'The rivers of blood', 27 November 1993.

13: 'Exit the dragon', 21 February 1997; 'For sale: Deng's many faces' & 'China pays its respects', 24 & 26 February 1997; 'End of the line for colony in Beijing's rail network', 24 June 1997; 'Power slips past the people' (Hong Kong 1842–1997), 26 June 1997; 'For some just another red bean bun day', 1 July 1997; 'New critics shine light on China's dark side', 3 June 1998.

14: 'Silent walls of China tell everyday tales of tragedy', 7 April 1995; 'A revolutionary out of his depth', 24 October 1996; 'Chinese whispers', 28 June 1997; 'Police block contact with dissident', 26 June 1998; 'New-age gurus seduce China', 14 June 1997.

Picture Acknowlegements

Photograph taken at Dazhai in 1971 by local photographer; print courtesy of Sally and Richard Greenhill.
   All other photographs were taken by John Gittings.

Glossary and Index of Names

Chinese

Index